Gifted Treasury Series
Jerry D. Flack, Series Editor

Integrating Aerospace Science into the Curriculum: K-12. By Robert D. Ray and Joan Klingel Ray.

Inventing, Inventions, and Inventors: A Teaching Resource Book. By Jerry D. Flack.

Lives of Promise: Studies in Biography and Family History. By Jerry D. Flack.

Mystery and Detection: Thinking and Problem Solving with the Sleuths. By Jerry D. Flack.

TalentEd: Strategies for Developing the Talent in Every Learner. By Jerry D. Flack.

Teaching Teenagers and Living to Tell about It: Gifted Students and Other Creatures in the Regular Classroom. By Pamela Everly.

TalentEd

Strategies for Developing the Talent in Every Learner

JERRY D. FLACK
University of Colorado at Colorado Springs

Illustrated by
Gay Graeber Miller

1993
TEACHER IDEAS PRESS
A Division of
Libraries Unlimited, Inc.
Englewood, Colorado

Copyright © 1993 Libraries Unlimited, Inc.
All Rights Reserved
Printed in the United States of America

No part of this publication may be reproduced, stored in a retrieval system, or transmitted, in any form or by any means, electronic, mechanical, photocopying, recording, or otherwise, without the prior written permission of the publisher. An exception is made for individual library media specialists and teachers who may make copies of activity sheets for classroom use in a single school. Other portions of the book (up to 15 pages) may be copied for in-service programs or other educational programs in a single school.

TEACHER IDEAS PRESS
A Division of Libraries Unlimited, Inc.
P.O. Box 6633
Englewood, CO 80155-6633
1-800-237-6124

Library of Congress Cataloging-in-Publication Data

Flack, Jerry D.
   TalentEd : strategies for developing the talent in every learner / Jerry D. Flack ; illustrated by Gay Graeber Miller.
   xiii, 249 p. 22x28 cm.
   ISBN 1-56308-127-X
   1. Creative thinking--Study and teaching. 2. Problem solving--Study and teaching. 3. Motivation in education. 4. Gifted children--Education. 5. Teaching. I. Title.
LB1590.5.F53   1993
370.15'4--dc20   93-15366
                                                                       CIP

P

> In order to keep this title in print and available to the academic community, this edition was produced using digital reprint technology in a relatively short print run. This would not have been attainable using traditional methods. Although the cover has been changed from its original appearance, the text remains the same and all materials and methods used still conform to the highest book-making standards.

This book is dedicated to George D. Summers.

Your friendship and support
are greatly appreciated and valued.

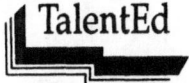

Contents

PREFACE xi

ACKNOWLEDGMENTS xiii

Introduction 1
   The TalentEd Teacher 3
   TalentEd Learning Environments 4
   The Role of the Library Media Specialist ... 4
   The Book: TalentEd Curriculum and
      Activities 5
   Notes 8

A Is for ABC Books 11
   Prodigious Proverbs 15
   Alphabet Grids 16
   Notes 18
   Teacher Resource 18

B Is for Biography 19
   A Day in the Life of _____:
      Learning About the Day You
      Were Born 22
   Biography Resources 23
   Notes 32
   Teacher Resources 32

C Is for Creativity Catalogues 33
   Note 35
   Teacher Resources 35

D Is for Daydreams 36
   Notes 40

E Is for Entrepreneurship 41
   Entrepreneurship 44
   Additional Entrepreneurship Activities .. 48
   Negotiating 49
   Negotiation Simulation 49
   Advertising 52
   Culminating Activity:
      Entrepreneurship Magazines 55
   Notes 55
   Teacher Resources 55
      Books 55
      Organizations 57

F Is for Fairy Tales 58
   Notes 67
   Teacher Resources 67

G Is for Garbage 69
   Academic Talent 75
   Communicating Talent 76
   Planning Talent 77
   A Celebrity Trash Drive 77
   Productive-thinking Talent 79
   Decision-making Talent 83
   Forecasting Talent 85
   Notes 88
   Teacher Resources 88

H Is for Hope...........................89
Notes 95
Teacher Resources 96

I Is for Invention......................97
What Is Innovation?................98
Linking Inventing and Problem Solving..99
    Mess Finding 99
    Data Finding 100
    Problem Finding 100
    Idea Finding 101
    Solution Finding 101
    Acceptance Finding............ 101
What to Invent?................... 102
Notes 102
Teacher Resources 103

J Is for Journals...................... 105
Notes 111
Teacher Resources 111
    Journals and Diaries........... 111
    Books About Journal Writing..... 112

K Is for Kingdoms.................... 113
Notes 116
Teacher Resources 117

L Is for Literature..................... 118
Fiction with Gifted Characters........ 120
Reading Lists 122
Ten Fine Books.................... 123
Book Sharing Ideas 124
Notes 127
Teacher Resources 127

M Is for Mystery..................... 129
Students as Mystery Writers.......... 139
Notes 141
Suggested Bibliography of
    Mystery Literature 141
    Primary Readers.............. 141
    Intermediate Readers........... 142
    Advanced Readers............. 143

N Is for Newspaper................... 146
Positive Self-concept 148
Fluency.......................... 148
Tolerance for Ambiguity............ 149
Flexibility 149
Persistence 150
Openness to Ideas................. 151
Intuition......................... 152
Independence 152
Originality....................... 153
Expressiveness 153
Elaboration...................... 154
Intelligence...................... 155
Sense of Humor................... 155
Perceptiveness 156
Problem Solving................... 156
Notes 157

O Is for Olympics.................... 159
Activities and Projects.............. 161
Olympic Facts..................... 167
    Ancient Olympics 167
    Summer Olympics.............. 167
    Winter Olympics.............. 168
Note 169
Teacher Resources 169

P Is for Pigs, Parody, and Puns......... 171
When Pigs Fly!................... 172
Parody........................... 176
Puns 178
Notes 180
Teacher Resources 180

Q Is for Questions.................... 181
Notes 186

R Is for Recipe....................... 187
Teacher Resource 188

S Is for Service....................... 189
Awareness........................ 190
Action 192
Notes 194
Teacher Resources 195

T Is for (No) Television 196
   Taming the Beast 197
   Notes 201
   Teacher Resources 201

U Is for Understanding a Word 203

V Is for Verse 207
   Haiku 208
   Cinquain 209
   Newspaper Verse 210
   Diamanté 210
   Cafeteria Verse 211
   Imagine Me Verse 212
   Limericks 212
   Impression Poems 213
   Personalized Verse 213
   Found Verse 215
   Concrete Poetry 215
   Notes 217
   Teacher Resources 217

W Is for Writing 219
   Teacher Resources 226

X Is for Classroom eXperts 227
   Notes 231

Y Is for DictionarY and EncYclopedia
   Stories 232
   Notes 234

Z Is for Zebras and Zoo Stories 235

AFTERWORD 237

INDEX 239

ABOUT THE AUTHOR 249

Preface

TalentEd: Strategies for Developing the Talent in Every Learner is the sixth volume in the Gifted Treasury series. In the same manner as previous volumes, this work focuses upon sharing important ideas, substantive curricula, valuable resources, and practical, easily implemented teaching strategies with teachers, administrators, library media specialists, parents, and other mentors of talented youth.

While previous volumes have found their center in topics such as mysteries, inventions, and aerospace science, this volume places special emphasis on process, especially the talent development process. It presents a plethora of topics—twenty-six to be specific—that may be utilized by teachers to address the talent development process. *TalentEd*,[1] an abridgment of *Talent Education*, is more than a name for a philosophy of education. It is also a descriptor of teachers and classrooms and teaching practices that represent excellence in the talent development process. The teaching ideas and strategies in this book represent a collection of winning educational strategies the author has observed, invented, and adapted across a lifetime spent in educating young people and attempting to do the very best job of creatively developing their talents.

The ideas, activities, and projects suggested herein are typical of those found in other volumes in the Gifted Treasury series. They work! The ideas have been tested and found to be worthy of replication. There are no age restrictions on these ideas and strategies. TalentEd teachers use these ideas equally well with five-year-old learners and twenty-five-year-old learners. The ideas are also versatile. The vast majority of the strategies in this volume will work as well in a high school science classroom as they will in a regular third-grade classroom.

The important role of the school library media specialist in the talent development process of youth is accentuated in this book as it is in all previous volumes of this series. School library media specialists are outstanding educators of talent, and should always be seen as indispensable allies of classroom teachers in the talent development process. Many opportunities for collaboration between classroom teachers and library media specialists are suggested in this book.

This book is very much attuned to current developments in American education. Literacy is paramount in the ideas and strategies suggested. Integrated learning and connections of big ideas across many disciplines are found in many of the thematic topics addressed in the twenty-six academic chapters. Diversity is stressed in every activity leading to the realization of the TalentEd philosophy. Academic excellence is the sine qua non of every chapter in this volume, and the fundamental importance of developing the gifts and talents of every student is embraced and applauded.

Finally, as with other volumes in the Gifted Treasury series, this book is not timebound. Ideas that have proved the test of time are shared. Ideas and issues that are currently being employed by TalentEd teachers are similarly showcased. Perhaps most of all, however, this book is about the future. It finds its heart in a vision of what education *can be*. TalentEd or Talent Education does not have to be, and definitely should not be, an exception; it can become the standard of the future.

Note

[1] The author first saw the term *TalentEd* used as the title of an Australian gifted education newsletter edited by Stan Bailey of the University of New England, Armidale, New South Wales. Used with permission.

Acknowledgments

Many friends, colleagues, and students contributed to the ideas and creative works that make up this book. The author wishes to extend thanks and appreciation to Linda Silverman and Dorothy Knopper of *Understanding Our Gifted*, Marvin Gold of *Gifted Child Today*, Lori Mammen of *Writing Teacher* and *THINK*, Patricia Broderick of *Teaching Pre-K-8*, and Theodore Callisto of United Educational Services for their support, cooperation, and permission in allowing the author to use writings that he first created for their publications.

The author further wishes to thank the many people who contributed writing, poems, and ideas, or made valuable suggestions for this book. They are: Hong J. So, Paddy Domier, Marilyn Schoeman Dow, Pamela Everly, Jeremy Johnson, Lindsey Thomas, Jason Oraker, Jim Keating, Dennis McCloskey, Pose Lamb, Gay Miller, Priscilla Barsotti, Anne Crabbe, Judy Ripley, Brett Rickman, Martha Dewey, Marie Sullivan, Dr. Bruce Rolfe, Brenda Sterner, Susan Brock, Mable Whitmore, and Emma Anderson.

Three additional people deserve the author's thanks and appreciation. Dr. Peg Bacon and Dr. Barbara Swaby provided enormous professional support for the author and are models of superb TalentEd teachers. George Summers provided many good meals, pleasant conversation, great walks, and moral support while the author worked on the pages of this book.

Finally, the author wishes to express great thanks to all the editors and support staff at Libraries Unlimited and Teacher Ideas Press. They make him appear to be a far better writer than he really is, and the wonderful staff make the Gifted Treasury series a source of great joy, pride, and pleasure in his life.

Introduction

> If your plan is for one year, plant rice;
> If your plan is for ten years, plant trees;
> If your plan is for 100 years, educate children.
> — Confucius

Given a choice among rice, trees, and educating children, the author will always choose to concentrate on the 100-year plan. *TalentEd: Strategies for Developing the Talent in Every Learner* finds its focus and center not only in its concern with the talent education and creative development of children and adolescents, but also in looking positively and hopefully toward the future. *TalentEd*, an abridgment of *Talent Education*, embraces a vision that all children can learn well and achieve excellence if provided with opportunity and challenge. Moreover, it looks to the next 100 years by concentrating on developing the knowledge, skills, and visions young people need in their preparation to be leaders and good citizens for the twenty-first century. As such, it especially accentuates hope for the future, and the roles individual choice and personal commitment play in creating good and fine tomorrows.

This book is very much about learning. The love of learning is a passion to be kindled and rekindled and ignited in young people. TalentEd teachers convey to them the message that one of the greatest treasures they can ever possess is a love of learning. T. H. White eloquently makes this point in *The Once and Future King*, the story of the legendary King Arthur. Wart, the young King Arthur, is saddened at the prospect of remaining a squire while his older companion Kay becomes a knight. Moved by his sorrow, Sir Ector sends the young Wart to Merlyn for cheering up. Merlyn wisely counsels Wart that the best way to overcome sadness is by learning something new.

> The best thing for being sad is to learn something. That is the only thing that never fails.
>
> You may grow old and trembling in your anatomies, you may lie awake at night listening to the disorder in your veins, you may miss your only love, you may see the world about you devastated by evil lunatics, or know your honor trampled in the sewers of baser minds. There is only one thing for it then — to learn. Learn why the world wags and what wags it. That is the only thing which the mind can never exhaust, never alienate, never be tortured by, never fear or distrust, and never dream of

regretting. Learning is the thing for you. Look at what a lot of things there are to learn—pure science, the only purity there is. You can learn astronomy in a lifetime, natural history in three, literature in six. And then, after you have exhausted a milliard lifetimes in biology and medicine and theocriticism and geography and history and economics—why, you can start to make a cartwheel out of appropriate wood, and spend fifty years learning to begin to learn to beat your adversary at fencing. After that you can start again on mathematics, until it is time to learn to plough.[1]

Merlyn is right. Learning to love learning is the most important gift any TalentEd teacher can share with young people.

This book is also very much about imagination. Imagine a whole classroom filled with eager, creative learners. Imagine a great school filled with talented youth. Imagine a great society that honors and prizes talent development. TalentEd is a way of imagining and then facilitating excellence in education.

What is TalentEd? First, know what it is not. It is not another critique of what is wrong with education in America. It is not another new kit that promises miraculous results. It is not a set of prescribed lesson plans or a curriculum model. Rather, it is a philosophy that believes learning should be exciting, expanding, challenging, positive, basic, hopeful, and unlimited. It is a belief that developing one's talent leads to excellence, achievement, and personal fulfillment.

TalentEd is a philosophy based on five general principles.

Excellence is paramount. The greatest gift teachers can give their students is a belief in excellence and confidence in their abilities to achieve excellence through the development of natural and acquired talent. It is the author's perception that too many American educators have lost sight of their primary strength and mission. They have forgotten what they do best: *teach*. The vast majority of educators have not been trained as social workers or guidance counselors or psychologists, and they often run amuck when they try to fill those roles. Of course, students' feelings about themselves are important. But, in the current national concern in education for self-concept, educators are ignoring the fact that life's sweetest victories come from tackling difficult problems and achieving success. The surest way to improve self concept is to teach young people to meet challenges head-on and triumph through the dint of hard work and commitment to excellence. Excellence is the province of teachers and mentors. Excellence is something teachers are fully trained to develop. TalentEd classrooms prize excellence and set high expectations for students. TalentEd rewards, not punishes, personal commitment, intrinsic motivation, and the drive for individual and team excellence.

The second principle of TalentEd is the belief that schools and classrooms should promote unlimited learning. This principle is founded on two inviolate beliefs: (1) All students can learn; and (2) All artificial barriers to learning must be removed. In TalentEd classrooms cognitive freedom exists. TalentEd teachers empower young people; they do not erect barriers to learning. All children are encouraged to develop their talent to the maximum. TalentEd teachers recognize the wisdom and truth found in Ashley Montagu's words: "Children are the most learning-hungry beings in the world."

The potential for learning and talent development in all students must be found and nurtured. *There is no other acceptable option*. Regardless of whether students are placed in homogeneously or heterogeneously populated classrooms or groupings, they should never *ever* be prevented from learning at their own appropriate rate of instruction. Flexible pacing of instruction needs to be the honored rule, not an exception to the rule. Individual student needs should never be sacrificed to administrative expediency. All parents send their children to school to learn, and all children come to school with a desire to learn. Children have both a fundamental right and a basic need to learn at a rate commensurate with their abilities. The bottom-line philosophy of virtually every public school system in America is that all students are accepted and embraced as they are, and that they will be afforded the very best education possible. This philosophy is accepted and instituted when students suffer from learning disadvantages, but the same philosophy is too frequently overlooked when students are unusually gifted, creative, or talented. Barriers to learning should be knocked down regardless of whether they are ill-conceived and undemocratic tracks that perpetuate failure in low-achieving students, or administrative barriers that prevent honors students from receiving rigorous and challenging educational experiences.[2]

The third principle of TalentEd is a strong belief in basic skills. The TalentEd philosophy subscribes to the belief that basic skills are fundamental, but goes beyond simplistic descriptions of what skills are basic, or the popular notion that basic knowledge may be learned only by rote. Literacy and the core beliefs of the whole language movement that embrace integrated, interdisciplinary, and holistic learning are central to TalentEd activities. The primacy of language is vital. Literacy in all forms—reading, writing, listening, and speaking—is practiced daily in TalentEd classrooms. Basic skills include more than literacy and numeracy, however. Basic skills include goal setting, time management, library research, creative and critical thinking, and problem solving. Students do need an extensive knowledge base. But the pursuit of talent excellence involves much more than the acquisition of facts. TalentEd students need to learn how to locate and use information in order to better solve problems that confront them and the society of which they are part. The twenty-six academic chapters in this book accentuate these core beliefs and provide challenging strategies to meet them. There is also a recognition among TalentEd teachers that the teaching of basic skills should be exciting, creative, and stimulating. Somehow, a notion has grown in the public imagination that scholastic work with the basics must be boring. Nothing could be further from the truth. The assignments, options, and approaches recommended in this book are proof that basic learning can and should be both challenging and exciting.

A celebration of diversity is also central to the TalentEd philosophy. As a means of instituting this fourth principle, good teachers try to find the special talent that each child possesses and then honor that talent. They see diversity as a strength and not as a distraction. They know that one of the roles of the TalentEd teacher in the talent development process is to promote individual fulfillment and not rank conformity. They recognize that it is impossible for any one person to corner the market on knowledge, talent, expertise, or wisdom. These teachers continually strive to celebrate uniqueness in all students. Strategies such as appointing classroom experts as described in chapter X are embraced by teachers who believe in the TalentEd philosophy. Such teachers are also knowledgeable about the wide variety of learning styles young people bring to school. They plan learning activities that address many varied and equally valued ways of learning and knowing. They routinely provide students with a menu of options for fulfilling classroom assignments and challenges that address different natural strengths, preferences, and abilities their students represent.

Hope is not only the subject of one of the twenty-six academic chapters in this book; it is the fifth guiding principle of the TalentEd philosophy. Positivism reigns in TalentEd classrooms. This does not mean TalentEd teachers are hopeless romantics or naive. Rather, leaders in TalentEd classrooms believe that miracles can happen if people believe in themselves, and individual and group excellence are prized. They are optimists. They believe in unlimited possibilities. They believe that learning is a positive and exciting enterprise. They believe in extending, expanding, and enhancing the lives of their students through conscious talent development.

The TalentEd Teacher

TalentEd teachers are joyous, they are enthusiastic, and they communicate enthusiasm for learning to their students. They share the wisdom of master teacher Marva Collins who tells her students, "Enthusiasm is the mainspring of the soul; keep it wound up and you will never be without power to get what you actually need."[3] Enthusiasm and the love of learning are apparent in every lesson TalentEd teachers present every day of the year.

Teachers who subscribe to the principles of the TalentEd philosophy very often see their professional role in a new light. They rarely, if ever, see themselves as mere dispensers of facts and basic information or as skills coaches. Rather, they work as partners, albeit *senior* partners, and facilitators with their students in complex and ongoing educational processes and learning cycles. They invite students to learn. They constantly provide a menu of student options, and provide students with many avenues for creative expression and talent development. TalentEd teachers foster in their students feelings of ownership in the learning process. They involve students in planning their own learning, and they provide students with many authentic choices.

TalentEd teachers are versatile. They teach contents and processes in a wide variety of ways. They also recognize that learning, even the most challenging learning, can and should be fun, and that joy and humor should never be far removed from daily interactions with their students.

These teachers also directly involve their students in evaluation plans. Evaluation is comprehensive, fair, multifaceted, ongoing, and driven by the desire of teachers to help students become the very best that they can be. TalentEd teachers believe in mastery learning. They recognize the fact that students learn best in safe and nonthreatening environments where they can profit from making mistakes. Mistakes are a necessary part of the learning cycle. Student-created and student-managed portfolios and student self-assessments are integral parts of the comprehensive evaluation process TalentEd teachers facilitate.

TalentEd Learning Environments

TalentEd teachers create classroom learning environments that are freeing and enabling rather than stultifying and restrictive. For example, the environment of a TalentEd classroom is very much a problem-finding, problem-solving laboratory where students are empowered through the skills they master. Learning is always relevant, fundamental, and integrated with existing knowledge and skills and across disciplines. The atmosphere in a TalentEd classroom reflects the acknowledgment that students need many kinds of learning experiences. Children and adolescents require solitude and time for reflection in the talent development process just as much as they need the positive socializing effects of small group and whole class experiences.

The author has used the activities and strategies in *TalentEd* in all types of learning environments. For seventeen years the author was a classroom teacher of primary, middle, and secondary students in the public schools of Michigan and Indiana. He has additionally worked for more than a decade with preservice and inservice teachers in Hawaii, Oregon, Missouri, Maine, Colorado, New Mexico, Nebraska, South Carolina, Utah, Ohio, Arkansas, Texas, Louisiana, Nevada, and British Columbia, and has seen these ideas implemented and given fair trials in many varying academic settings. The teaching and learning strategies will work in any learning environment. The activities may be used with individual students, small groups, or whole classes. They can be utilized in mainstream classrooms, in honors classes, in Super Saturday classes for gifted and talented children, in special seminars, and in home and parochial school settings.

The Role of the Library Media Specialist

For many years the author has argued the case for the indispensable role the school library media specialist should play in the education of gifted, creative, and talented students.[4] It is absolutely essential that library media specialists be active partners in the development of student talents. Many of the strategies recommended in this book work especially well in school library media centers and with the valued input or direction of school library media specialists. Print and nonprint resources are abundant in many of the topic areas addressed in this book such as invention, garbage and the environment, mysteries, newspapers, and the Olympic Games. School library media specialists are wonderful in helping both students and teachers locate valuable references and resources in these and other topic areas.

In both philosophy and practice, TalentEd is very much about empowering students to achieve excellence. One of the proven ways to realize this goal is to help young people learn *how* to learn. In her classic work, *The Making of a Scientist*, researcher Ann Roe reveals that a major contribution premier scientists credit for their eventual choices of careers in scientific research, and to which they attribute eventual success in those careers, was the discovery early in their student lives "of the possibility of finding out things oneself."[5] In other words, learning how to learn and learning how to find things out.

Library media specialists can teach students how to find resources and how to critically evaluate the resources once found. They can share their very considerable research skills in teaching students how to design, plan, and carry out research studies. Moreover, library media specialists typically have the equipment and the training to further help students channel the knowledge derived from their research into creative works such as audiovisual presentations.

Library media specialists can also share their love of books with talented students and provide the type of guided study of literature recommended in chapter *L* of this book.

The Book: TalentEd Curriculum and Activities

While this introduction addresses the underlying philosophy of Talent Education and suggests broad guidelines for its implementation, the bulk of the text is given over to highly specific teaching and learning strategies that creative teachers will recognize or want to adopt. This is chiefly a book of ideas and strategies, and all of them work! Every strategy, idea, activity, and project in this book has been tried and found successful either by the author or by other teachers who embrace the philosophy of TalentEd and believe in the infinite capacity children and adolescents have for learning and for thriving on excellence and challenge.

Although Talent Education is a philosophy rather than yet another curriculum model, it does embrace and utilize effective models of curriculum design and delivery. Models that are easily implemented and that have considerable bearing on the talent development process are recommended in several chapters. Howard Gardner's conception of multiple intelligences is discussed and Calvin Taylor's Multiple Talents model is utilized in the classroom teaching and learning strategies discussed in chapter *G*. The use of Bloom's *Taxonomy of Cognitive Objectives* is explored in the discussion of questioning strategies found in chapter *Q*. The author's own descriptive curriculum model for critical thinking and problem solving is found in chapter *M*, and Anne Crabbe's dynamic model for enhancing creativity is highlighted in chapter *N*. One of many fine creative problem-solving models is used to explore the topic of inventions and inventing in chapter *I*.

The diagram on pages 6-7 provides a visual overview of these activities and strategies. At one glance, teachers can see the wide variety of topics, activities, strategies, and models addressed in the book. Curriculum webs are extremely versatile and may constitute yet another teaching technique that TalentEd teachers will desire to use with their students when introducing or reviewing topics found in this book, such as inventions, mysteries, newspapers, the Olympic Games, and the environment. Webbing prepares students for learning. With webs or concept maps, teachers can ascertain the prior knowledge students possess, as well as visually represent to students the breadth and depth of a topic to be studied. In chapter *M* the author uses a mystery web (fig. M 2) to represent the many possible directions learning about mysteries may take. Students can examine the many types of sleuths created by mystery authors; they can examine the etymology of crime vocabulary; they can examine the world of real-life crime; and they can use the metaphor of mystery or puzzlement as a springboard to investigations of mysteries and conundrums found in disciplines as diverse as archaeology, psychology, and forensic medicine.

(Text continues on page 8.)

6 Introduction

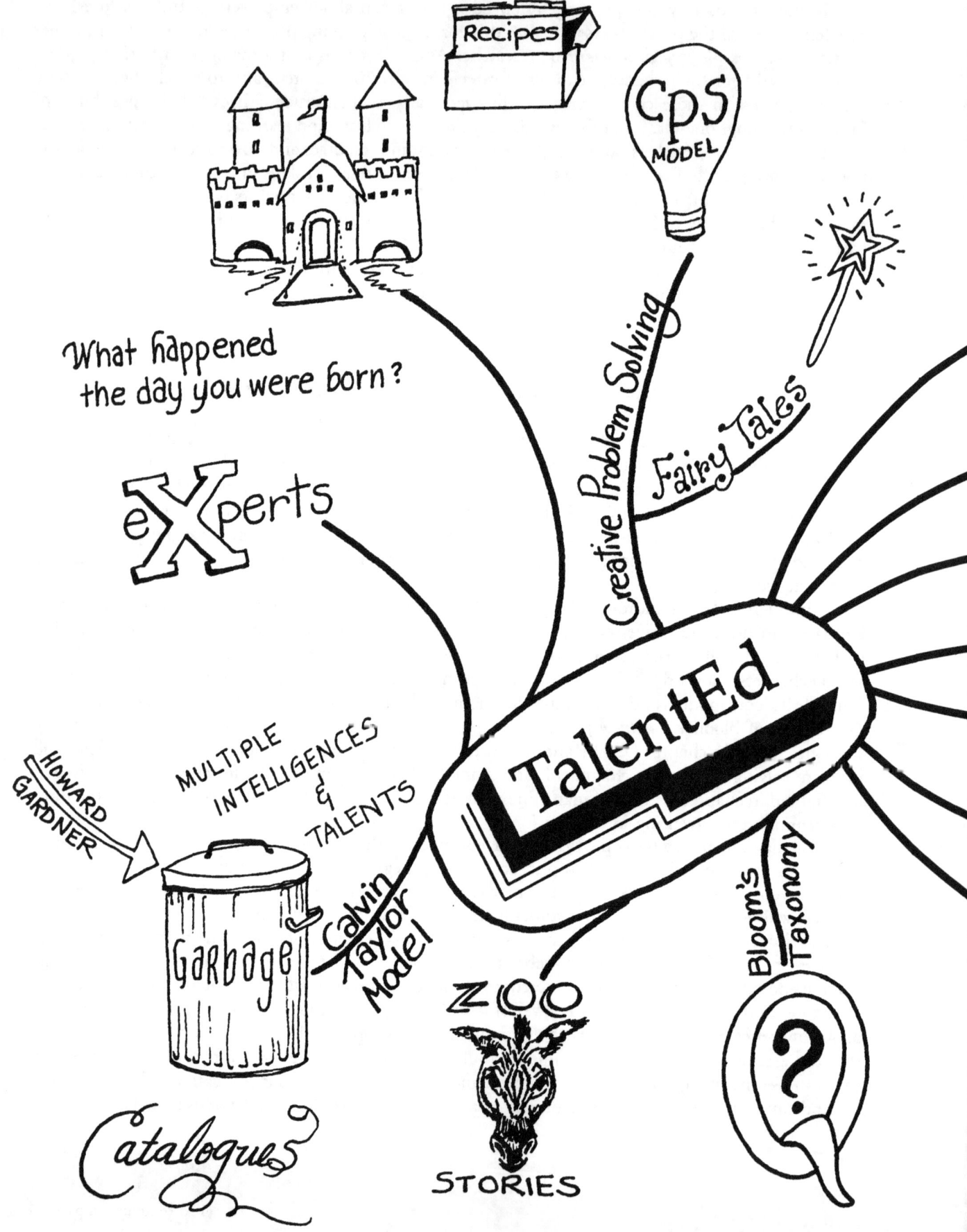

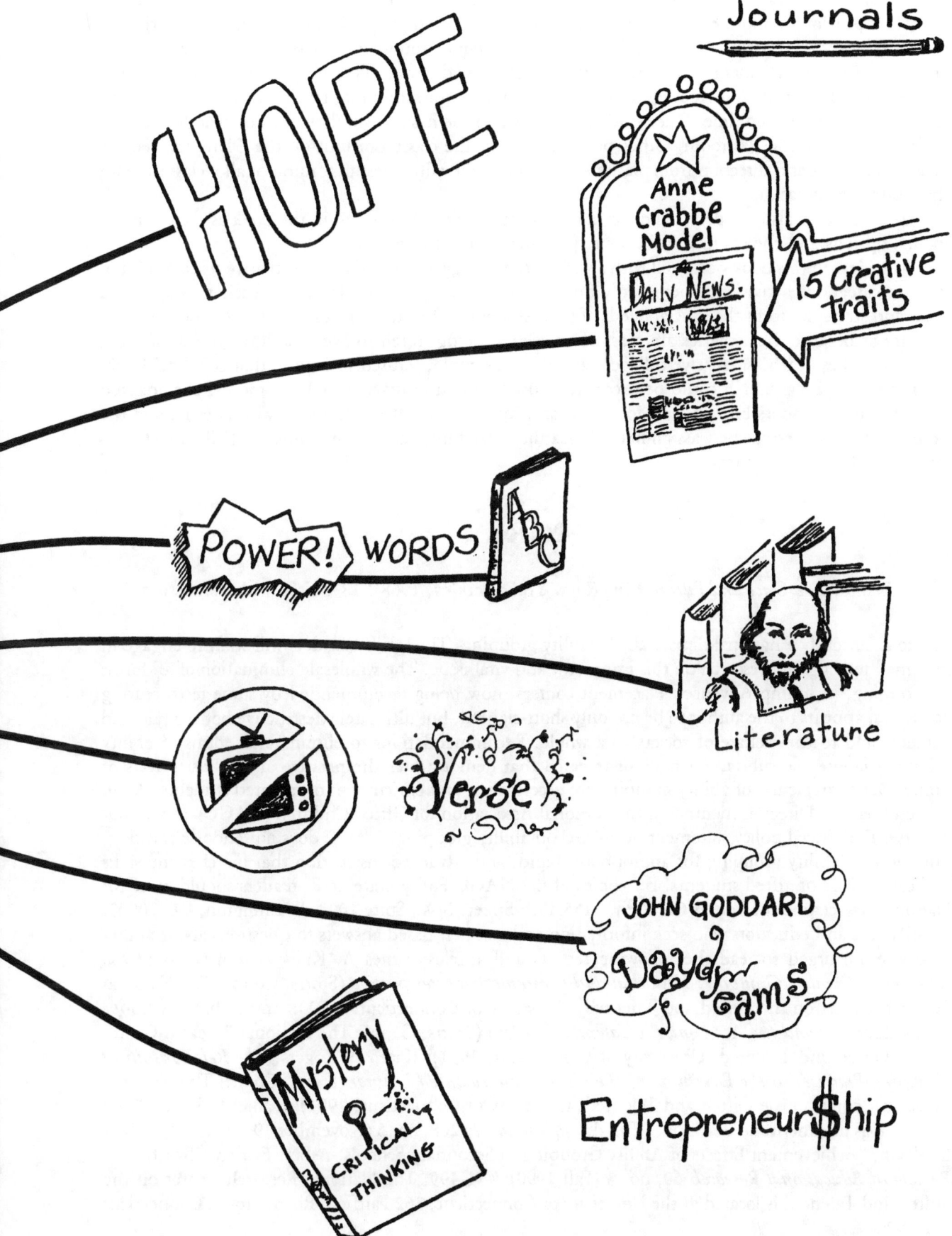

Many of the ideas and projects found in this book accentuate the school and home partnership in the talent development process, and underscore the much desired parental support and collaboration on which TalentEd classrooms depend. The ideas and activities found in this book vary greatly in the amount of time commitment and allotment needed to be made by both teachers and students. Activities such as journal writing and creating a list of daydreams require minimal teacher directions and little expenditure of classroom time. Once students understand the basic tasks, they can work comfortably on their own outside the classroom. Other projects, such as the classroom unit on the Olympics, require substantial input and direction from teachers, as well as their willingness to commit or allot class time for the student explorations.

Teachers may also use personal discretion in using the activities found in the book as class requirements, options and choices to fulfill class requirements, and as extra credit.

The ideas in this book work well with a wide variety of age groups. Wise and creative teachers do not label or categorize activities as being only for one age or ability group. TalentEd teachers adapt good ideas and strategies to fit the special needs of their students. They do not quickly dismiss strategies that have merit because the activities are most often seen as being suited to age or ability groups different from those they teach. A creative college teacher, for example, refused to believe that the ABC books recommended in chapter A could be successfully used only in primary school classrooms. She adapted their use to her honors English class for third- and fourth-year college students, who later named the experience the semester's best assignment. Versatility, flexibility, and adaptability are hallmark characteristics of TalentEd teachers.

Notes

[1] T. H. White, *The Once and Future King* (New York: Berkley, 1968), 183. Used with permission.

[2] There is currently a national debate about ability grouping. Thoughtful readers will want to engage in informed reading and research on this important and vital issue. The wholesale elimination of all forms of grouping, including Advanced Placement courses, now being recommended by some restructuring advocates, appears to the author to be not only short-sighted, but ultimately destructive both to talented students and to the welfare of society as a whole. Recommendations to eliminate all forms of ability grouping ignore the substantial body of research that demonstrates the positive and robust effects of limited yet strategic use of ability grouping for acceleration and enrichment of talented students. As an elected Board of Directors member of the National Association for Gifted Children (NAGC), the author endorses the official policy statement of NAGC on ability grouping. NAGC does not endorse tracking, but endorses ability grouping for appropriate, rapid, and advanced instruction that matches the skills and capabilities of gifted students. For copies of the NAGC Policy Statement, readers should write to: National Association for Gifted Children, 1155 15th Street, NW, Suite 1002, Washington, DC 20005.

Parents and educators who seek information and research-based answers to questions about ability grouping are urged to read the following reports and articles: James A. Kulik, *An Analysis of the Research on Ability Grouping: Historical and Contemporary Perspective* (Storrs, Conn.: The National Research Center on the Gifted and Talented, University of Connecticut, 1991); Ann Robinson, *Cooperative Learning and the Academically Talented Student* (Storrs, Conn.: The National Research Center on the Gifted and Talented, University of Connecticut, 1991); Karen B. Rogers, *The Relationship of Grouping Practices to the Education of the Gifted and Talented Learner* (Storrs, Conn.: The National Research Center on the Gifted and Talented, University of Connecticut, 1991); Daniel J. Singal, "The Other Crisis in American Education," *The Atlantic Monthly* 268, no. 5 (November 1991): 59-74; Robert E. Slavin, "Achievement Effects of Ability Grouping in Secondary Schools: A Best Evidence Synthesis," *Review of Educational Research* 60, no. 3 (Fall 1990): 471-499. The National Research Center on the Gifted and Talented is located at the University of Connecticut, 362 Fairfield Road, Storrs, Connecticut 06269-2007.

[3] For a description of the brilliant teaching of Marva Collins and the messages she communicates to her students, see Marva Collins and Civia Tamarkin, *Marva Collins' Way* (Los Angeles: J. P. Tarcher, 1990).

[4] For further discussion see Jerry D. Flack, "A New Look at a Valued Partnership: The Library Media Specialist and Gifted Students," *School Library Media Quarterly* 14, no. 3 (Summer 1986): 174-179.

[5] Ann Roe, *The Making of a Scientist* (New York: Dodd, Mead, 1952), 82.

# Is for ABC Books

Motivating students to become abecedarians is an important first step in developing their talent. Words! Words! Words! One of the absolutely sure ways to help students develop their talent is by helping them build their vocabularies. The truth of this declaration may be seen in a profound statement by Newbery Medal-winning author Madeleine L'Engle (*A Wrinkle in Time*). She makes the case for the fundamental importance of words in our lives in this passage from her published journal *A Circle of Quiet*.

> The more limited our language is, the more limited we are; the more limited the literature we give to our children, the more limited their capacity to respond, and therefore, in their turn, to create. The more our vocabulary is controlled, the less we will be able to think for ourselves. We do think in words, and the fewer words we know, the more restricted our thoughts. As our vocabulary expands, so does our power to think. Try to comprehend an abstract idea without words: we may be able to imagine a turkey dinner. But try something more complicated; try to ask questions, to look for meaning; without words we don't get very far. If we limit and distort language, we limit and distort personality.[1] (Excerpt from *A Circle of Quiet* by Madeleine L'Engle. Copyright © 1972 by Madeleine L'Engle Franklin. Reprinted by permission of Farrar, Straus & Giroux, Inc.)

Words are one of humankind's most potent forces. Words are vital in developing the talents of young people.

Bright students love big words; they enjoy building their vocabularies and adding new words to their personal lexicon. The love students have for new words is a splendid opportunity for teaching students about reference tools such as specialized dictionaries and thesauri.

There are many fine word-building activities. The personal favorite of the author is the ABC book. ABC books are perfect examples of the kinds of assignments and prompts TalentEd teachers can give students that speak to the diversity of learning skills, talent, creativity, and interest found among students in typical classrooms. The alphabet book provides a generic structure within which all students can function. Structure is provided, but the pattern does not become a straight jacket that stifles creativity. The structure is found in the broad format. Each student, or each cooperative learning group, may be assigned a twenty-six-letter alphabet book on any topic the teacher or students choose. The way each student or group executes the broadly given assignment may vary tremendously according to the investment of time, talent, creativity, and task commitment.

Begin by sharing with students some of the incredibly marvelous alphabet books that may be found in libraries and bookstores. The first alphabet book the author ever used with students was *The Abecedarian Book* by Charles W. Ferguson. Ferguson's book is advertised as follows: "An alphabet book of big words for adults with the curiosity of children and the capacity of adults."[2] The reader quickly learns what the author intends. The *A* word is *antediluvian*, and the reader learns that *abecedarian* is a 300-year-old word describing a person who is either learning or teaching the alphabet. The *M* word is *malapropism*, and the *O* word is *onomatopoeia*.

Working with library media specialists, teachers can present an assortment of outstanding ABC books to students, from which they can derive ideas for themes and motifs for their own alphabet books. Outstanding alphabet books of note include these:

Anno, Mitsumasa. *Anno's Alphabet: An Adventure in Imagination*. New York: HarperCollins, 1979.

Each letter is painted as if finely carved from wood, but a second look reveals that each painting is an optical illusion. Only one-half of letter *M*, for example, is shown; the other half is a mirror image.

Aylesworth, Jim. *The Folks in the Valley: A Pennsylvania Dutch ABC*. Illus. by Stephano Vitale. New York: HarperCollins, 1992.

Illustrations that make use of Amish and Mennonite folk art motifs add much to an alphabetical highlighting of Pennsylvania Dutch activities such as making jam, quilting, and chopping wood.

Base, Graeme. *Animalia*. New York: Harry N. Abrams, 1986.

Base, an Australian illustrator, has created what may well be the most exquisite ABC book ever published. Each page is beautiful to look at and also contains all manner of animals and objects that begin with one of the twenty-six alphabet letters. Each page is also headed with an alliterative line such as "Beautiful blue butterflies basking by a babbling brook." Besides a magnificently colorful butterfly, readers will find a bear, bassoon, baboon, beetle, and bicycle on the *B* page. The illustrator also hides himself, as he might have appeared as a young boy, in every picture for readers to find as a further challenge.

Bowen, Betty. *Antler, Bear, Canoe: A Northwoods Alphabet Year*. Boston: Little, Brown, 1991.

Beautiful color engravings provide a childlike view of the year in the north country of Minnesota.

Coon, Alma S. *Amy, Ben, and Catalpa the Cat*. Illus. by Gail Owens. Williamsburg, Va.: Colonial Williamsburg Foundation, 1990.

The alphabetical adventures of a boy and girl and a cat in the Williamsburg George Washington knew are told in beautifully illustrated verse.

Cox, Lynn. *Crazy Alphabet*. Illus. by Rodney McRae. New York: Orchard Books, 1990.

The trouble starts when a bird eats an apple. Of course, a cat chases the bird, and that cat is chased by a dog. Every letter does something to the letter that precedes it in this "house that Jack built" kind of funny madness.

Downie, Jill. *Alphabet Puzzle*. New York: Lothrop, Lee & Shepard, 1988.

> Readers are invited to peer through windows and use visual clues to guess what objects represent each alphabet letter in Downie's beautiful illustrations.

Elting, Mary, and Michael Folsom. *Q Is for Duck: An Alphabet Guessing Game*. New York: Clarion Books, 1980.

> Why is *Q* for duck? Because ducks go *Quack*. The sounds and behaviors of animals are portrayed via the alphabet in this clever book. Older students can make similar ABC books for their younger siblings, or sixth-grade students can make such books for their first-grader buddies with whom they are paired.

Fisher, Leonard Everett. *The ABC Exhibit*. New York: Macmillan, 1991.

> Besides depicting the alphabet with such objects as icebergs, balloons, and jugglers, the artist's paintings are wonderful introductions to the elements of color, shape, and light.

Geiset, Arthur. *Pigs from A to Z*. Boston: Houghton Mifflin, 1986.

> Seven sibling pigs seek to build the perfect tree house. Each etching contains the seven little pigs and five versions of the given alphabet letter.

Hausman, Gerald. *Turtle Island Alphabet: A Lexicon of Native American Symbols and Culture*. New York: St. Martin's Press, 1992.

> From Arrow and Basket and Cradle to Zigzag, Hausman shares Native American stories and poems to reveal the symbols and wisdom of Native American beliefs.

Hepworth, Cathi. *Antics! An Alphabetical Anthology*. New York: G. P. Putnam's Sons, 1992.

> A charming, beautifully illustrated ABC book based on word play with ants. Readers meet *Ant*ique, Immig*rants*, *K*ant, Rembr*ant*, and S*ant*a Claus among others of the distinguished ant family.

Hoban, Tana. *A, B, See!* New York: Greenwillow Books, 1982.

> Remarkable photographic images of many objects for each alphabet letter.

Kellogg, Steven. *Aster Aardvark's Alphabet Adventures*. New York: Mulberry Books, 1987.

> Wonderfully drawn animal adventures and clever alliteration are found on every page. TalentEd teachers will find Kellogg's book to be useful in introducing the lesson found in chapter *Y*.

Levitt, Paul M., Douglas A. Burger, and Elissa S. Guralnick. *The Weighty Word Book*. Longmont, Colo.: Bookmakers Guild, 1985.

> A delightful ABC book that makes wonderful use of puns. The origins and meanings of "big" words are explained through delightful stories and clever puns.

Limscott, Jody. *Once Upon A to Z*. Illus. by Claudia Porges Holland. New York: Doubleday, 1991.

> Wonderful lessons in alliteration. Each ABC page tells a story using only words beginning with the featured letter of the alphabet. Each story stops in the middle, so to speak, and is continued by the next letter in the alphabet. Vivid, bright illustrations. *Once Upon A to Z* may be used as an introduction to the activity prescribed in chapter *Z*.

Lobel, Anita. *Alison's Zinnia*. New York: Greenwillow Books, 1990.

> Twenty-six girls, from Alison to Zena, give twenty-six flowers, from amaryllis to zinnia, to one another. Beautiful floral paintings add to the magic of this book.

MacDonald, Suse. *Alphabetics*. New York: Bradbury Press, 1986.

> The artist finds new and expansive ways of seeing in this ABC book. The letter *C* becomes a clown's mouth, and a pair of *X*s become xylophone sticks.

Martin, Bill, Jr., and John Archambault. *Chicka, Chicka, Boom, Boom*. Illus. by Lois Ehlert. New York: Simon & Schuster, 1989.

> Alphabetical rhyme chants that beg to be read aloud. The letters race each other to the top of a coconut tree. One packaged version of the book contains an audio cassette with the text read and sung by Ray Charles.

Musgrove, Margaret. *Ashanti to Zulu: African Traditions*. Illus. by Leo Dillon and Diane Dillon. New York: Dial Books for Young Readers, 1976.

> The alphabet is used to portray the traditions of twenty-six African peoples in this Caldecott Medal-winner.

Owens, Mary Beth. *A Caribou Alphabet*. Brunswick, Maine: Dog Ear Press, 1988.

> This book celebrates the reintroduction of caribou to the state of Maine after an absence of eighty years.

Paul, Ann Whitford. *Eight Hands Round*. Illus. by Jeanette Winter. New York: HarperCollins, 1991.

> Traditional patchwork patterns are explained and illustrated for children, from the anvil pattern for *A*, and zigzag for *Z*. Eight Hands Round is the illustrated quilt pattern for the letter *E*.

Shirley, Gayle C. *C Is for Colorado*. Illus. by Constance Rummel Bergum. Helena, Mont.: ABC Press, 1989.

> *A* is for aspen and *Y* is for yucca, and there are twenty-four more letters representing Colorado sights, products, and tourist attractions that reveal much about the centennial state. Each letter is introduced with a poem.

Van Allsburg, Chris. *The Z Was Zapped*. Boston: Houghton Mifflin, 1987.

> All manner of mayhem occurs to the alphabet letters in this twenty-six-act play directed by Van Allsburg.

One of the first kinds of alphabet books the author's students created was "big word" alphabet books. Students plunged into the large, unabridged dictionaries in the school library media center and came up with the biggest words they could find for each of the letters of the alphabet. They then drew illustrations for their newly acquired big words, or cut appropriate illustrations from old magazines and junk mail picture files kept in the classroom for just such occasions.

Alphabet books are remarkably versatile in their uses, and students love to create them. They can be used effectively when students create autobiographical alphabet books: "Me from A to Z: 26 Reasons Why I Am a Great Person"; or as bouquets to their families: "The Nelsons: 26 Superlatives." ABC books can be about daydreams, wishes, goals (see chapter *D*), or heroes. Alphabet books can be used equally effectively as capstones to cognitive units of instruction. When completing a unit on state history, endangered species, or oceanography, students can summarize what they have learned with, say, Ohio or California books, A to Z, or collaborative ABC books about endangered species and oceans. In the latter, for example, Tom notes, defines, and illustrates all the oceanic terms beginning with *B* (e.g., baleen, barnacle), while Sharon tackles the *Q* words (e.g., quadrant, quay). Primary-age students who are studying animal homes might create an ABC book of drawings and definitions of burrows, caves, dens, puddles, and warrens. Creative primary teachers may ask their students to make their drawings poster size and compile all the pages together into a Big Book of animal homes.

When the author's students finished reading *The Taming of the Shrew*, they knew that one project option they had was the creation of Shakespearean ABC books. Students may also create an ABC book as a form of service. For example, with only modest adult guidance and supervision, talented students can design, execute, and duplicate ABC books about their school or community to be given to new members of the community or new students at the school. Some students may be inspired to create an ABC rap or chant on a given theme or subject, or merely to celebrate the alphabet letters themselves as Bill Martin, Jr., and John Archambault do in *Chicka, Chicka, Boom, Boom*.

It goes without saying that any good alphabet book is not complete without illustrations, so students have an added creative workout in determining the visual style and format their ABC books will have. Incidentally, do not think ABC books are just for elementary students. A TalentEd college English professor in Massachusetts regularly assigns ABC books in her freshman honors writing class. When students evaluate her class at the end of the semester, they routinely vote the alphabet book their favorite assignment of the course.

Prodigious Proverbs

ABC books are especially versatile, but they are not the only tools TalentEd teachers may use to stretch and build the vocabulary power of their students. One of the fun and challenging activities students enjoy is the creation of their own prodigious proverbs. Using dictionaries and thesauri, students rewrite famous proverbs using "big" words and phrases. Their intent is to create proverbs that are sufficiently difficult to stump their peers. Here are a few examples. The translation of the proverbs is found at the end of the chapter.

> Legal tender is the mathematical operation of all malignancy.
>
> A continuously moving rock congregates no green, plant-like organisms.
>
> All that scintillates is not necessarily a soft, precious element.
>
> The thirst for knowledge led to the feline's demise.
>
> You cannot make a larva fabric currency bag out of a female swine's organ of listening.

An especially delightful sampling of small children's impressions of proverbs is found in *Don't Cross Your Bridges Before You Pay the Toll*. Children are given the first half of famous proverbs and complete them with their own creative endings. For example, one child informs readers that a penny saved is "not much." Each thought is also illustrated by its author.

Alphabet Grids

Another alphabet activity students enjoy involves the creation and completion of alphabet grids related to classroom subjects under study. A subject of study is written, one letter at a time, down the left-hand margin of a page, the vertical axis of the grid. Across the top of the page, the horizontal axis, a variety of broad topic headings related to the subject are listed. Draw the remaining horizontal and vertical lines to complete the grid. The task for students is to fill in all the resulting squares with words that match the topics called for in the columns, and that begin with the letters of the subject found on the vertical line. A sample grid on the subject content of Canada is shown partially completed in figure A.1. Wise TalentEd teachers plan far in advance. When teachers know what topics and units are forthcoming, they can suggest to their students that they create alphabet grid frameworks for their classmates to complete as an activity in the forthcoming unit.

Rudyard Kipling said, "Words are the most powerful drug used by mankind." Letters and words are certainly the building blocks of meaning and making sense of the world. TalentEd teachers who provide students with lots of language experiences, and who challenge their students to constantly be about the business of learning and using new words, are giving students an invaluable gift. The TalentEd classroom is alive with literacy, the celebration of words, and word-based activities.

> Speech is civilization itself. The word, even the most contradictory word, preserves contact. It is silence which isolates.
> —Thomas Mann

Fig. A.1. Alphabet grid of Canada.

	CITIES	FAMOUS WOMEN	FAMOUS MEN	RIVERS	PRODUCTS	HISTORICAL SITES
C	Calgary	Emily Carr		Coppermine River		Capilano Suspension Bridge
A						
N					Nickel	
A						
D			John Diefenbaker			Argillite Sculptures
A						Dawson

From *TalentEd: Strategies for Developing the Talent in Every Learner.* © 1993 Teacher Ideas Press, P.O. Box 6633, Englewood, CO 80155-6633

Notes

[1] Madeleine L'Engle, *A Circle of Quiet* (New York: Farrar, Straus & Giroux, 1972), 149. Used with permission.

[2] Charles W. Ferguson, *The Abecedarian Book* (Boston: Little, Brown, 1964), dust jacket.

Teacher Resource

Stark, Judith Frost. *Don't Cross Your Bridges Before You Pay the Toll.* Los Angeles: Price Stern Sloan, 1985.
    First-graders' encounters with the meaning of proverbs.

<u>Answers to prodigious proverbs:</u>

Money is the root of all evil.

A rolling stone gathers no moss.

All that glitters is not gold.

Curiosity killed the cat.

You cannot make a silk purse from a sow's ear.

# Is for Biography

> The art of Biography
> Is different from Geography
> Geography is about maps,
> But Biography is about chaps.
>
> —Edmund Clerihew Bently
> *Biography for Beginners*

Of course, biography is about ladies as well as chaps, and it is a wonderful subject for gifted, creative, and talented students. Happily, bookstores and library media centers today are filled with excellent biographies and autobiographies of both women and men of diverse races, ethnic groups, and nationalities. Encounters with excellent biographies offer students countless opportunities for important reflection. Biographies offer youth both illumination and inspiration. Students can identify with such famous people as Eleanor Roosevelt and Martin Luther King, Jr., who have known isolation and who have shared the feeling of "being different." They can be inspired by the heroic efforts and successes of individuals like Marie Curie and Thomas Edison, who worked hard and long to achieve success. Biographies about talented people at work increase the understanding young people have about history and vocations and avocations. Biographies of Annie Oakley and Georgia O'Keeffe inform students about the colorful eras in which the subjects lived, while biographies of Sally Ride speak to careers in space science.[1]

Biography should be everpresent in a TalentEd classroom. This genre serves as an exemplary supplement to almost any text and as enrichment in any content area. Texts that lack significant rigor for bright students, or that represent too few women and minorities, may be augmented with modern biographies. Through the biography genre, youths may enhance their knowledge of science, mathematics, art, music, architecture, and a host of other subjects by reading biographies of people who solved problems and achieved success in these fields.

Three salutary things have occurred in biographies published for youth in recent years. First, the inexcusable dearth of biographies about women, especially in nontraditional roles, and minorities has largely been corrected.[2] Second, many of the biographies penned today present their subjects free of the didactic hero worship so common in past biographies for children and adolescents. Subjects are presented as complete human beings who are capable of errors in judgment, making mistakes, and suffering defeats, as well as having life successes. A third notable feature of contemporary biography is the scholarship modeling of the authors that is presented to young readers through their works.

Abraham Lincoln

Exemplary works that demonstrate these benefits include Russell Freedman's *Lincoln: A Photobiography*. Freedman provides extensive documentation that includes lists of Lincoln historical sites, prominent books about Lincoln, acknowledgments for picture credits, and a thorough index. Stephanie Sammartino McPherson's biography of nineteenth-century astronomer Maria Mitchell, *Rooftop Astronomer*, is one of the excellent new biographies about women scientists. Yet another stellar example of these positive trends is *Native American Doctor: The Story of Susan LaFlesche Picotte* by Jeri Ferris, which tells the heroic story of a physician who treated her own people, the Omahas, as well as non-Indians, in the prairie lands of nineteenth-century Nebraska. Newbery Medal-winning author Joan W. Blos tells the colorful story of Denver's Molly Brown in her picture book biography *The Heroine of the Titanic*. Blos presents her subject as a true heroine, but also as a human being who often embellished the truth and was capable of error as well as heroics.

Biography studies provide young people with a marvelous array of creative project possibilities. As a response to their reading of outstanding biographies, students can generate first-rate creative projects to demonstrate their own learning and simultaneously enhance the learning of other students. The following are but a few starting points teachers may wish to recommend to challenge youth as they encounter first-rate biographies.

Suggest to students and parents that they jointly read a biography as a family project. Discussion of last night's reading will definitely spark exciting breakfast-table conversation. Utilizing this approach allows students the opportunity to see their parents modeling a positive behavior, reading, and also allows students to be near someone familiar with whom they can share ideas and ask relevant questions.

Each state is allowed two statues in the U.S. Capitol Rotunda. Colorado is one state that currently has only one statue in the Rotunda. Other states are also represented with just one statue. Based on their readings of biography, ask students to determine what person would be the best candidate for their state to enshrine. If the students' state of residence already has two statues, propose the following alternative: Congress has determined that not nearly enough women and minorities have been represented in the statuary of the U.S. Capitol Rotunda. Each state may add a new statue of a woman or a minority person. Whom should your state choose to honor? Write a summary of the accomplishments of the person nominated.

TalentEd teachers can select a critical era (e.g., the 1960s, World War II, the Civil War) and work with the library media specialist to locate a representative list of biographies of people who made a significant difference during the chosen time. Categories may include: artist, athlete, entrepreneur, environmentalist, entertainer, writer, statesperson, musician, mathematician, and scientist. Ask each student in the class to read a biography of one of the subjects who lived in the chosen time period. Class discussions then can be built upon understandings of how people from various walks of life functioned within and viewed the same historical time frame.

Ask students to place themselves in the position of a biographical subject. Ask each reader to find a crisis situation in which the subject had to resolve a conflict in which two rights were in opposition, making a completely satisfactory decision virtually impossible. How did this person resolve the conflict? How might the student have approached and handled the same conflict?

Introduce a bit of geography into a biography unit. Ask students to create passports for such interesting biographical subjects as Charles Darwin, Helen Keller, Winston Churchill, Christopher Columbus, and Jane Goodall.

As more and more students in class read biographies, begin a classroom (or school) letter exchange in which students who have read different biographies write letters to each other, assuming the identities of their favorite biographical subjects. "Henry Ford" can write a letter to "Georgia O'Keeffe" about his latest invention, the Model T.

Young readers may enjoy being biographical games detectives. Ask a bright and resourceful reader to find out what kinds of games and entertainments her favorite biographical subject played when he or she was young. The student then engages in some original research, learns how to play the game, and teaches it to her contemporary classmates.

The world as a quilt. As a possible culminating classroom activity, following students' reading of many biographies, ask each student to create one square for the quilt featuring the person he or she found most fascinating. Each square can symbolize at least one important event in the subject's life. Once the quilt is completed, students can use it as the focal point of a discussion about what can be learned from the study of biography.

Students can also create a biographical quilt about their chosen subject. Dramatic events, words, and symbols from the life can be highlighted in their own drawings, which can be stitched or fastened together to resemble a patchwork quilt.

The author's favorite TalentEd biography (or autobiography) assignment involves asking students to create birthday time capsules for themselves, family members, or friends. The following passage from the author's book *Lives of Promise: Studies in Biography and Family History* describes a biography assignment that his students loved.[3] The research skills development, creativity, and critical thinking they learned in the process of completing the project were outstanding.

A Day in the Life of _____: Learning About the Day You Were Born

What is the most important day in a life, yet the one about which most people know the least? It is that special day each student first greeted this world. Students were so busy getting used to bright lights, loud noises, the sharp slap of the doctor's hands on their bottoms, and the "oohs" and "aahs" of admiring nurses, doctors, parents, and grandparents that they just did not have time to read the newspaper or watch the evening newscast to keep track of what was going on in the world on their first day on this planet.

Children and adolescents often dislike history when it is perceived as a collection of dry, stale, and seemingly irrelevant dates and facts. But history and historical research can really come to life for students when they have a relevant purpose and a personal stake in the study. One of the most enduring and exciting assignments teachers can give them is the task of surveying the history and events connected with the special day each of them was born.

This activity is not only a fun, challenging, and relevant assignment, it is also a grand opportunity to introduce students to the use of reference tools that may be new to them, such as library microfilm and microfiche. This assignment serves another valuable function. It provides a satisfactory alternative to the popular family biography or family genealogy projects used in so many classrooms across the country. In the culture today, many children and adolescents are adopted, are foster children, are refugees, or are the children of single parents. Asking children to research their family trees may cause some of them to experience pain and discomfort and to feel different and left out. Such an assignment may prompt the wrath of a parent, who justifiably charges that the school community has no business prompting a child to explore sensitive and highly private family situations. Educators should never paint a child into a corner, so to speak. TalentEd teachers always provide alternatives. The Day in the Life project is a highly suitable alternative project to family history inquiries and family biographies.

Encourage students to create as thorough and as complete a picture of the day each was born as possible. First, brainstorm with students all the kinds of things they might learn about their special day. Students should be able to generate a substantial list of pertinent items. The following is but a brief sample of the kinds of research questions they might wish to pose:

What world, national, state, and local news dominated the headlines?

Who held the elective offices of president, governor, mayor?

What were the best-selling stocks in the stock market?

What was happening in the world of entertainment?

What were the best-selling movies, books, songs?

    How much did it cost to go to the movies?

    What were the most popular television programs?

    What was the price of *Time* magazine?

What were the weather conditions and forecast?

What were Dear Abby and Ann Landers saying about the mores and morals of society?

What projections were made in the horoscope?

> What types of products were most commonly advertised in display advertisements in newspapers and magazines?
>
> What was the average cost of an apartment rental listed in the classified advertisements in newspapers?
>
> What were the prices of common goods and services (e.g., gas, milk, bread, a box of cereal, a pair of jeans, automobile tires, etc.)?
>
> Was any special season in progress (baseball's World Series, deer-hunting season, Mardi Gras, etc.)?

Creative students will no doubt suggest additional kinds of information to collect to create their personal time capsules. The information students seek does not have to be exclusive to the exact day and year each was born. Through the skillful use of resource materials available in good libraries, students can further enrich their final products by answering research questions like these.

> What historical events occurred on the same day throughout recorded history?
>
> What famous people were born on the same day throughout history?
>
> What is the origin and meaning of my given name and surname(s)?

Once students have exhausted the list of possible items of information to collect about their very special day, they are ready next to determine how and where to find the information they need to create a quality, in-depth profile. Here the library media specialist can be of tremendous help to students. That research expertise will prove invaluable. Some of the following resources may prove to be especially useful. Teachers should note that students will more than likely have to utilize out-of-school library facilities to locate much of the desired information.

Most public libraries have both local newspapers and the *New York Times* on microfilm. They will also have popular periodicals such as *Time*, *Newsweek*, *Sports Illustrated*, *Ladies Home Journal*, *Ebony*, *Seventeen*, *The Saturday Evening Post*, and *The New Yorker* in bound volumes or on microfilm. For a minimal fee most libraries can provide photocopies of pages from both newspapers and periodicals that will save students hours of note taking. *Chase's Annual Events: Special Days, Weeks & Months*, a delightful reference resource, highlights the festivals and events that occur on each of the 365 days of the year in the United States. It includes such esoteric events as hog-calling contests and Groundhog Day celebrations. The following resources may assist TalentEd teachers and library media specialists in enabling students to successfully complete a Day in the Life projects.

Biography Resources

Selected books and a video history include:

Carruth, Gorton. *What Happened When: A Chronicle of Life & Events in America*. New York: Harper & Row, 1989.

> An essential collection of facts and dates from the year A.D. 986 to the present. Broad categories of Civil Rights, Architecture, Business and Industry, and Fashion subsume additional topics such as crime, books and publishing, politics and government, suffrage, technology, women, sports, and education. Each of the years of the twentieth century is well documented.

Chase's Annual Events: Special Days, Weeks & Months: An Almanac and Survey of the Year. Chicago: Contemporary Books, 1989.

> Each of 365 daily entries lists the famous people born on that day as well as the special events and celebrations that occur throughout the nation. Persons born on July 11 would note that they share their date of birth with John Quincy Adams, actor Tab Hunter, and boxer Leon Spinks. July 11th festivals include Anthony Wayne Day (sponsored by Wayne State University in Detroit); National Cheer Up the Lonely Day, on which citizens are encouraged to visit shut-ins and the lonely in hospitals and nursing homes; Chesapeake Turtle Derby (celebrated in Baltimore); and the beginning of the Choctaw Indian Fair (celebrated in Philadelphia). On July 11, 1987, Matej Gaspar was born in Zagreb, Yugoslavia. At his birth he was proclaimed the five billionth inhabitant of Planet Earth.

Frewin, Anthony. *The Book of Days*. London: St. James's Place, 1972.

> Herein are the significant historical events that have occurred throughout history on each of 366 days (February 29th is included) of the year. Each entry additionally lists all the eminent persons who were born or died on that day. For example, readers whose birthdays fall on April 6 learn that they share their birthdays with Maximilien de Robespierre of French Revolution fame; that an earthquake in London badly damaged St. Paul's and other churches on April 6, 1580; and that the composer Igor Stravinsky died on this day in 1971.

Gregory, Ruth W. *Anniversaries and Holidays*. Chicago: American Library Association, 1975.

> Each day of the year is accompanied by a list of all the famous and eminent persons born on that same day. Special feasts and celebrations for each day are also described. July 12 is the birthday of George Eastman, American inventor of cameras; Sir William Osler, physicist; and Henry David Thoreau, author of *Walden* and other works. It is also Family Day in South Africa, Orange Day in Northern Ireland, and the anniversary of the authorization by Congress of the Congressional Medal of Honor (1862). In Portugal, July 12 is the occasion for the celebration of Our Lady of Fatima. Tennessee celebrates July 12 as a legal holiday commemorating the birthday of Nathan Bedford Forrest, American cavalry commander in the Confederate army.

Grun, Bernard. *The Timetables of History: A Horizontal Linkage of People and Events*. New York: Simon & Schuster, 1991.

> Grun does not list days of the year, but he provides a year-by-year account of significant developments in seven areas: history and politics, literature and theatre, religion and philosophy, the visual arts, music, science and technology, and daily living. Through the use of this excellent resource tool students can learn about the year of the birth of the subject they choose to profile.

Korn, Jerry, ed. *This Fabulous Century*. New York: Time-Life Books, 1970.

> Time-Life Books has created a pictorial time capsule view of each of the decades of the twentieth century. The major personalities, culture, music, fads, sports, and dominant historical, economic, and political events of each decade are profiled with the stunning photographic essays that made *Life* magazine famous throughout much of this century.

Smith, Elsdon C. *New Dictionary of American Family Names*. New York: Harper & Row, 1973.

> Smith provides information about both given names and surnames commonly found in the United States. George Summers, for example, could learn that the derivation of his last name is English, and refers to the *summoner*, the petty officer who warns people to appear in court. George would further learn that his given name is from the French and Welsh and means either "descendant of a farmer" or a "dweller at the sign of St. George."

The Video History of Our Times. Norwalk, Conn.: Easton Press Video.

Easton Press Video produces hour-long videos highlighting the major events, fashions, and trends of each year from 1930 through 1969. Unfortunately, the video cassettes may not be purchased individually. They are marketed as part of a video club package shipped to subscribers every other month. Check video stores and public library video collections for possible availability of individual years. Easton Press Video, 47 Richards Avenue, Norwalk, CT 06857, 1-800-367-4534.

Withycombe, Elizabeth Gidley. *Oxford Dictionary of English Christian Names*. New York: Oxford University Press, 1973.

This is but one of many books found in the reference section of a well-stocked library that will provide information about the origin and meaning of names. In this volume, for example, a student may learn that *Diana* is the Latin name of the moon goddess (in Greek it's *Artemis*) and find a history of the use of the name in European countries since the Renaissance.

Your Birthday. New York: Natalis Press, 1990.

Natalis Press has produced a series of 365 books, one for each day of the year, highlighting historical events that occurred on each given day. The birthdates of famous persons born on that particular day, as well as information on constructing a family tree, are provided.

Authentic birthdate newspapers and magazines are available from many sources. Used bookstores are always good places to search for such items. One popular mail-order catalogue, *Wireless*, offers newspapers from various cities and from dates as far back as 1886. For complete details, write to *Wireless*, P.O. Box 64422, St. Paul, Minnesota 55164-0422. The JCPenney store catalogue also contains information for ordering birthdated newspapers.

Of course, students should not forget to engage in some good interviewing of their relatives to collect additional information. They may want to ask what grandmothers and grandfathers were doing the day they were born. They will want to ask Mom to describe the day as she recalls it. If possible, find out the name of the obstetrician who assisted with the delivery. Again, if these questions pose serious problems or invasions of privacy for some students, they can easily be omitted. Alternatively, students can be encouraged to ask their teachers if they recall what the teachers were doing on the given day.

Hallmark stores now offer reasonably priced computer printouts that provide some of the information called for in the preceding lists. Natalis Press has also produced a series of 365 small books, titled *Your Birthday*, that also highlight events in history for each day of the year. However, these profiles of days are not personalized and contain primarily national and international news and cultural events. They may be a good beginning point for students, but no student's search should begin and end in a Hallmark store or with a prepackaged book! One of the real benefits of this project is the skill of research practice and expertise students develop while using the library media center.

Once students have found all the answers they need to complete their profiles, they should assemble the data in the most creative package they can develop. In cooperative learning groups, students may brainstorm all types of products that might be created. There is no one correct way to produce a day-of-birth time capsule. Most students compile scrapbooks consisting of a narrative account of their special day, complemented with photocopies of newspaper front pages, stock market citations, advertisements, weather maps, and the like. The availability of excellent software packages such as "The Newsroom" and "Publish It!" make it possible for students to create professional-looking, special edition newspapers to celebrate or commemorate the day each has chosen.[4]

One innovative junior high school girl chose to create a time capsule not about herself, but about her mother, who was born in the late 1930s in the era of radio soap operas, big bands, Depression prices, and the looming war in Europe. After collecting print materials, she also hunted for and located audiotapes of selected soap operas, "Our Gal Sunday," "Helen Trent," and Glenn Miller records. She enlisted the support of several friends who helped her compile an hour-long audio cassette tape for her mother's birthday present. The hour began with the news report of the special day in 1938. This was followed by a commercial advertising the latest sales on women's dresses at the local dry goods store. Next, it was time for an episode in the continuing saga of "Helen Trent," whose adventures were occasionally interrupted to allow for on-the-air advertising of soap products and the weather report. Before turning the program over to Glenn Miller music, still another advertisement told listeners what was playing on the double bill at the local movie theatre that night: *Snow White and the Seven Dwarfs*, and *Boys Town* with Spencer Tracy. In all, the cassette program was a magical time capsule that both surprised and enchanted the student's most fortunate mother.

Nancy, an eighth-grade student, spent several weeks completing this audio time capsule. Teachers can make the Day in the Life project either a long- or short-term project, depending on the time opportunities or constraints. One TalentEd teacher uses this project as the desired outcome of a relatively short field trip experience. She takes her students to the large, city center branch of the public library. There a media specialist introduces the high school students to the reference section of the library and explains how to access and utilize microfilm copies of newspapers. Then the students have three hours to find out all they can about the day they were born. Within a few days of the field trip, students are expected to complete a short, creative paper highlighting what they learned. Hong J. So, a young man who was born in Busan, Korea, wrote the poem "Death and Life" after just such a field trip. Hong J. So says of his earliest years, "I was born the last child of six; four sisters and two brothers, in a family with a thriving private business. But by the time that my family came to the United States from Korea on April 6, 1978, all we had were just bare essentials and a dream. A dream of bettering our lives in this great nation."[5]

Death and Life

Scattered clouds above my head
On a muggy day in July.
I think it's gonna rain.

Riots breaking out in Chicago,
Governor calls the National Guard.
No suspects but two people killed.

I was born on this day,
This day of joy and happiness—
Unknown hero catches a boy
Fallen from three story building.

I arrived here on this day,
This day of pain and sorrow—
A youth's life has ended,
Fallen from the Garden of the Gods.

No cares in this world,
Just an infant knowing nothing.
Horoscope reveals that I should
Assist those in trouble.

No connections in this world,
Just a child ready to grow up.
Paper reveals that I should
Study toward stage, government.

The headlines on the paper
Show the violence on the other side,
Most missions flown in Nam.

As I go on reading the paper, I
Come to advertisements:
Fancy two-pant suit for $49.95.

What will people do tonight?
See "Navarone," "The Sound of Music,"
Or Dinah Shore, in person.

I was new born on this day,
This day of peace and violence.
People in tranquility,
But countries at war.

I was blessed on this day,
This day of death and life.
People dying all over the world
And I was born on this day.

The biography time capsule/birthday book project is fun and challenging for students of all ages and grade levels. Once students are introduced to the existing library media resources and taught how to retrieve needed information correctly and efficiently, older students will be able to function nicely on their own. Younger students may need the assistance of a parent, grandparent, mentor, or older sibling to provide transportation to the library and to help retrieve and successfully use library resources such as microfilm files. More than a few younger gifted students have joyfully conspired with an older sibling or a parent, and worked with a stealth that would be the envy of Sherlock Holmes, to produce a time capsule for a lucky parent as a birthday, Mother's Day, or Father's Day gift.

Many delightful and creative alternative uses and product outcomes derived from this project have been shared with the author. A Colorado Springs, Colorado, TalentEd school principal saves future students the time and trouble of completing this project. Whenever a teacher in his building or a family friend has a baby, he and his wife go to the local newsstand and buy several newspapers of the day and a wide assortment of current magazines. They place all these items in a suit- or dress-box and wrap it neatly. They enclose a gift card for the new baby that contains this request: "Open this box on your seventeenth birthday!"

The time capsule project can also be completed as a class project. In one Colorado school that was celebrating its twenty-fifth year of existence, the kindergarten teacher had her class work as a group (with lots of delighted parent involvement) to create a mural that visually displayed what the world had been like twenty-five years earlier on the day the school first opened. A group of teachers in still another building created a wonderful retirement gift as a loving farewell to their principal. On the day the principal retired, the teachers presented both a slide show and a memory book containing all the salient and important events that occurred in the world on the very first day she stepped into a classroom to begin her teaching career. A Day in the Life time capsule can also be used to celebrate anniversaries, graduations, and many other special occasions. The author has found it one of the most satisfying gifts both to create and to give to friends and relatives. The person who creates the gift has a great deal of fun researching the data needed for the project, learns a lot about history in the process, and has the opportunity to employ an enormous amount of creativity in the development of the final product. The lucky person who receives this gift of love is deeply touched and forever grateful.

Figures B.1-B.4, pages 28-31, may be shared with students as possible approaches they may wish to take in preparing the final products they create for the Day in the Life biography project.

Biography is the only true history.
—Thomas Carlyle

(Notes follow on page 32.)

Fig. B.1. Scrapbook Item.

Joan Marie (Andrus) Locker: This Is Your Story

This is your book, your story. It is a book about you and a chronicle of the special day (and year) you were born. You were preoccupied with other matters on May 19, 1944, so here in review is your story on May 19, 1944.

It was a good year, made even more special by your birth. War news, of course, dominated the headlines. American troops were invading the Italian peninsula, heading for Rome. In England, General Eisenhower was preparing for the D-Day invasion less than a month away. In the Pacific theatre of war, American troops were nearing the Philippines. British General Montgomery was on the cover of *Life* magazine and Dr. Alexander Fleming, the discoverer of penicillin, was on the cover of *Time* magazine.

If you had been listening to the radio that day, you would have heard the "Kate Smith Show" and "Amos and Andy." You might also have been interested to learn that the New York Yankees baseball team lost to the St. Louis Browns, 6-5. The win elevated the Browns to first place in the American League. In fact, both St. Louis teams, the Browns and the Cards, led their respective leagues at the end of the day, May 19. Both teams went on to face each other in the fall in an all-St. Louis World Series, which the Browns won.

If the hospital nursery played music for new arrivals, you probably heard "Mairzy Doats" or "I'll Be Seeing You" on the radio. You might also have heard a review of *A Tree Grows in Brooklyn*, a popular, best-selling book in May 1944. If you had been a bit older, you could have gone to the movies with your Mom and Dad. Perhaps you would have seen *Going My Way* or *The Song of Bernadette*, two of 1944's biggest movie hits.

Children across America were planting victory gardens, and rationing was a fact of life. Had you been of working age, you might have had a job as a waitress, earning $18.00 a week. A three-piece maple bedroom suite would have cost your parents $74.95. Your Mom's grocery bill might have included these items:

   1 lb. coffee, 27 cents

   Northern Toilet Tissue, four rolls for 18 cents

   24 oz. jar of peanut butter, 33 cents

   Spareribs, 21 cents/lb.

   Leaf lettuce, three bunches for 10 cents

   Iodent Tooth Powder, 37 cents

Maybe your parents would invest in the stock market to begin building a nest egg for your eventual college tuition. On May 19, 1944, Sinclair Oil, Packard, and Willys were big stocks to buy.

All in all, much was occurring on May 19, 1944. It was a great day, made even more special by your appearance on the scene.

Fig. B.2. Historical record.

May 19th in History

Throughout history, many significant events have occurred on May 19.

Anne Boleyn was beheaded in 1536. The Spanish Armada set sail from Lisbon in 1588. Napoleon created the Order of Legion of Honour in 1802. There was an attempted assassination of Queen Victoria by William Hamilton in 1849. Irene (Asteroid 14) was discovered by J. R. Hind in 1851. Tolosa (Asteroid 138) was discovered by M. Perrotin in 1874. Oscar Wilde was released from Pentonville Prison, 1895. The Tonga Islands were annexed to Great Britain in 1900. The U.S. Emergency Immigration Act was passed in 1921.

In Turkey, May 19 is the celebration of Youth and Sports Day. Lady Astor, the first woman member of England's Parliament, was born on this day in Virginia in 1879. Ho Chi Minh, revolutionary leader of North Vietnam, was born on May 19, 1890. Frank Capra, successful Hollywood film director, was born in Palermo, Italy, on this day in 1897. Malcolm X (Malcolm Little), U.S. Black Muslim leader, was born in Omaha, Nebraska, on May 19, 1925.

The following people died on May 19: James Boswell, the great biographer of Samuel Johnson; American author Nathaniel Hawthorne; William Gladstone, English Prime Minister; Thomas Edward Lawrence, popularly known as Lawrence of Arabia; Ogden Nash, American humorist; and Charles Ives, American composer.

The most famous event in recorded history, of course, was the birth of Joan Marie Andrus in Denver, Colorado, on May 19, 1944.

Fig. B.3. Simulated news article.

DENVER POST

MAY 19, 1944　　　　　　　　　　　　　　　　　　　　Section A, Page 1

WORLD'S CUTEST BABY IS BORN!

The world's cutest baby was born this morning at General Hospital at 4:30 a.m. Doctors and nurses were completely baffled when little Joan Marie Andrus entered the world. "I have never seen such a beautiful baby," stated head nurse Ruth Swenson. Dr. Arthur Lopez, the attending physician, announced triumphantly, "I am sure that I will win the Nobel Prize for medicine for the delivery of this marvelous baby. She is precious!"

The proud mother and father, John and Louise (Arbeta) Andrus, of 657 E. Lehigh Avenue, were equally pleased with the birth. "We're so proud and happy," said Mrs. Andrus. "She is going to grow up to be a wonderful person," beamed the proud new father.

Word of the incredible birth did not immediately affect the baseball standings in either the National or American Leagues, but word is circulating that composer Aaron Copland has already begun work on a new symphony honoring the birth of the baby. Teen idol Frank Sinatra may also record a popular song called "I'm in Love with Joan Marie."

From across the country and around the globe, the famous and the infamous commented on the birth. In Washington, D.C., President Roosevelt said, "This is a day that shall be long remembered." His constant companion, Fala, added, "Arf! Arf!" The president's opponent in this year's election, Republican Presidential Candidate Thomas E. Dewey, could not resist adding a comment. "Joan Marie's birth is a miracle, just like my victory over FDR will be this November."

In England, General Eisenhower and General Patton saw this new birth as a good omen for the planned "D-Day" invasion of Europe. "This birth could really turn the tide of victory for the Allied Forces," said a jubilant Eisenhower. At London's Number 10 Downing Street, Winston Churchill interrupted his war cabinet meeting to add his note of congratulations to the Andrus family. "Surely, the birth of this beautiful baby will inspire our troops to fight ever more nobly and bravely."

Meanwhile, on the continent itself, Hitler screamed in Berlin, "*Dieser mein ungeschehen machen*" (This will be my undoing).

Back in the U.S.A., Betty Grable wondered if the newborn beauty would constitute a threat to her own popularity as a pin-up girl with American soldiers. "She does have beautiful legs," Grable grumbled nervously.

Locally, Governor James Bradley spoke from the capitol steps. "I proclaim this great day 'Baby Joan Day!'" Not to be outdone, Denver Mayor Ralph Edwards said he would consider naming the newest city park the "Baby Joan Playground."

Baby Joan was unperturbed by all the attention. She simply slept. (See related story on B1.)

Fig. B.4. Flashback predictions.

DENVER POST

B1   Colorado Features

Denver Seer Sees Baby Joan's Future

Only minutes after the sensational birth of Baby Joan Marie Andrus, *Denver Post* reporters interviewed Denver seer Claire Voyant in hopes of sharing with the anxiously waiting world glimpses of the baby's future.

"I see many, many events of great significance in her forthcoming life. At two, she will charm Santa Claus. At five, she will attend Webster Elementary School and be a kindergarten wonder. Some will be jealous of her many talents and tease her for being the teacher's pet. She will be active in Girl Scouts and win first place in the fifth-grade spelling bee. She will attend Wilson Junior High School and South High School. She will like sports and will be a blue-ribbon swimmer. She will also be an honor-roll student. In her senior year, she will be in the Homecoming Queen's court.

"In 1962, she will attend the University of Colorado at Boulder. There she will major in elementary education. (Her years of being a teacher's pet will finally pay off.) There she will meet James Douglas Locker, whom she will marry in 1967. They will have three children. The youngest, Alison, will one day create a time capsule about her life and the day she was born.

"All in all, I predict a wonderful life for Joan Marie."

At this point, Miss Claire Voyant's crystal ball began to cloud over and she said she could discern only one final prediction. "This beautiful baby will grow up to be a beautiful and wonderful wife, mother, and teacher. She will bring beauty to all who know her."

■■■

Notes

[1] Some of the material in this chapter originally appeared in the author's book *Lives of Promise: Studies in Biography and Family History* (Englewood, Colo.: Teacher Ideas Press, 1992), and in Jerry D. Flack, "In Search of Serendipity," *Understanding Our Gifted* 4, no. 4 (March-April 1992): 17-18.

[2] The National Women's History Project is a fine source of biographies about women, and especially minority women. National Women's History Project, 7738 Bell Road, Windsor, CA 95492-8518.

[3] See Flack, *Lives of Promise*, 85-94.

[4] "The Newsroom" is published by Springboard Software, Inc., 7807 Creekridge Circle, Minneapolis, MN 55435. "Publish It!" is published by Timeworks, Inc., 444 Lake Cook Road, Deerfield, IL 60015.

[5] Hong J. So, letters to author, October 19, 1989. Used with permission.

Teacher Resources

Blos, Joan W. *The Heroine of the Titanic*. New York: Morrow Junior Books, 1991.

Ferris, Jeri. *Native American Doctor: The Story of Susan LaFlesche Picotte*. Minneapolis, Minn.: Carolrhoda Books, 1991.

Freedman, Russell. *Lincoln: A Photobiography*. New York: Clarion Books, 1987.

McPherson, Stephanie Sammartino. *Rooftop Astronomer: A Story of Maria Mitchell*. Minneapolis, Minn.: Carolrhoda Books, 1990.

C Is for Creativity
Catalogues

Many TalentEd teachers share the author's trait of being genuine, grade A, certified pack rats. The classrooms of these pedagogical collectors always overflow with "treasures" that other, more temperate and tidy souls have discarded. Not too many years ago, the author kept a table in the corner of his classroom that overflowed with trade catalogues his colleagues and weary mail carriers gladly tossed his way. Examining the mountain of L. L. Bean, Neiman-Marcus, Eddie Bauer, and Abercrombie & Fitch catalogues, an idea began to emerge and take shape. Why not have students create their own catalogues? The following day the idea was presented to students, and they were off and running as designers, copy writers, editors, illustrators, and advertising departments all rolled into one.

Each student was asked to create a catalogue. Each catalogue was to have a central theme, ten to twelve well-described items, and as much original artwork as possible. Examples of unique catalogues were shared with students. The library media specialist supplied a facsimile reproduction of the *Sears, Roebuck & Co. 1908 Catalogue No. 17*. A neighbor shared a copy of *His & Hers: The Fantasy World of the Neiman-Marcus Catalogue*, an anthology of some of the most fantastic items that have appeared in Neiman-Marcus catalogues over the years, such as a $600 Monopoly game made of fine chocolate and a pair of his and her ostriches. Colleagues supplied unique catalogues such as the *Pork Avenue Collection*, devoted to pig enthusiasts, and the *Journal of Academic T-Shirts*, a collection of casual wear for intellectuals and eggheads.[1]

The selection and development of the theme and its related catalogue items was a boon to creative productivity for students. A serendipitous bonus of the catalogue creation project is the improvement and refinement of students' writing skills. Even verbally gifted students benefit from practice in learning to write with clarity, precision, and conciseness. Writing copy for their catalogues engages students in an activity that requires them to focus on exactness and precision in the use of words. In many cases students need to move beyond simple descriptions of appearance. They are required to describe in detail how a catalogue item works or is operated.

The catalogue assignment is similar to the ABC books described in chapter *A*. A generic framework is provided for students. Once they have sampled several catalogues, all students have a good idea of what is expected of them in order to assure success. How students respond to the challenge is largely a matter of their personal creativity and the level of their personal commitment to excellence.

C Is for Creativity Catalogues

The final products are likely to be highly creative. One of the author's students, an eight-year-old boy, created a catalogue of mechanical birds that included the rare "chocolate chickadee" as well as the more common "jail bird." Another third-grade student created *Robots Galore*, a robot catalogue complete with robots designed to cook, wash windows, make music, answer telephones, pick up children's bedrooms, and do homework. A fourth-grade student created a catalogue of survival items future colonists may need to settle Mars. A middle-school student's *Dream Homes Catalogue* was created in the manner of the free real estate catalogues typically found at the entranceway to grocery stores. The contents of her catalogue featured elaborate and detailed drawings of unique homes that might be found around the world: a Chinese houseboat, cliff dwellings at Mesa Verde, an Alaskan igloo, and a Bavarian castle. The *Dream Homes Catalogue* even contained the ubiquitous and pesky tear-out coupon readers could complete and mail to receive further information on unique real estate options.

Students' themes ranged far and wide. Young bibliophiles created catalogues related to their favorite authors and books. A sixth-grade girl created *The Judy Blume Catalogue* that offered readers items suitable for favorite characters from Judy Blume books. The *All Creatures Great and Small Catalogue* gave readers many choices of items representative of Yorkshire Dales, and the practice of veterinary science. A second student borrowed James Herriot's title for her catalogue of items with playful names. Her *All Creatures Great and Small Catalogue* featured books and other items about little creatures. Readers could purchase Aphida Christie mysteries, the children's classic *Worm in the Wallows*, Old Lice after-shave lotion, and gourmet food items such as spaghetti and mothballs and French flies.

Students need not work alone if teachers desire that they work in pairs or small groups. Two of the author's students worked together to create a parody of camping supply catalogues. Tony and Damon's catalogue featured items such as the Instant Pollution Kit, which contained a mixture of cans, paper, dead animals, foul smells, and an oil slick. The city camper only had to add contaminated water and stir. The catalogue was alphabetically indexed, and even featured a tourist-trap map that showed campers where to find quicksand, Dead Fish Bay, the snake pit, a tarantula farm, Sam's Rendering Works, Garbage Mountain, Sewer Falls, and the not-so-posh International Spittoon Hotel for Drifters and Drunks and Bums.

Theme catalogues may also be tied into class readings, topics, and projects. Students reading Shakespeare's *Romeo and Juliet* can create catalogues that might have aided either Elizabethans or Verona residents to complete their shopping. Social studies students examining Civil War history may create Union or Confederate catalogues. Science students studying the weather can design catalogues for meteorologists.

A TalentEd first-grade teacher in Colorado asks each of her students to create one page for the class catalogue devoted to the works of Bill Martin, Jr. Students accent words, colors, animals, and characters from their favorite Bill Martin, Jr., stories and poems.

Serendipity may be lurking around, just waiting to be discovered in the latest delivery of junk mail and mail-order catalogues. Do not throw those catalogues away. Turn them into teaching and learning experiences for TalentEd kids.

Note

[1] Hog Wild, *The Pork Avenue Collection*, 7 Faneuil Hall Market Place, Boston, MA 02109. Outer Products, *Journal of Academic T-Shirts*, Box 88, Lafayette Hill, PA 19444.

Teacher Resources

Marcus, Stanley. *His & Hers: The Fantasy World of the Neiman-Marcus Catalogue*. New York: Viking, 1982.

A sampling of the best items found in the celebrated department store's catalogue.

Schroeder, Joseph J., ed. *Sears, Roebuck & Co. 1908 Catalogue No. 17*. Northfield, Ill.: Digest Books, 1971.

A facsimile edition of the "Great Price Maker."

# Is for Daydreams

> Nothing happens unless first the dream.
> —Carl Sandburg

The TalentEd classroom should be a place where dreams are encouraged and honored. As Eleanor Roosevelt said, "The future belongs to those who believe in the beauty of their dreams."

John Goddard is a man whose life exemplifies the meaning of Mrs. Roosevelt's words. He has led a life of grand adventure. Born in 1924, he has lived by the philosophy, "To dare is to do ... to fear is to fail."[1] When he was fifteen years old, John Goddard took the time to set 127 goals or daydreams for himself, including exploring the Nile River, climbing Mount Ararat in Turkey in search of Noah's Ark, and reading the entire *Encyclopaedia Britannica*. John Goddard graduated from the University of Southern California where he majored in psychology and anthropology. He has climbed many of the world's highest mountains and explored many of its most vital rivers. He is a member of the Royal Geographic Society of England and the Adventurers' Club of Los Angeles. In 1978, John Goddard was named the Encyclopaedia Britannica's Gold Medal Winner in Exploration. He has chronicled one of his greatest adventures, his 4,145-mile traverse of the world's longest river, in *Kayaks Down the Nile*, published by Brigham Young University Press in 1979.

A list of John Goddard's 127 daydreams and life goals appears in figure D.1.[2]

For many years the author gave a copy of John Goddard's daydreams to each of his students early in the school year for perusal and discussion. Students then were given two weeks to create their own lists of fifty goals or daydreams. Typical student responses included items like these:

1. Argue a monumentally important case before the Supreme Court.
2. Pitch a no-hitter in the World Series.
3. Play football in a major New Year's Day Bowl game.
4. Become the first woman president of the United States.
5. Learn to fly an airplane.
6. Compose a song that wins a Grammy award.
7. Find the lost continent of Atlantis.
8. Have access to 1,000 acres of wilderness land.
9. Solve a puzzling mystery or crime.
10. Read the *Bible* from cover to cover.

Fig. D.1. John Goddard's daydreams and goals.

Explore:
1. Nile River*
2. Amazon River*
3. Congo River*
4. Colorado River*
5. Yangtze River, China
6. Niger River
7. Orinoco River, Venezuela
8. Rio Coco, Nicaragua*

Study Primitive Cultures In:
9. The Congo*
10. New Guinea*
11. Brazil*
12. Borneo*
13. The Sudan*
14. Australia*
15. Kenya*
16. The Philippines*
17. Tanganyika (now Tanzania)*
18. Ethiopia*
19. Nigeria*
20. Alaska*

Climb:
21. Mt. Everest
22. Mt. Aconcagua, Argentina
23. Mt. McKinley
24. Mt. Huascaran, Peru*
25. Mt. Kilimanjaro*
26. Mt. Ararat, Turkey*
27. Mt. Kenya*
28. Mt. Cook, New Zealand
29. Mt. Popocatepetl, Mexico*
30. The Matterhorn*
31. Mt. Rainier*
32. Mt. Fuji*
33. Mt. Vesuvius*
34. Mt. Bromo, Java*
35. Grand Tetons*
36. Mt. Baldy, California*

37. Carry out careers in medicine and exploration*
38. Visit every country in the world
39. Study Navajo and Hopi Indians*
40. Learn to fly a plane*
41. Ride horse in Rose Parade*
42. Iguacu Falls, Brazil*
43. Victoria Falls, Zimbabwe*
44. Sutherland Falls, New Zealand
45. Yosemite Falls*
46. Niagara Falls*
47. Retrace travels of Marco Polo and Alexander the Great*

Explore Underwater:
48. Coral reefs of Florida*
49. Great Barrier Reef, Australia*
50. Red Sea*
51. Fiji Islands*
52. The Bahamas*
53. Explore Okefenokee Swamps and Everglades*

Visit:
54. North and South Poles
55. Great Wall of China
56. Panama and Suez Canal*
57. Easter Island
58. The Galapagos Islands
59. Vatican City*
60. The Taj Mahal*
61. The Eiffel Tower*
62. The Blue Grotto, Capri*
63. The Tower of London*
64. The Leaning Tower of Pisa*
65. The Sacred Well of Chichen Itza, Mexico
66. Climb Ayers Rock in Australia*
67. Follow River Jordan from Sea of Galilee to Dead Sea

Swim In:
68. Lake Victoria*
69. Lake Superior*
70. Lake Tanganyika*
71. Lake Titicaca, South America*
72. Lake Nicaragua*

73. Become an Eagle Scout*
74. Dive in a submarine*
75. Land on and take off from an aircraft carrier*
76. Fly in a blimp, balloon, and a glider

From *Happy Birthday to U.S.*, by Murry Suid and Roberta Suid. Copyright © 1975, Addison-Wesley.

* Indicates daydream or goal has been realized

(Figure D.1 continues on page 38.)

Fig. D.1 – *Continued*

77. Ride an elephant, camel, ostrich and bronco*
78. Skin-dive to 40 feet and hold breath for two-and-a-half minutes underwater*
79. Catch a ten-pound lobster*
80. Play flute and violin*
81. Type 50 words a minute*
82. Make a parachute jump*
83. Learn water and snow skiing*
84. Go on a church mission*
85. Follow the John Muir trail
86. Study native medicines and bring back useful ones*
87. Bag camera trophies of elephant, lion, rhino, cheetah, cape buffalo, and whale*
88. Learn to fence*
89. Learn jujitsu*
90. Teach a college course*
91. Watch a cremation ceremony in Bali*
92. Explore depths of the sea*
93. Appear in a Tarzan movie
94. Own a horse, chimpanzee, cheetah, ocelot, and coyote
95. Become a ham radio operator
96. Build own telescope*
97. Write a book*
98. Publish an article in *National Geographic Magazine*ial
99. High-jump five feet*
100. Broad-jump 15 feet*
101. Run mile in five minutes*
102. Weigh 175 pounds stripped*
103. Perform 200 sit-ups and 20 pull-ups*
104. Learn French, Spanish, and Arabic*
105. Study dragon lizards on Komodo Island
106. Visit birthplace of Grandfather Sorenson in Denmark*
107. Visit birthplace of Grandfather Goddard in England*
108. Ship aboard a freighter as a seaman*
109. Read the entire *Encyclopaedia Britannica*
110. Read the *Bible* from cover to cover*
111. Read the works of Shakespeare, Plato, Aristotle, Dickens, Thoreau, Rousseau, Hemingway, Twain, Burroughs, Talmage, Tolstoi, Longfellow, Keats, Poe, Bacon, Whittier, and Emerson*
112. Become familiar with compositions of Bach, Beethoven, Debussy, Ibert, Mendelssohn, Lalo, Milhaud, Ravel, Rimsky-Korsakov, Respighi, Rachmaninoff, Paganini, Stravinsky, Toch, Tschaikovsky, Verdi*
113. Become proficient in the use of a plane, motorcycle, tractor, surfboard, rifle, pistol, canoe, microscope, football, basketball, bow and arrow, lariat, and boomerang*
114. Compose music
115. Play *Clair de Lune* on the piano*
116. Watch fire-walking ceremony in Bali and Surinam*
117. Milk a poisonous snake*
118. Light a match with a .22 rifle*
119. Visit a movie studio*
120. Climb Cheops' pyramid*
121. Become a member of the Explorers' Club and Adventurers' Club*
122. Learn to play polo
123. Travel through Grand Canyon on foot and by boat*
124. Circumnavigate the globe*
125. Visit the moon
126. Marry and have children*
127. Live to see the 21st century [he was born in the first half of the 20th century]

*Indicates daydream or goal has been realized.

Students were required to consult atlases, encyclopedias, gazetteers, and other library resources to find the correct spelling of the names of exotic locales. The assignment also asked students to go a step further and imagine that one of their dreams had already been realized. One young woman's daydream becomes vividly imagined in the following writing sample.

The Dream

The mist parted and I looked around. There she stood in a fancy costume in the middle of a rink. The eyes of countless spectators were focused on her. I looked up and saw five colored rings above her head, suspended from the ceiling. She looked just like me. Carefully, still in my nightgown, I stepped onto the ice and moved toward the girl in the fancy costume. I had the feeling that she sensed that I was there, but neither she nor the crowd could hear or see me. I whispered "Good luck" to her. Suddenly, music began to play and I rushed to get out of her way.

Gliding, spinning, leaping over the ice, the girl was like a butterfly floating on air, barely touching the surface. Her jumps were beautiful and poised. She completed a double-axel with a perfect landing just as the lush music came to an end. Silence hung in the air for a second before bursts of cheering and whistling erupted from the large crowd in the auditorium.

The crowd grew quiet in anticipation as the marks from the judges began to flow from the loud speaker. "Six point 0, 6.0, 6.0, 6.0, 6.0, 6.0...." The crowd roared its approval. The girl who was me shook her head, fearing she had misunderstood. Her coach embraced her and exclaimed, "A perfect score. I am so proud of you!"

"Perfect score," the girl repeated to herself. And, then the scene changed. The mist parted and I had just enough time left to see the girl on the highest podium with the gold medal around her neck as the sound of "The Star-Spangled Banner" began to be heard.

The mist folded over, accompanied by a comforting blackness. The girl in the nightgown and the girl in the fancy costume became one, and I slept the sleep of peace.[3]

The daydreams assignment offers students a challenge to think about the creative ways in which they want to spend their lives. When the students turn in their lists of fifty daydreams and goals, a wise teacher makes a copy of each student's paper and places it in the student's writing folder. The lists students create are most revealing. They allow TalentEd teachers to better know the dreams and aspirations of their students. The assignment also helps teachers personalize education. When teachers know more about the daydreams their students have, they can recommend new books and articles to students who have indicated an interest in a given topic, for example, about space. The same teacher can also tell another student, who has evidenced an interest in the Galapagos Islands and its incredible fauna, about a public television special that is on the horizon dealing with that fascinating place. Teachers can also connect students who reveal similar interests in travel, careers, and avocations.

The student writings also reveal much about the creativity and writing talents of students. Provide students with possible suggestions, but leave plenty of room for individual creativity to surface. Students may write about one of their dreams coming to fruition via a front-page news story, or perhaps a *Sports Illustrated* or *Newsweek* cover story. They can pen journal or diary entries like the example shared here. Another student who may not want glory and fame may elect to keep her achievement a secret, and her writing will take the form of a top-secret document for the eyes of the President only.

Lots of variety can surface in the ways different teachers utilize the daydream assignment. One creative Vancouver, British Columbia, teacher has her students make posters based on their daydreams. She also discovered some insightful information about her students' values in the process as she reveals in these comments:

"My students made daydream books over a period of two months. We edited them and they have since been made into laminated posters. It is interesting to note that the students' daydreams have been honed from the acquisition of Porsches and Lamborghinis to the very core of their needs. One of my students, Tony, a foster child, finally abandoned the luxury cars and wrote that he wanted to be loved by one person forever. Shortly after, Tony was legally adopted. I, too, wrote a daydream book and enjoyed the opportunity to clarify my own life goals."[4]

Perhaps a fitting closing note for this chapter is a notion put forth by one of America's greatest patriots that is worth sharing with youth to underscore the importance of their possession of dreams for the future.

> I like the dreams of the future better
> than the history of the past.
> —Thomas Jefferson

Notes

[1] John Goddard, *Kayaks Down the Nile* (Provo, Utah: Brigham Young University Press, 1979), 319.

[2] Murry Suid and Roberta Suid, *Happy Birthday to U.S.* (Menlo Park, Calif.: Addison-Wesley, 1975), 53-54. Used with permission.

[3] Natasha Marin, "The Dream." Used with permission.

[4] Carol Smallenberg. Personal correspondence.

E Is for Entrepreneurship

The current interest that the private business sector is taking in education translates into a golden opportunity for TalentEd teachers to secure the talent and resources of business leaders in their communities in developing tomorrow's business leaders today. A study of entrepreneurship can also be a wonderful occasion for involving the cooperation and participation of parents in the education of students. Through almost any classroom, the teacher can locate many enterprising parents who will be willing to share their business acumen and experiences with students. Perhaps one parent owns her own television repair shop, while another busy parent works part time selling Mary Kay cosmetics or Amway products.

The word *entrepreneur* was coined in 1755 by French economist R. Cantillon and is derived from the French word *entreprendre*, meaning "to undertake." An entrepreneur is one who creates a business undertaking. A study of entrepreneurship is a superb opportunity for students to read, examine, and learn about creativity in action. Every day someone says, "Hey, I have a good idea. I know of a service or product that the people need. I am going to create my own business."

Of course, creating a business involves a lot more than just wishing it were so. Commitment and opportunity are necessities if the entrepreneur's dream is to become a reality.

Entrepreneurship is a fine way for TalentEd teachers to share the history of America's great free enterprise system with youth. It is also a fine opportunity for businessmen and businesswomen to share in the exciting work of educating young people. There are also many fine programs and resources that exist to help teachers and parents introduce students to the exciting world of entrepreneurship.

An initial activity in an entrepreneurship unit can be a student inquiry wherein each student chooses an entrepreneur—past or present—to study. Figure E.1, page 42, lists people whose entrepreneurial efforts are worthy of student investigation. A list of recommended resources students may consult for information in research for entrepreneur reports is found at the end of the chapter. The works of Nathan Aaseng, Steven Caney, and Mary Ellen Snodgrass are especially helpful. Figure E.2, page 43, is a reporting form teachers may desire to share with their students.

Fig. E.1. Famous entrepreneurs and their product or business.

Wally Amos	Famous Amos Cookies
Melitta Bentz	Coffee maker
Joshua Lionel Cowen	Model trains
Walt Disney	Animation
John Dryden	Prudential Insurance
Henry Ford	Automobile
Dan Gerber	Baby food
Robert de Graff	Pocket books
Cliff Hillegass	Cliff Notes
Steve Jobs	Apple Computers
Dr. John Kellogg and W. K. Kellogg	Kellogg's Cereals
Ray Kroc	McDonald's
Edwin Herbert Land	Polaroid Cameras
Sir Thomas Lipton	Lipton Tea Company
George Parker and Charles Parker	Parker Bros. Games
C. W. Post	Post Cereals
John D. Rockefeller	Standard Oil Company
Margaret Rudkin	Pepperidge Farm
Harland Sanders	Kentucky Fried Chicken
Richard W. Sears and Alvah C. Roebuck	Sears, Roebuck
Levi Strauss	Levi's jeans and other clothing
Sarah Breedlove Walker	Cosmetics
Sam Moore Walton	Wal-Mart
Aaron Montgomery Ward	Montgomery Ward
William Wrigley, Jr.	Chewing gum

■ ■ ■

E Is for Entrepreneurship 43

Fig. E.2. Entrepreneur fact-finding form.

Name of entrepreneur_____

Early history

    date of birth:

    birthplace:

    childhood experiences:

    education:

Adult life

    Best-known innovation or product:

    Company founded:

Impact of entrepreneur: How has the product or service changed society

Additional points of interest

Source of information

———————————————— ■ ■ ■ ————————————————

From *TalentEd: Strategies for Developing the Talent in Every Learner*, © 1993 Teacher Ideas Press, P.O. Box 6633, Englewood, CO 80155-6633

Entrepreneurship

One of the primary objectives of an entrepreneurship unit may be the realization of student-created businesses. Regardless of whether they open a one-time-only lemonade stand or develop a thriving desktop publishing company, students who create their own businesses have the potential to learn much about their own talents and skills, profits and losses, the free enterprise system, and the personal commitment and dedication it takes to succeed in the marketplace.

Marilyn Schoeman Dow is an international creativity consultant for schools and businesses and creator of the YES! Program of Young Entrepreneurs Symposia for Young Enterprising Students. She states that talented fifth- and sixth-grade students she works with in entrepreneurship projects learn and exercise skills that include time management, goal setting, critical thinking, career planning, research, leadership, ethics, innovation, creative problem solving, decision making, and building self-esteem.

In the YES! Program fifth- and sixth-grade students develop a business plan; create business cards, letterhead, stationery, and brochures; and present their business plans to symposia attended by business and community leaders, parents, and educators. One class of young entrepreneurs met with the governor of Washington State and appeared with him in a photograph on the cover of the Sunday magazine of the *Seattle Times*. The governor issued a special proclamation honoring the students and their entrepreneurship work. Many of the students are inspired to proceed with the implementation of their business ventures. Student businesses included the following:

Musik!	Live music for parties
Pounding Hooves	Clean, pick, polish horses' hooves
Silly Suds	Hand-carved soap animals
Petorama City	Pet care for small animals
Jon's Nursery	Plants in personalized pots
Crafty Leather	Personalized handmade leather crafts
Puffy Pillows	Handmade personalized decorator pillows
Lopsided Lollipop	Handmade cards and gifts
Yards Unlimited	Yard and lawn care
Mexican Recipes	Mexican cookbooks
Cards by Pony Express	Greeting cards delivered on horseback

As a preliminary activity to setting up their own businesses, students should complete an entrepreneurship selfstudy, a model for which is in figure E.3. The questions in a selfstudy should focus upon each student's strengths, personal likes, and the potential for business success in the marketplace. From the completed selfstudies, students should be able to determine whether they have the time, skills, and desire to create a business, and whether or not needs exist in the community for the products or services they want to provide. If students answer in the affirmative, then they can proceed to create their own business plans. Allow students time to share their business plans with the entire class or in cooperative learning groups. It may be fun to have students vote prizes to the most imaginative business plans and for those they believe to have the greatest potential for success.

Fig. E.3. Entrepreneurship selfstudy.

Name:

Age:

1. List your hobbies and leisure-time activities:

2. What skills and talents do you possess (e.g., speak a foreign language, play piano, word processing skills)?

3. Do any of your hobbies, leisure-time activities, skills, or talents suggest possible business opportunities? If yes, which?

4. List the products and services on which you most frequently spend money:

5. List five businesses where you most frequently spend money:

6. Are there any products or services you have trouble locating?

7. Are there products and services in your neighborhood that appear to be overpriced? If so, which?

8. Do your answers to questions 4-7 suggest possible markets for products or services you might offer? If yes, explain.

9. Do you prefer to work indoors or outdoors?

10. Do you prefer to work alone or with one or more partners?

11. With what age group(s) do you most enjoy working?

    5-12   13-17   18-25   26-59   60+

12. How many hours a week can you budget to starting and maintaining your own business?

13. Consider some of these student-created businesses:

    baby-sitting and child care   desktop publishing

    gardening and lawn care   tutoring   music lessons

    shopping service   pet care   photography

    T-shirt or greeting card design, production, and sales

    used book sales   cooking and baking

    household and garage cleaning

    Now, brainstorm a list of products or services you might be able to offer to one or more of the consumer age groups you indicated in question 11 above.

(Figure E.3 continues on page 46.)

Fig. E.3—*Continued*

14. Is there a potential market in your neighborhood or community for the products or services you have listed?

15. List friends, relatives, neighbors, and other acquaintances who own their own businesses.

    What questions might you ask these contacts about starting your own enterprise?

16. How might you advertise your potential business (e.g., posters, flyers, bulletin board notices)?

    Where might you advertise your potential business (e.g., grocery story, church, and YMCA bulletin boards, house-to-house distribution)?

17. What name will you give your business?

18. Outline your business plan or feasibility study. Consider the following:

    - information
    - product or service
    - name of business
    - potential market
    - start-up costs and investments (e.g., initial supplies, advertising)
    - ongoing expenses (e.g., cost of art supplies)
    - standard charges for products or services (e.g., hourly rate for baby-sitting)
    - number of hours a week you plan to devote to business
    - number of hours you need to work to make a profit

    Consider all expenses and all sources of income. Does your proposed business have a good opportunity for making a profit? Is the potential profit a fair exchange for the amount of time and energy your proposed enterprise will cost you?

    If you decide the last question in the affirmative, when do you plan to start your business?

The following is a very special entrepreneurship success story written by Marilyn Schoeman Dow.[1]

An Entrepreneurship Success Story:
The Sitter with the Art Bag

Karen said she wanted to be an entrepreneur. She was already a baby-sitter so she created her niche in the market by becoming the Sitter with Art Bag. After designing and hand-delivering her bright green business brochure, the phone jumped off the wall with client calls. Parents were eager to have Karen care for their children because when she comes to babysit, the children don't watch television, they do art projects. She created easy art projects for younger kids, and more difficult projects for older children. She found a retired art teacher in the neighborhood who mentored her as she selected art projects and materials.

Karen charged $1.50 per hour. Every seventh time she babysat was free to her customers. She sent cards to her clients' children on their birthdays. She established a card file on each child so that no child did the same project twice.

Her accounting was done on file cards. Karen used a five-column system that included a column each for income, expenses, savings, church tithe, and salary. Whatever money remained after her tithe became her salary.

The fifth-grader started her business in April. In August she had already hired a Santa Claus for a Christmas party for her clients. In March she made up a flier for her ten best clients offering them three free hours of baby-sitting in her home, with her mother joining them.

The business was so successful that Karen began considering expanding into two other areas. One was a referral service for sitters to handle the overflow demand for her services. The other was a baby-sitter training program.

In June her mother called me to say, "Marilyn, you've been instrumental in getting Karen's business started. I thought you would like to know that I promised her if she made $1,000.00 in her first year, I would give her some kind of special reward. Well, she made $1,070.00. Can you join us for lunch to celebrate!" What a joyous event it was!

Karen's accomplishment was remarkable, even if there had been no profit. She inspired many people through her interaction with children and adults and through her amazing success. Karen was a keynote speaker at the Young Entrepreneurs Symposium where the response to Karen's story was overwhelming. Word continues to spread. More students, parents, educators, and business people are exploring ways to get youth involved in business because of Karen's success story.

> Whatever you can do,
> or dream you can,
> begin it. Boldness
> has genius, power, and
> magic in it.
> —Johann Wolfgang von Goethe

Additional Entrepreneurship Activities

TalentEd Throughout the entrepreneurship unit, students should keep an entrepreneur's journal. When they read business articles, hear an entrepreneur speak, or plan strategies for their own businesses, they can put their notes and observations in their journals. The journal serves as a repository for all the notes, ideas, and observations students have during the unit.

TalentEd Tabitha Ruth Wexler, better known as "Turtle," is the central character in Ellen Raskin's Newbery Medal-winning novel *The Westing Game* (New York: Avon Books, 1978). She becomes a very successful entrepreneur. After reading her story, ask students to imagine "Turtle" joins forces with one of the famous entrepreneurs listed in figure E.1. What is the primary product or service of their corporation? How did these two meet? Does their company have a special corporate image such as leadership in fighting discrimination? Does the company have a unique marketing or advertising program? If so, how does it operate? Write the story of this company and the functions of its two chief executive officers (CEOs) through a stockholders report, a cover story for *Fortune* magazine, or in another creative manner.

TalentEd Invite students to interview local entrepreneurs in order to discover the benefits and drawbacks of owning your own business. Students may create question schedules with inquiries such as these: Why did you create your own business? How did you get started? What product or service do you provide? How many people do you employ? What marketing or business goals do you have? What are the drawbacks of owning your own business? What are the pleasures? Do you have any specific recommendations for people who want to create their own business?

Students can combine the responses they receive into articles for the class entrepreneurship magazine or make oral presentations of their findings to the class.

TalentEd Ask students to select a common tool or instrument in their environment such as a pen, notebook, or backpack. Give them five minutes to brainstorm all the possible uses they can think of for the items named. Did they think of some highly creative and unusual uses? A good test of potential for entrepreneurial success is creativity. Can students find new uses for old products? Can they think of new combinations? Success usually begins with new and fresh ideas.

TalentEd Encourage students to research the lives of young entrepreneurs, past and present. Such figures may include Thomas Edison, Steve Jobs, Cornelius Vanderbilt, Samuel Colt, and Jean Paul Getty. Students can share their findings through poster demonstrations, bulletin board displays, or via articles in the class entrepreneurship magazine.

TalentEd Taking a clue from the ideas suggested in chapter *A*, assign small groups of students the task of creating an ABC book on entrepreneurship, free enterprise, or consumer economics. Possible words might include *assets, advertising, banks, credit, checks, dividends, economy, federal income taxes, insurance, jobs, loans, liability, monopoly, quality, savings, values, Xerox,* and *zeal.* Of course, students need to explain the relationship of each of these things to their chosen theme. Xerox may represent an example of a free enterprise corporation that thrives on innovation. Profits cannot be declared until after federal income taxes have been paid. Quality products and services may be the key ingredients in the entrepreneurship success equation.

Negotiating

A successful entrepreneur must be able to negotiate. Any study of entrepreneurship may be a fine occasion for helping students develop and enhance their negotiation skills. The following negotiation simulation is fun for students to play and instructive in teaching them the art and skill of learning to negotiate. When students have played this simulation, they are more likely to better appreciate the art of negotiating, gain respect for good negotiators, understand the types of behaviors that play a key role in successful negotiations, and understand that negotiating involves taking risks.[2]

Negotiation Simulation

Divide the class into an even number of groups (e.g., 2, 4, 6, 8) that have a membership of not more than four. One-half of the groups will play the role of buyers for toy stores, and the other half of the groups will be sellers representing toy manufacturers. Make an overhead transparency of figure E.4, page 50, and show it to the entire class. Explain that this is a model of the brand new Super Sensational Toy. Provide each team with one hard copy of figure E.4. Give the sellers' instructions (fig. E.6, p. 51) *only* to the selling teams. Give the buyers' instructions (fig. E.5, p. 51) *only* to the buying teams. Give each team fifteen minutes to meet and to determine the buying or selling strategy that each will use. Each team is free to determine what it thinks the toy can and should do, and the buying or selling price for which each team will negotiate. *All* teams should consider the following questions during their fifteen-minute planning period.

What is the highest price we will pay/sell?

What is the lowest price we will pay/sell?

What concessions can we make or request?

What behaviors should we look for in the buyers/sellers?

What negotiating strategies might we successfully employ?

After the buying and selling groups have met for fifteen minutes, assign teams of buyers and sellers to meet and begin their negotiations. Allow paired teams approximately thirty minutes to negotiate and attempt to reach a satisfactory purchase/sales agreement. After about twenty minutes, it is a good idea to provide a break during which all the teams go back into a huddle, determine the progress they are making, and decide if any strategy changes need to be made. After the buying and selling teams have completed ten more minutes of negotiations, reconvene the entire class. Ask each group to report whether or not they succeeded in negotiating a deal. Once all groups have reported, debrief by talking about what behaviors helped the groups successfully negotiate. What behaviors or positions, or both, led to a stalemate? Who was the leader of each team? What behaviors did he or she exhibit? What did students learn about negotiating from the simulation?

Try the negotiations simulation again at a later date with a new product. Indeed, challenge creative students to propose and draw new products to use for the negotiations simulations.

(Text continues on page 52.)

50 *E* Is for Entrepreneurship

Fig. E.4. Super Sensational Toy.

Fig. E.5. Instructions to buyers.

You need this toy to satisfy customer demands.

You know that the sellers have a good reputation for the quality of their products and the fairness of their dealings.

You can buy at least 1,500 **Super Sensational Toys** with no fear of ending up with surplus merchandise.

You can realize a profit if you pay no more than $21.50 per item.

You have shopped extensively and you really believe this toy is among the best offered to toy stores this season.

─────────── ■ ■ ■ ───────────

Fig. E.6. Instructions to sellers.

You must sell as many **Super Sensational Toys** as possible for your company to have a successful marketing season.

Your asking price is $30.00 per toy, but you can ask more or less.

You have not previously done business with the buyers' company.

Advertising

One possible creative venture related to the study of entrepreneurship might be a study of advertising. Once entrepreneurs have developed ideas, products, or services, they need to attract consumers. It is not enough just to create a better mousetrap. The inventor/entrepreneur has to sell lots of mousetraps to have a successful business.

Advertising is a particularly appropriate area of study for youth because children and adolescents comprise a major target population for advertisers. First, youths have their own money to spend. Second, they have influence in how their family spends money. Finally, they represent a tremendous future market. Manufacturers of cereal, soft drinks, and jeans, for example, want to create brand loyalty among consumers who have sixty-plus years of purchasing power ahead of them.

Ask students to clip especially striking advertisements from magazines and newspapers and affix them in their entrepreneurship journals. Ask students to list and describe in their journals highly effective commercials they have heard or seen on radio and television. At the next class session have students share the best and most creative examples of advertising they have found. Categorize student responses according to the advertising techniques used. Share examples of advertising practices with students. Some of the major techniques are:

Star power: Rock musicians, actors, sports figures, and other famous people promote the use of the product or service.

Example: Michael Jackson loves Tubby Bunny Bubble Gum.

Snob-appeal: Ownership of the product or service launches the possessor into a special, elite class.

Example: Really popular kids always choose Tubby Bunny Bubble Gum.

Bandwagon: Everybody is using the product or service; don't be left out.

Example: Don't chance the shame of being the only kid in your class who doesn't chew Tubby Bunny Bubble Gum.

Emotional response: Appeal to sentiment (e.g., patriotism, guilt, love).

Example: Make this Valentine's Day special. Buy Tubby Bunny Bubble Gum to say "I Love You" to that extra-special person in your life.

Convincing statistics: Impress potential customers with numbers.

Example: Four out of five dentists recommend Tubby Bunny Bubble Gum for brighter, healthier teeth.

Jingle: Catchy musical pieces serve as memory-joggers for consumers.

Example (sung to a perky tune):

"Don't be Dumb! Dumb! Dumb!
Chew Tubby Bunny Bubble Gum!"

What additional advertising techniques can students describe? Ask students to brainstorm the various media utilized by advertisers. In addition to newspapers, magazines, radio, and television, what other media are used? Student responses may include the Yellow Pages, bulk-rate mail, flyers, and billboards.

As students begin to enjoy learning about advertising, it may be an appropriate time to invite advertising specialists to share their work with the class. The public relations officer for the school system might make an excellent guest. How does he or she promote education in the community? Representatives from advertising agencies may also be willing to share ideas and resources with students.

When students become more knowledgeable about various forms of advertising, form groups of four students. Each group should select a product or service they desire to promote. Students may select a product or service that one of them is developing for the entrepreneurship project. Alternatively, they may also create an entirely new product like Tubby Bunny Bubble Gum.

Each advertising agency group should complete a service contract with the entrepreneur for whom they will be working. Figure E.7 is one example. The teacher receives a copy.

Fig. E.7. Advertising contract.

Advertising Contract

Date:

Name of advertising agency:

Name of entrepreneur:

Product or service to be advertised:

Target population(s):

Media or medium to be used:

Specific television programs, periodicals, and so on to be used:

Advertising techniques to be used:

Slogans, jingles, and other special effects to be used:

Advertising product or artifact to be created:

Signatures of advertisers:

_____   _____   _____   _____

_____ ■ ■ ■ _____

From *TalentEd: Strategies for Developing the Talent in Every Learner*, © 1993 Teacher Ideas Press, P.O. Box 6633, Englewood, CO 80155-6633

E Is for Entrepreneurship

Once groups have determined the specifics of their advertising campaign, they should proceed to develop at least one artifact of the campaign. Multiple options may be suggested. Students may create a large poster representative of a giant billboard or a display ad. They may create a video of a television commercial they have planned. They may create an improvisation that portrays an element of the public reaction to their advertisement (e.g., a toddler pestering his mother to purchase Tubby Bunny Bubble Gum). Creative students will no doubt think of a wealth of other possibilities.

After allowing ample time for planning and production, have students share their advertising artifacts with the class. Give plenty of positive feedback to students, noting that the acts of creation and presentation always involve risk-taking. Ask the student audience to discern the target population of the artifact as well as the advertising techniques used.

If students desire to proceed into further adventures in advertising, teachers can suggest the ideas and activities listed below. The student activities are written as directions for ease of use by educators. Students may create advertisements for their own entrepreneurship projects or for existing products and services. In the latter case, they may want to present their ads and other creative products to local businesses or service organizations such as the United Way.

1. Create a jingle for a new product or existing service.

2. Collect a variety of advertisements representing different advertising techniques.

3. Rewrite, rescript, or redesign your least favorite television or display ad.

4. Design a means to test truth in advertising. How, for example, might you determine if a particular paper towel is truly more absorbent than competing brands? Conduct a test and reveal the results to classmates or in your class magazine, *The Entrepreneur.*

5. List the many different types of advertising you have noted: television, radio, newspaper, magazine, flyers, Yellow Pages, and so on. Use your detective skills to determine how you can find out the relative cost of advertising in each of these different media. What is the most expensive medium of advertising? Which is the cheapest? What are the rationales given to justify the greater costs of the more expensive media? Which media are most effective? How is effectiveness determined? Chart or graph the results of your research.

6. Be a good advertising detective. Find an agency or business that needs some advertising. Perhaps it is your 4-H Club, scouting group, or church. Maybe your library media specialist needs help in educating the community about many new library media services. Possibly your Aunt Jeanne has just opened a catering service and needs greater exposure for her business. How can you help? Once you have found an individual or group that can utilize your advertising skills, determine what kind of advertising your customer desires. Plan and execute an advertising campaign for your client.

7. Design and create a poster or bulletin board advertisement for a classroom or library media center service or product.

8. Design a logo for your class. Investigate the possibility of creating class T-shirts using your logo.

9. Become the classroom yellow pages chief. Ask each classmate to choose a skill, talent, or self-created product he or she would like to advertise in the classroom yellow pages. Be sure to provide specific instructions as to the designated size and length of ads allowed as well as the data each ad should contain. Review student submissions with your teacher. Assemble the ads and publish your classroom yellow (or purple, green, or pink) pages.

10. Create a parody of a well-known advertisement found in television, newspaper, radio, or magazine advertising. The parody should underscore the uniqueness of the original advertisement.

Culminating Activity: Entrepreneurship Magazines

Throughout the entrepreneurship unit, TalentEd middle and secondary students should be reading articles about the business world in such diverse publications as *Fortune*, *Forbes*, *Success*, *Black Enterprise*, *Business Week*, *Inc.*, *Entrepreneurial Woman*, and *New Business Opportunities*. Local businesses may be happy to donate or loan copies of such periodicals for classroom use.

As a culminating activity of the entrepreneurship unit, students can create their own business magazine. Their periodical can serve to showcase interviews they have had with business people, articles about their own entrepreneurship efforts, interesting highlights from their entrepreneur reports, and other entrepreneurship news. The magazine may also serve as a vehicle for displaying the creative advertisements each student or student group creates. Students may even wish to include business news about their success in negotiating for the Super Sensational Toy. Students may use one of the many software packages for newspaper and magazine formatting to create a professional-looking classroom business periodical.

Notes

[1] The author wishes to thank Marilyn Schoeman Dow for sharing the success story of one young entrepreneur. For additional information about the YES! Program, entrepreneurship seminars, and other products and programs for young people, contact Marilyn Schoeman Dow, ThinkLink, Schoeman Dow & Associates, 2515 39th Avenue SW, Seattle, WA 98116-2501, (206) 937-1626. Her book *Young Authors Conference: Kids Writing for Kids* ($14.95, plus $1.75 shipping & handling) contains recommendations for teaching entrepreneurship concepts.

[2] The negotiations simulation was suggested to the author by Paddy Domier of Glenwood, Minnesota.

Teacher Resources

BOOKS

Aaseng, Nathan. *Better Mousetraps: Product Improvements That Led to Success*. Minneapolis, Minn.: Lerner Publications, 1990.

Success stories of Eastman Kodak, Rolls-Royce Motors, Tupperware, and Pepperidge Farms.

_____. *Close Calls: From the Brink of Ruin to Business Success*. Minneapolis, Minn.: Lerner Publications, 1990.

This book tells the success stories of Heinz, Folger's, 3M, Hallmark, and Woolworth, among others.

_____. *From Rags to Riches: People Who Started Businesses from Scratch*. Minneapolis, Minn.: Lerner Publications, 1990.

The success stories of JCPenney, Hewlett-Packard, Sears, Roebuck and Company, Apple Computer, and Marriott.

———. *The Problem Solvers: People Who Turned Problems into Products*. Minneapolis, Minn.: Lerner Publications, 1989.

> The stories of John Deere, Edwin Land, Dan Gerber, and other entrepreneurs are revealed.

Barkin, Carol, and Elizabeth James. *Jobs for Kids*. New York: Lothrop, Lee & Shepard Books, 1990.

> Two experienced children's authors tell young people how to choose work they will enjoy and how to profit from their efforts. Many practical hints are provided, including determining how much to charge for one's products and services.

Caney, Steven. *Steven Caney's Invention Book*. New York: Workman Publishing, 1985.

> Half of this fine book is devoted to entrepreneurship stories.

Drew, Bonnie, and Noel Drew. *Fast Cash for Kids*. Hawthorne, N.J.: Career Press, 1991.

> The authors define an entrepreneur and then provide 101 ideas kids can utilize to become one. Suggestions are given on such diverse enterprises as creating bird feeders, being a golf caddie or a birthday clown, and creating a garage-cleaning business.

Dunnan, Nancy. *Entrepreneurship*. Englewood Cliffs, N.J.: Silver Burdett Press, 1990.

> A complete handbook for young people on starting a business. The author includes information on how to write a business plan, raise seed money, keep accurate records, and keep everything legal.

Kent, Calvin, ed. *Entrepreneurship Education: Current Development, Future Directions*. New York: Quorum Books, 1990.

> Articles on entrepreneurship in education at the elementary and secondary levels as well as college programs. The popular *Mini-Society* elementary program is discussed.

McDiarmid, Teena. *The CHP Book of Making Money*. Niagara Falls, N.Y.: CHP Books, 1988.

> A book for children about earning and managing money. The author suggests such business projects as a dog-washing business, home delivery of advertising flyers, snow removal services, and birthday party planners.

Snodgrass, Mary Ellen. *Late Achievers: Famous People Who Succeeded Late in Life*. Englewood, Colo.: Libraries Unlimited, 1992.

> The stories of Sarah B. Walker, Wally Amos, Mary Kay Ash, Harland Sanders, Ray Kroc, and Sam Walton are revealed.

Vare, Ethlie Ann, and Greg Ptacek. *Mothers of Invention: From the Bra to the Bomb, Forgotten Women and Their Unforgettable Ideas*. New York: William Morrow, 1988.

> Stories of remarkable women inventors and entrepreneurs.

ORGANIZATIONS

Junior Achievement, Inc.
National Headquarters
45 East Clubhouse Drive
Colorado Springs, CO 80906-4477
(719) 540-8000

Career Press, Inc.
180 Fifth Avenue
P.O. Box 34
Hawthorne, NJ 07507

Learn to Earn Program
National 4-H Council
7100 Connecticut Avenue
Chevy Chase, MD 20815
(301) 961-2934

Joint Council of Economics Education
432 Park Avenue South
New York, NY 10016
1(800) 338-1192

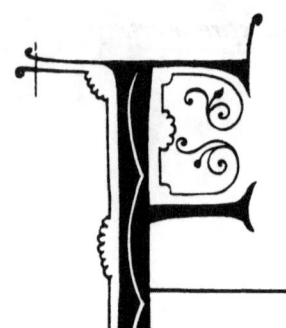

F Is for Fairy Tales

Once upon a time a wise person asked Albert Einstein what kind of reading fare should be given to young people who hoped to have careers in science. Einstein purportedly responded, "Why, fairy tales, of course."

Actually, Einstein could have made the same prescription for all careers. A creative teacher can teach virtually any content or process through the use of fairy tales. The same holds true of parents who wish to enrich their children's lives. To teach well, the teacher (or parent) must first engage the learner, and there are few motivators as powerful as the allure of the classic fairy tales.

The author has found fairy tales to be an excellent vehicle for teaching creative problem-solving strategies. For example, when introducing a creative problem-solving model (see chapter *I*, pages 99-102), dilemmas that might confront classic fairy-tale characters may be used effectively as sample problems. What might Little Red Riding Hood do if there was no woodsman nearby when she went to visit her grandmother? Since the content of the tale is familiar, the students are free to concentrate on the creative problem-solving steps.

First, students can analyze the situation. What facts do they know about Little Red Riding Hood's situation? Second, they can define the key problem facing Little Red Riding Hood. Once the key problem has been identified, students can brainstorm ideas about how Little Red Riding Hood might save herself and her grandmother. Once they have a list of alternatives, the students next propose criteria to use in evaluating their alternatives. Criteria might include: Will the proposed solution be ecologically sound? Can the proposed solution be quickly implemented? The final stage should find the students formulating a detailed plan of action to implement their proposed best solution.[1]

Children and adolescents love these lessons and learn valuable problem-solving skills quickly. Teachers who are interested in problem-solving strategies might try these additional prompts: How might the Three Bears Goldilocks-proof their house? How might Cinderella and her stepsisters learn to resolve their differences and live happily together?

The creative thinking abilities of fluency, flexibility, originality, and elaboration, defined in chapter *N*, may also be taught and reinforced using fairy-tale content. Fluency and entrepreneurial skills receive attention when TalentEd students simulate business planning as they engage in developing the nation's first all-children's mall, Cinderella City. Students can brainstorm the kinds of businesses they will invite to participate in their venture. New mall tenants might include Rapunzel's Hair Care, Little Red's Candy Basket, Alice's Card Shop, and Prince Charming's Formal Wear. While the entrepreneurs are busy concocting capital-raising schemes and planning the grand-opening festivities, the class architects can generate blueprints for the mall, and the designers can draw interior sketches for each of the mall's businesses.[2]

Students may also exercise fluency skills in generating many ideas for a classroom newspaper based on a fairy-tale motif or design. What kinds of newspaper news items, weather forecasts, sports stories, advice columns, classified advertisements, and stock market reports can be fashioned from fairy-tale data? Once they have generated many possible ideas, the class journalists can create a delightful and highly original edition of *The Black Forest Times*. Perhaps the top news story will be about the grand opening of the new Cinderella City Mall.

Students can observe flexibility in the diversity found in the many versions and tellings of a single fairy tale. A classic tale for such an exploration is "Little Red Riding Hood." The story of the little girl who invites trouble when she fails to obey her mother's instruction to be wary of strangers most likely traces its origins back to France's seventeenth-century storyteller, Charles Perrault. The Brothers Grimm told a similar tale more than a century later. Even today new versions of "Little Red Riding Hood" are being told. Students can receive a fine introduction to comparative literature by examining some of the many versions of this classic cautionary tale for children. Students may examine nearly three centuries of worldwide tellings of this classic story, collected by Jack Zipes in *The Trials and Tribulations of Little Red Riding Hood*. The stories in this anthology range from Perrault's French tale penned in 1697 to the humorous American version written by James Thurber.

60 F Is for Fairy Tales

Two diverse modern versions, representing East and West, may be compared by students. Trina Schart Hyman's 1983 *Little Red Riding Hood*, based on the Grimm version, was named a Caldecott Honor Book. In 1990, artist Ed Young won the Caldecott Medal for his Chinese version of the tale, *Lon Po Po*. A particularly useful tool for illustrating such comparisons is the Venn diagram, and figure F.1 highlights some of the similarities and differences found in these two tales.

Fig. F.1. A Comparison of *Little Red Riding Hood* **and** *Lon Po Po*.

Additional Venn diagrams might be used to compare the two wolves found in James Marshall's delightful retellings of *Little Red Riding Hood* and *The Three Little Pigs*. An alternate approach would be a comparison of the wolf in Marshall's *The Three Little Pigs* with the wolf Jon Scieszka created in *The True Story of the 3 Little Pigs by A. Wolf*. Diversity itself can be explored through examining the many strong ethnic and national female models found in folktales and fairy tales from around the world. See Suzanne Barchers's *Wise Women: Folk and Fairy Tales from around the World*.

Originality is practiced by students who create a new line of greeting cards based on fairy-tale themes to be sold in Alice's Card Shop at the Cinderella City Mall. What fairy-tale themes, characters, and allusions can they use to celebrate birthdays, graduations, and other special occasions? In a similar fashion, students can exercise their originality by creating a twelve-month calendar with a fairy-tale motif, also to be sold at Alice's. Each of the twelve picture panels may be a scene from a different classic tale.

Examples of artistic originality may be seen in the lush illustrations Fred Marcellino conceived for Malcolm Arthur's translation of Charles Perrault's *Puss in Boots*, and in the illustrations Trina Schart Hyman and Ed Young created for the previously cited *Little Red Riding Hood* and *Lon Po Po*.

Students can also observe other people's originality by examining some delightful retellings of classic fairy tales. In *The True Story of the 3 Little Pigs by A. Wolf*, Jon Scieszka gives the wolf a forum to tell his side of the story. He went to the first little pig's house of straw only to borrow a cup of sugar. Could he help it if his sneezing fit destroyed the little pig's home? *The Frog Prince Continued* is another whimsical treatment of a fairy tale in which Scieszka explores the proposition that perhaps the princess and the frog did not live happily ever after in the palace. He strikes a third time with *The Stinky Cheese Man and Other Fairly Stupid Tales*. Fiona French brings Snow White into the modern era marvelously in *Snow White in New York*. In a most clever twist, Bernice Myers tells the story of a young man who yearns to be a football star in *Sidney Rella and the Glass Sneaker*. Students will quickly see the resemblance between Sidney's story and that of Cinderella. Once students have read and enjoyed these creative stories, they will be motivated to create their own innovative retelling of classic fairy tales.

Story is not the only form such retellings and reflections can take. Fairy tales can inspire the creation of poems. Here, the word *wolf* is written vertically and then used as the focal point for a poem the wolf himself might write:

Why me?
am I the **O**nly villain?
it gets **L**onely always
being the **F**all guy!³

Junior scientists and inventors can meet fairy-tale problems with original responses. Ask these students to design and construct a scale model of a vehicle that could take Cinderella to the ball in the event that her fairy godmother fails to show and work her magic on the pumpkin. Young scientists can also research different approaches to planting and raising beans that Jack and his mother plant.

Creative questions can prompt original responses among students. What might have happened if Jack had planted carrot seeds instead of beans? In what ways might the story of the princess and the frog be different if the princess had turned into a frog when she kissed the frog prince? How might Cinderella and Prince Charming have experienced a different life if the prince had had a significant physical disability?

Even reluctant student writers show enthusiasm when they are asked to create fractured fairy tales. This writing activity is an excellent elaboration activity. To set the stage for fracturing, first give each student three or four index cards. On each card, they should write a simulated dictionary entry of a slang word or phrase. An example might look like this: Turkey (noun), someone or something that is flawed; for example, "That movie is a real *turkey*." Collect all of the cards, alphabetize them, and create a slang dictionary that students can use as they rewrite classic fairy tales with modern, and invariably comic, turns. Artistically talented students can achieve similar effects with pictures. They can illustrate Sleeping Beauty's story, or any other fairy tale, in the fashion of the latest teen music or dress craze.

Romance plays a big role in fairy tales. A lovely princess and a handsome prince meet, fall in love, wed, and live happily ever after. As an elaboration exercise, invite students to engage in some family research. How did their grandparents meet, court, and marry? The end result of their research can be an original fairy tale written about their grandparents. The final product makes a terrific anniversary present for grandparents.

One of the most delightful book creations in the past several years is *The Jolly Postman, or Other People's Letters* by Janet Ahlberg and Allan Ahlberg. Riding his bicycle, a jolly English postman delivers letters to fairy-tale characters that include the Three Bears, Cinderella, and B. B. Wolf, Esq. B. B. (Big Bad) Wolf's letter is delivered in care of Grandma's Cottage and consists of a letter from the law firm of

Meeny, Miny, Mo & Co., which informs Mr. Wolf that their client, a Miss Riding Hood, protests the wolf's wearing of her grandmother's clothing and orders Mr. Wolf to vacate her grandmother's cottage immediately.

Many opportunities exist for expanding and elaborating upon the ideas put forth in *The Jolly Postman, or Other People's Letters*. Students can assume the roles of the characters who receive mail from the Jolly Postman, and can create return letters for the Jolly Postman to pick up and deliver to others. B. B. Wolf's response to the firm of Meeny, Miny, Mo & Co. might look like this:

Harold Meeny, Attorney
Meeny, Miny, Mo & Co.
Deep Woods, Grimm City

Dear Mr. Meeny,

I have received your RUDE, accusing letter. Enclosed please find the signed lease for this property. If this harassment from you and Miss R. Riding Hood does not cease immediately, I will instruct my attorney, Mr. Mal Practice, of the firm of Shy Ster, Mal Practice, and F. Lee Bailiff, to sue for damages.

Legally yours,

B. B. Wolf

Enclosure

TalentEd students can write more letters for the Jolly Postman to deliver to fairy-tale characters who do not appear in *The Jolly Postman, or Other People's Letters*. They can also create dramatic improvisations involving the delivery of other goods and services using the prompts in figure F.2 for idea starters. Instruct students to choose one item from each column. Working in groups, they should create a three-minute pantomime or improvisation presenting a possible outcome based on their choices.

Fig. F.2. Prompts for fairy-tale improvisations—Black Forest deliveries.

Fairy-tale Characters	Item Delivered	How Delivered
Three Bears	Mail	Jolly Postman
Cinderella	Pizza	Storks
Snow White	Flowers	United Parcel Service
Red Riding Hood	Furniture	Harley Davidson
Jack & The Beanstalk	Baby	School bus
Rapunzel	TV and stereo	Semitrailer

Fairy tales are so versatile that they can even be used to teach reading skills. The author created the following reading lesson to acquaint middle school students with text patterns found in expository material.

Explain to students that there are four main models, or patterns, of writing found in their textbooks and other expository material. Main ideas may be stated at the beginning, middle, or end of a paragraph. In some cases, the main idea is so important that it is stated twice; first, at the beginning of a paragraph, and then restated in different words at the end. The particular model an author chooses will then dictate the placement of the supporting details that anchor the main idea. The four major writing formats can be illustrated with the schematics in figure F.3.

In model A, the main idea is stated first, and supporting details follow as sustaining evidence. In model B, this order is reversed. In model C, some of the supporting details precede the placement of the main idea. The main idea is stated halfway through the paragraph, and then followed by still more supporting evidence. Model D resembles model A; the first sentence states the main idea. Due to the importance of the main idea, however, it is rephrased in a summary statement in the final sentence of the reading passage.

Fig. F.3. Models of text writing.

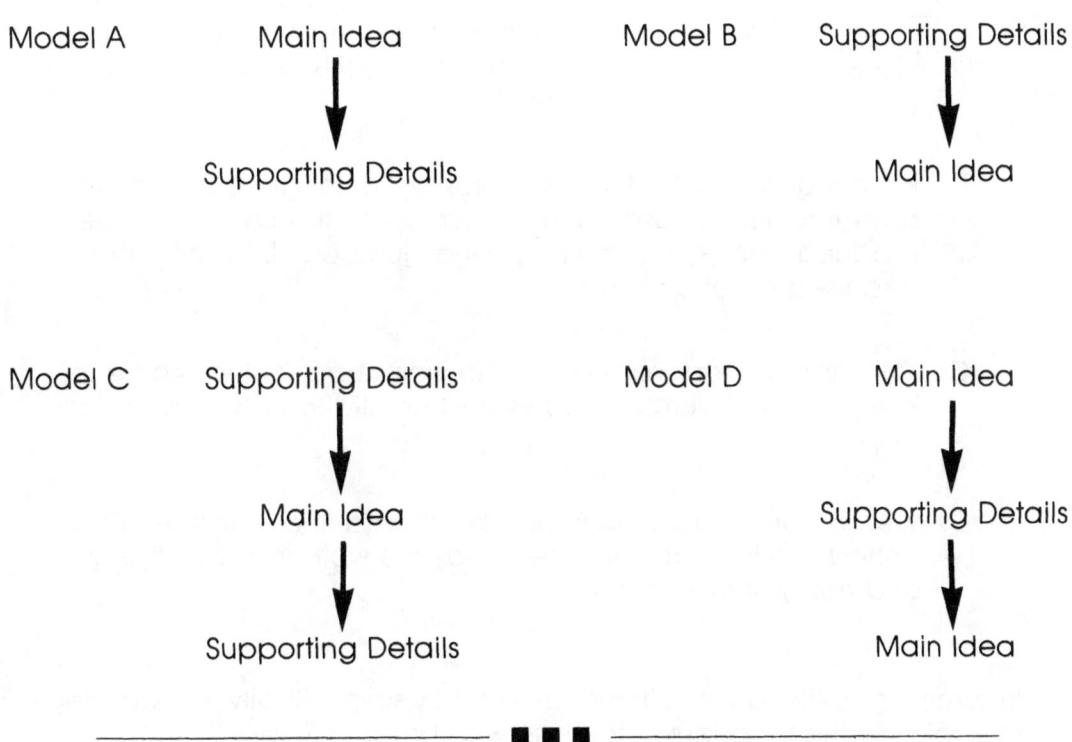

Once students understand the four models, ask them to read the four quite different versions of "Little Red Riding Hood" shown in figure F.4, pages 64-66. The students' task is to read the four versions and match each with the model, A, B, C, or D, that it represents. The correct answers are found at the end of the chapter, page 68.

(Text continues on page 67.)

Fig. F.4. Variations on a theme.

The writing in the following four versions of "Little Red Riding Hood" illustrates four models of expository writing. The problem for you to solve is this: Which version, 1, 2, 3, or 4, goes with which model?

1. Completing his investigation of the wolf-slaying in nearby Woodsville yesterday, local police chief John Doe said the case once again proved that those who break the law suffer in the end. Doe was referring to the wolf slain by the local woodcutter, Joe Badaxe. Police pieced together the case from assorted findings.

   A. The deceased wolf apparently discovered Miss R. Riding Hood tripping through the woods with a basket of goodies.

   B. He allegedly tricked her into taking a longer path to her grandmother's house, then he hurried to the same cottage, subdued the grandmother, and jumped into her bed, disguised in her clothing.

   C. Miss Riding Hood walked into the wolf's trap, but was able to keep out of his lurching paws and simultaneously scream for help.

   D. Woodsman Badaxe was nearby, heard the screams, and rushed into the cabin in time to slay the wolf and save the girl and her grandmother.

In summing up the case, Officer Doe proudly said, "Finally, the woods are safe; let this be a lesson to those who break our laws."

F Is for Fairy Tales 65

2. Above all else, let it be said: Crime doesn't pay! A certain wolf learned this recently when he tried to outsmart a young lady in an attempt to obtain her basket of goodies. While on her way to her grandmother's house to deliver food, the wolf spied the little girl and, upon discovering the contents of the basket she was carrying, he put into effect his plan to steal the basket. He rushed to the grandmother's cottage, overcame the grandmother, and hopped into her bed, disguised in her clothing. Shortly thereafter, the girl arrived and was puzzled to note that her grandmother looked strange. Her mother had advised her of her grandmother's illness, but this, thought the girl, was ridiculous. The young girl made several comments about the strange appearance of her grandmother (really the wolf), finally touching upon the size of her teeth. At this point, the wolf leaped from the bed and threatened to eat the child and her basket of goodies. All sorts of confusion reigned. The girl screamed and ran about. The wolf did likewise, chasing the young girl. Meanwhile, a nearby woodsman heard the strange goings-on, rushed to the scene, and saved the day by bashing the wolf's brains. The little girl and her grandmother were happily reunited.

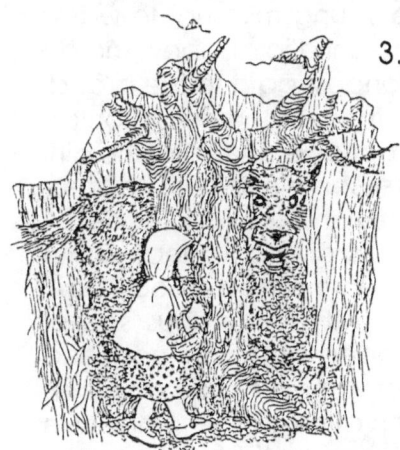

3. Man, like a long time back, you hear, there was a wolf that thought he was really bad. He tried to outsmart a neat-looking chick who wore red threads. He met the chick in an awesome place in the woods. Noticing that she had a basket of goodies, he laid some jive on her about what a hip day it was for a walk. Well, the chick fell for the dude's plan and took the long road to her granny's pad while this bad wolf dude trucked on over to the old lady's place, mean and fast. There he caught the old woman off-guard (she was groovin' on "General Hospital"), tied her up, and threw her in the closet. Then he put on some of the old lady's rags and hopped into her bed. The wolf thought that he was really bad. He said, "Man, I'm really cool and I'm gonna surprise little old red cap!" But, the wolf was to learn differently. He was about to find out that being bad doesn't always pay off. Meanwhile, the chick kept

(Figure F.4 continues on page 66.)

From *TalentEd: Strategies for Developing the Talent in Every Learner*, © 1993 Teacher Ideas Press, P.O. Box 6633, Englewood, CO 80155-6633

Fig. F.4. — *Continued*

coming through the woods and finally arrived at her granny's cottage. She took one look at the mess in granny's bed and knew it was a bad scene. The wolf didn't look like her granny at all. She let out some really loud vibes and a nearby woodsman rushed to her aid and wasted the wolf. Then the chick, her granny, and the woodsman had a real bash.

4. Many years ago, a large carnivorous mammal, frequently referred to as a wolf, meanly tricked and then attacked a young girl for the sole purpose of obtaining her basket filled with edibles, which would satisfy his hunger. He learned of the nutritious ingredients of the basket when he happened to cross the path of the young girl as she leisurely strolled through the same fertile, wooded area. The young lady had been sent into the woods by her mother to visit her ailing grandmother. It was hoped that the combined pleasure of receiving the basket of food and seeing the pretty young girl in her smart red costume would revive the ailing woman's spirits. The mother had specifically told the young miss not to waste time in the woods, but the wolf persuaded the child to disobey and do otherwise, sending her on the prettiest but longest path to the grandmother's humble abode. In the meantime, the wolf hurriedly took a shortcut and arrived at the elderly woman's cottage ahead of the girl. He forced the grandmother into a closet, dressed himself with appropriate garments from the woman's wardrobe, and took to her bed.

Soon the young lass arrived and immediately noted that something was wrong. She questioned the person in the bed about "her" strange appearance, finally commenting on the enormous size of "her" dentures. On this signal, the wolf leaped from the bed and began to chase the girl. The young lass screamed loudly and thus attracted the attention of a nearby conservation officer who, with great courage and boldness, faced the wicked wolf, slew him, and reunited the two frightened women. There are many stories of deceit and villainy known to man. Nevertheless, no story shows more clearly than this one that wickedness fails and goodness triumphs over evil.

■ ■ ■

There's virtually no end to the creative way teachers can use fairy tales. It is not surprising that Einstein recognized the value of fairy tales in developing creative minds through the speculation and sense of wonder they provoke. Fairy tales really are magical. TalentEd teachers wisely use them often and in imaginative ways.

Notes

[1] The use of fairy tales to teach creative thinking is further explored in Jerry D. Flack, *Once Upon a Time: Creative Problem Solving Through Fairy Tales* (East Aurora, N.Y.: D.O.K. Publishers, 1985).

[2] Many of the creative ideas suggested here appeared in Jerry D. Flack, "Those Fabulous Fairy Tales," *Teaching Pre-K-8* 20, no. 3 (November/December 1989): 64-67.

[3] See Flack, *Once Upon a Time*, 31.

Teacher Resources

Ahlberg, Janet, and Allan Ahlberg. *The Jolly Postman, or Other People's Letters*. Boston: Little, Brown, 1986.
  A delightful and creative work of art keyed to classic fairy tales. The author-illustrator team has also produced *The Jolly Christmas Postman*, Boston: Little, Brown, 1991.

Arthur, Malcolm, trans. *Puss in Boots*. Illus. by Fred Marcellino. New York: Farrar, Straus & Giroux, 1990.
  Perrault's tale of a sagacious and faithful cat is lavishly illustrated by Fred Marcellino in this Caldecott Honor Book.

Barchers, Suzanne, ed. *Wise Women: Folk and Fairy Tales from around the World*. Illus. by Leann Mullineaux. Englewood, Colo.: Libraries Unlimited, 1990.
  A collection of 61 folktales from around the world features strong, clever, and thoughtful women.

French, Fiona. *Snow White in New York*. New York: Oxford University Press, 1986.
  Glorious illustrations assist in the modern retelling of a classic tale.

Hyman, Trina Schart. *Little Red Riding Hood*. New York: Holiday House, 1983.
  Magical illustrations greatly enhance Hyman's retelling of the Grimms' version of this tale.

Marshall, James. *Little Red Riding Hood*. New York: Dial, 1987.
  A witty and charming telling of the classic tale of warning to children.

──── . *The Three Little Pigs*. New York: Dial, 1989.
  The poor wolf never has a chance when pitted against Marshall and his porcine hero.

Myers, Bernice. *Sidney Rella and the Glass Sneaker*. New York: Macmillan, 1985.

>Children of all ages delight in this modern adaptation of the Cinderella story wherein a young boy enjoys the hero's role.

Scieszka, Jon. *The Frog Prince Continued*. Illus. by Steve Johnson. New York: Viking, 1991.

>The author and illustrator have great fun contemplating what life in the palace might be like for the princess and the frog after the initial thrill of romance is gone.

———. *The Stinky Cheese Man and Other Fairly Stupid Tales*. Illus. by Lane Smith. New York: Viking, 1992.

>In this spoof of several classic fairy tales, famed characters get in each other's way and into each other's fairy tales.

———. *The True Story of the 3 Little Pigs by A. Wolf*. Illus. by Lane Smith. New York: Viking, 1989.

>The wolf finally gets an audience and tells his side of his confrontation with the three pigs.

Young, Ed. *Lon Po Po*. New York: Philomel, 1989.

>China is the setting for Young's gorgeous paintings and retelling of "Little Red Riding Hood."

Zipes, Jack. *The Trials and Tribulations of Little Red Riding Hood*. South Hadley, Mass.: Bergin and Garvey, 1983.

>A collection of Little Red Riding Hood tales representing more than 300 years of storytelling.

Answers to figure F.3:

1. Model D
2. Model A
3. Model C
4. Model B

Is for Garbage

Garbage might appear to be an unseemly topic, but there are educational riches to be mined in student investigations and projects focused on this broad subject. Garbage is an important topic of environmental studies, a subject of considerable contemporary inquiry. Archaeologists examine the garbage of the past. Today's junk will yield many stories in some future age. The possibilities are limitless for stimulating reading, writing, problem solving, and acting that students can be engaged in when studying the many aspects of garbage and the environment. The topic of garbage is approached in this chapter using one of the most effective models of curriculum design available to teachers today. Calvin Taylor's Multiple Talents model is popular with teachers because of its focus on finding and developing the many talents that students have, beyond traditional academic subject areas, such as math and English. It is a versatile model that can be applied to virtually any content focus. To illustrate its considerable potential value to TalentEd teachers, the study of garbage found in this chapter is modeled on the Multiple Talents model. For a discussion and two examples of the application of the model, please read the following.

One of the finest and most easily implemented teaching models is Calvin Taylor's Multiple Talents design. Dr. Calvin Taylor, professor of psychology at the University of Utah, completed his doctoral work at the University of Chicago under the direction of L. L. Thurstone, one of the twentieth century's foremost researchers on the nature of intelligence. Dr. Taylor extended and applied Thurstone's factor analysis work with intelligence in creating his own model of multiple talents.[1] In turn, Taylor's work has been applied and greatly popularized by Dr. Carol Schlichter of the University of Alabama in a nationally replicated model that has come to be known as Talents Unlimited.[2] Readers may further note similarities between Taylor's theory of multiple talents and the more recent scholarship of Howard Gardner and his evolving theory of multiple intelligences.[3]

First articulated in the 1960s, Calvin Taylor's model of multiple talents included six talent areas: academic, planning, productive thinking, decision making, forecasting, and communicating. More recently, he has added three other talent categories: discerning opportunities, human relations, and implementing.[4]

The heart of the Multiple Talents model is a deliberate and conscious attempt to urge educators to move beyond a solitary focus upon academic talent. Taylor provides a multidimensional view of giftedness. In his many writings, Taylor argues persuasively that educators reach more students, and prepare all students better, when they teach using a multiple talents focus: "If we limit ourselves to cultivating merely one talent (academic), only fifty percent of our students will have a chance to be above average in classes. Across six talents, about ninety percent will be above average and almost all other will be nearly average in at least one talent area."[5]

Moreover, Taylor claims, when educators cultivate other talents and cease to focus exclusively on academic talent, they may actually see, over time, growth in academic success by students who have not previously enjoyed such success. Accomplishments in talent areas such as forecasting and productive thinking build students' self-esteem and confidence, and tend to facilitate their growth in academic talent.

The Multiple Talents model should appeal to TalentEd teachers for at least two reasons. First, the use of the model invites educators to develop a broader and more inclusive definition of gifted, talented, and creative students. Taylor does not just focus upon one identifiable talent, academic; rather, he argues that schools should focus upon a variety of talents that are generally recognized by society as being of need and value. From a clinical standpoint, it is quite appropriate to provide accelerated and extremely rigorous programs for five to ten percent of the student body that are academically talented. Despite some heroic efforts to the contrary (Jaime Escalante of *Stand and Deliver*), it is probably not overly realistic to assume that a significantly larger population of students would choose programs of acceleration. However, a great many students will benefit from the increased self-esteem that may well be the result of exposure to multiple talents instruction. The student who barely makes the grade in English or mathematics classes may shine when the classroom focus shifts to communicating, productive thinking, and planning.

A second plus of the Multiple Talents model is that it focuses attention on the whole child or adolescent. Whereas traditional "academics-only" approaches concentrate exclusively upon students' schoolhouse learning, multiple talents instruction provides an environment in which students are provided with opportunities and encouragement to develop all their talents.

Concrete examples of how these two benefits may be realized are found in two student profiles. Carlotta's reading level is below her school grade placement, and her report card marks are in the *C* and *D* range. She is struggling in math and often appears disappointed that she cannot achieve better grades in school. She wants to succeed. She enjoys her English class, but rarely does better than *C* work on spelling tests and grammar work. One day her English class reads a story about Amelia Earhart's life and disappearance. Knowing of her love for creative dramatics, the teacher asks Carlotta if she would like to produce and direct a class dramatic presentation based on the Amelia Earhart reading. Throughout the next two weeks, Carlotta's talents flourish. She works with one of her academically talented classmates to create a script that displays polished writing and an absence of misspellings. She uses her decision-making talent to determine which scenes from the story to accent, and to choose the best cast possible. She plans all the rehearsals, skillfully juggling students' various schedules. She effectively communicates with the cast members, reminding them of the clothing they need to wear and the props they must furnish. Almost single-handedly, Carlotta produces and directs a highly entertaining play about Amelia Earhart that is enjoyed not only by her only English class, but by other classes as well. Because her special and unique talents are recognized, valued, and *developed*, Carlotta's English grade improves to an *A*. A wise teacher realized that focusing upon her areas of strength first would help Carlotta improve her accomplishments in nearly all other areas, including the academic.

John is academically gifted. He appears to have a positive self-concept and seems to enjoy school. He is mostly successful in all academic areas and receives *A* and *B* grades with apparent ease. The *B* grades are not the result of academic challenge. They reflect the many assignments John has lost or forgotten to complete. John's teachers complain that although he is bright and mostly a joy to have in class, they become frustrated with him because he never seems able to plan beyond the moment at hand. The critical point in John's story is that a potentially serious problem looms on the horizon, if his weakness in the area of planning talent is not addressed and corrected. As he matures and his academic work becomes increasingly more demanding, he will not be able to afford to miss key assignments. His lack of skill and success in planning may ultimately dominate his behavior and spoil his chances for success, even in his strength area, academic talent.

In these two profiles, readers should see at least two of the many ways this model can be used positively in the instructional guidance of youth. Exposure to a wide variety of activities and strategies across many talent areas is good for all students. However, students who already are stars in the academic arena, and who feel good about their school experiences as a result of this success, may definitely profit from increased exposure to opportunities to build confidence in areas where they are not so gifted. Conversely, students who display weaknesses in exclusively traditional academic settings may find new confidence when educators consciously find their talent areas, and provide more opportunities for success.

Notes

[1] Calvin W. Taylor, "Cultivating Simultaneous Student Growth in Both Multiple Creative Talents and Knowledge," in *Systems and Models for Developing Programs for the Gifted and Talented*, Joseph S. Renzulli, ed. (Mansfield Center, Conn.: Creative Learning Press, 1986), 306-351.

[2] Carol Schlichter, "Talents Unlimited: Applying the Multiple Talent Approach in Mainstream and Gifted Programs," in *Systems and Models for Developing Programs for the Gifted and Talented*, Joseph S. Renzulli, ed. (Mansfield Center, Conn.: Creative Learning Press, 1986), 352-390.

[3] Howard Gardner, *Frames of the Mind: The Theory of Multiple Intelligences* (New York: Basic Books, 1983).

[4] C. June Maker, "Calvin Taylor: Multiple Talent Approach," *Teaching Models in the Education of the Gifted* (Baltimore, Md.: Aspen Systems, 1982), 293-325.

[5] Calvin W. Taylor in Rita Cipalla Bobowski, "The Care and Feeding of Talent," *American Education* 14, no. 8 (October 1978): 44.

G Is for Garbage

Figure G.1 provides educators with a list of action descriptors for each of Taylor's six critical talent areas: academic, planning, productive thinking, decision making, forecasting, and communicating. It parallels the list of action verbs educators can use when translating the *Taxonomy of Educational Objectives: Cognitive Domain*, edited by Benjamin Bloom, into classroom teaching practices (see figure G.2). Curriculum planning is greatly enhanced when these models are used in tandem to develop units of instruction. The action verbs from Bloom's Taxonomy may be used as question stems and activity prompts to facilitate student learning across the entire spectrum of cognitive activities that are typically found in traditional academic talent settings. Taylor's model, as expressed in the list of six descriptors in figure G.1, serves to remind educators to provide experiences for students that move them beyond academic talents into other significant talent domains.

Fig. G.1. Calvin Taylor's Multiple Talents model.

Academic Talent	Communicating Talent	Planning Talent
Classify	Demonstrate	Coordinate
Collect	Sketch	Designate
Select	Perform	Implement
Recall	Inform	Budget
Map	Translate	Arrange
Identify	Propose	Initiate
Name	Explain	Plan
Locate	Announce	Organize
Memorize	Show	Provide
Diagram	Articulate	Develop

Productive-thinking Talent	Decision-making Talent	Forecasting Talent
Compose	Compare	Project
Alter	Value	Extrapolate
Change	Determine	Propose
Design	Defend	Perceive
Modify	Discriminate	Imagine
Reverse	Disclose	Hypothesize
Rewrite	Rate	Assume
Originate	Conclude	Predict
Construct	Assess	Contemplate
Create	Judge	Explore

■ ■ ■

Fig. G.2. Bloom's *Taxonomy of Educational Objectives: Cognitive Domain.*

Knowledge	Comprehension	Application
Define	Discuss	Illustrate
List	Explain	Demonstrate
Recall	Review	Translate
Name	Report	Sketch
Repeat	Locate	Dramatize
Memorize	Identify	Operate
Cite	Generalize	Complete
Recognize	Translate	Solve
Report	Summarize	Show
Label	Illustrate	Practice

Analysis	Synthesis	Evaluation
Analyze	Create	Judge
Experiment	Design	Compare
Contrast	Construct	Evaluate
Diagram	Compose	Rate
Inspect	Propose	Select
Solve	Plan	Assess
Differentiate	Redesign	Decide
Interpret	Hypothesize	Verify
Classify	Translate	Rate
Categorize	Imagine	Determine
Dissect	Fashion	Appraise

■ ■ ■

There is, admittedly, some overlapping. The Taylor model includes academic talent that closely corresponds to Bloom's knowledge and comprehension categories. The synthesis category of Bloom's Taxonomy is similar to Taylor's productive-thinking talent category. Nevertheless, by keeping both lists close at hand while writing curricula, educators are reminded to stretch students academically, as well as to create opportunities to move students beyond academic areas and into other valuable talent development areas.

Dr. Taylor's recently added talent areas of discerning opportunities, human relations, and implementing are not included in figure G.1. Although these are certainly valid talent areas, it is the author's belief that they can be addressed and subsumed within the first six talents. That is, discerning opportunities appear to be attributes of forecasting talent, human relations activities fall into the category of effective communication, and implementing talent is part of a broad understanding of planning.

74 G Is for Garbage

It should be recognized that the use of the Multiple Talents model does not mean teachers have to plan five times more activities for students than they do when planning for the traditional academic talent classroom. Rather, the use of this model serves as an invitation or inducement to provide students with incentives and more opportunities to *use* the information and data they acquire in new domains and applications in the academic talent arena, and in ways that are often personally more meaningful and satisfying. The following sections discuss applications for the first six of Taylor's talent areas.

Academic Talent

Academically talented students perform well those tasks traditionally associated with schoolhouse learning in society. Such students are typically identified for programs for gifted and talented youth. They are students who function extremely well in the academic domain. Academically talented students are able to

1. collect and classify information,

2. name parts,

3. compile lists,

4. record correct data, and

5. build a substantial knowledge base.

One could easily add such phrases as "research significant topics," "map important data," and a host of other descriptors of traditional scholastic behaviors and pursuits.

In examining the fascinating topic of garbage, there are many avenues of knowledge-based building, research, and inquiry that talented students may pursue. They may initially collect, read, and learn more about garbage and environmental issues from service organizations (e.g., the Sierra Club) and government pamphlets, books, and periodicals. One of the most interesting publications is the magazine titled *Garbage: The Practical Journal for the Environment*. *Garbage* features articles on the history of garbage; timely and relevant articles about pollution and recycling tips; and information about individuals, companies, and government agencies that are working to solve problems created by garbage. For further information about this periodical, contact *Garbage: The Practical Journal for the Environment*, 2 Main Street, Gloucester, Massachusetts 01930. Another periodical of note is *E: The Environmental Magazine*, published by Earth Action Network, Inc., 28 Knight Street, Norwalk, Connecticut 06851.

Legal eagles may engage in an academic pursuit to ferret out information about legal matters related to refuse. There have been many lawsuits and legal actions involving pollution and damage to the environment. Students may learn about the Environmental Protection Agency, its history, its duties, and its effectiveness. What are the local and state laws respective to litter on streets and highways? Students may be interested to learn that in 1988, the United States Supreme Court, by a 6-2 vote, ruled that police may freely sort through a person's trash without a search warrant. In an insightful comment about the importance of garbage, Chief Justices William Brennan and Thurgood Marshall stated, "A single bag of trash testifies eloquently to the eating, reading, and recreational habits of the person who produced it."[1]

The Justices' remarks suggest yet another academic pursuit. Just how much garbage do people create? A provocative and insightful assignment involves asking students to monitor their own trash, or that produced by their families, over a given period of time, such as one week. One Colorado Springs, Colorado, science teacher gives each of her students large plastic trash bags on the Monday of a given week when the students are examining environmental issues. The students must carry the trash bags with them for a week, depositing in them all the trash they create throughout that time. On Friday of the given week, the students weigh the trash they have created, analyze the contents, and categorize the types of trash found. Invariably, students are surprised by the volume of trash they collect in just one week.

A New Jersey elementary teacher asks her students to examine trash created by their families for one month. Students itemize and list the contents, and note those things that might be recycled or used in other ways. One example of the search for new uses involves the ubiquitous plastic bread bag. Once the bread has been consumed, the crumbs found in the bag can be shared with birds. The plastic bag might be used for collecting the week's coffee filters and grounds. A second look may indicate that the coffee grounds could also be recycled in the garden, leaving only the plastic wrap and the coffee filters.

Class historians may want to examine how technology has changed the kinds of garbage that exist. A good student investigation would include a comparison of the kinds of trash and refuse that existed in 1900 in the United States, and a comparison of 1900 conditions with those of today. Further inquiries might look at changing ways of hauling or disposing of trash across a century of industrial technology and progress. Historians may also want to determine who some of the pioneers have been in the fields of waste management and recycling.

Students with a love for words may compile a glossary of terms for use by their classmates. An inquiry may begin with a search for the derivation of the word *garbage*. A student-generated glossary may include terms such as: *air*, *dump*, *ecology*, *environment*, *garbology*, *habitat*, *landfill*, *litter*, *nature*, *pollution*, *refuse*, *trash*, *waste*, and *wildlife*.

Still other students may want to consult books such as Lynne Cherry's *A River Ran Wild* and John Javna's *Fifty Things Kids Can Do to Save the Earth* in order to better learn about individual action and responsibility with respect to the environment.

Communicating Talent

Students who have a talent for communicating are those who exhibit fluency with words, thoughts, and ideas, or who transmit messages to others with a high degree of effectiveness. Students who are especially adept in communications are able to

1. tell a story,

2. express feelings,

3. recount an adventure,

4. summarize information, and

5. paint a picture.

Communication talent is not limited to verbal exchanges. Students may impart information as well as attitudes (e.g., enthusiasm) expressively through many media, such as art, drama, and pantomime.

Students may communicate information and feelings about the subject of garbage in myriad ways. Perhaps one inquisitive student can interview the mayor or the city's pollution watchdog about steps currently being taken in the community to handle waste efficiently and effectively. The student utilizes good communication skills both in the first stage, interviewing, and in the second stage, reporting or sharing what he or she has learned. Other creative youths may attempt to convince their classmates to develop greater recycling habits through the creation, production, and showing of a video they create and share. Perhaps their video will emphasize the three Rs of environmental concern: reduce, reuse, and recycle. Students interested in gauging public support for recycling efforts may canvass their neighborhood to find out how often citizens are engaged in recycling efforts. Results of the canvass may be communicated via the use of graphs, maps, charts, and other visuals.

Many of the ways students can communicate effectively involve writing skills. Students may write letters to the editor suggesting ways all citizens in the community can alleviate waste problems. Similar letters might be forwarded to the school board about ways and means to reduce waste in the schools.

A creative means of communicating concern for the environment may be expressed through the use of imaginative writing. Students can write obituaries for items of trash or refuse they find on the school grounds. The obituaries might conclude with suggestions for ways that the lives of other objects might be saved through recycling.

Students can imagine themselves as members of the animal kingdom. What message do they want to communicate to humans? What items of trash or garbage pose particular threats? What plea might an otter, bear, whale, hummingbird, or duck deliver to humankind? What might be the most effective way of communicating the message?

Students who communicate best when afforded the use of props may want to first create puppets or marionettes from recycled garbage, such as rolled-up newspapers or paper towel tubes (for arms and legs), leftover string from packaging, and empty plastic milk jugs (for the heads). Once a puppet or marionette is created, students can use the puppet to voice a message of environmental concern to fellow classmates.

Students may work in cooperative groups to create ABC banners, posters, or books about the twenty-six ways, one for each letter of the alphabet, that people can become more garbage-conscious and more environmentally responsible.

Planning Talent

Students exhibiting planning talent are those who can get the job done. They are students who are able to

1. convert ideas into action plans,

2. implement strategies,

3. budget time and resources,

4. organize separate tasks into a meaningful whole, and

5. designate tasks and responsibilities.

Many are the gifted and talented students with great ideas who crash their ships of opportunities and expectations on the rocks of procrastination! Perhaps no student is as frustrating to teach as the one with great talent who continually disappoints self, parents, and teachers with half-hearted efforts and incomplete assignments. These students have great potential, but it is never realized. Of course, such behavior patterns often lead to unsatisfactory adult life patterns.

Students need to be taught how to become effective planners. They are not born with such skills. Studies of garbage, trash, and creative recycling provide ample opportunities to help students acquire, sharpen, and practice planning talents. One of the most imaginative and effective means of doing this is through the use of the celebrity trash drive.

A Celebrity Trash Drive

In an age when students may have cellular phones and 800 and 900 telephone numbers at their ready disposal, letter writing has become a lost art. Students lack experience with letter-writing skills and may well undervalue their relevancy and importance. The Celebrity Trash Drive is a highly motivating and highly effective way to teach kids the importance of letter-writing skills. Each student chooses three to five favorite famous people, and uses letter-writing skills to request an item of trash from each celebrity for a class display and possible auction. One creative class in Utah secured funds for an overnight class field trip by soliciting celebrity trash, displaying it for a week in the school's activity center, and auctioning it off during an extended lunch period, with the school principal serving as the auctioneer. Because most celebrities are not easily reached in person or by telephone, the best communication medium is a letter of request. As students do not want to appear illiterate in the eyes of their idols, they will pay attention to learning proper letter-writing skills.

Begin by letting students know that a 50 percent response rate on surveys and requests is considered a good or high rate of return. Therefore, they will not want to select only one celebrity. Rather, they should choose a minimum of three to five people to whom they will send requests. The school library media specialist will be a special resource in helping students locate addresses of authors, politicians, movie and television stars, and recording artists. Most authors may be contacted through their publishers. Local radio or television stations may also be able to provide the addresses of entertainers or, at least, the addresses of major talent agencies who represent them. Periodicals such as *TV Guide* often provide addresses of favorite programs as well as network television addresses. The many editions of *Who's Who* generally provide the addresses of the subjects profiled. A good brainstorming activity may be the listing of other resources students might examine to locate addresses of celebrities.

Discuss with students the form of letters of request and purpose of their letters. Discuss the main parts of a letter including the letterhead, if school stationery is used (highly recommended), the date line, inside address, salutation, body, complimentary close, and signature. Also talk about the specific purpose and function of their letters. The following questions and prompts may be put to students.

> What is the purpose of your letter? State this in your first draft.
>
> What is the best way to say what you need to say?
>
> What is the best way to say what you would like to say?
>
> How much overlap is there between the latter two things?
>
> In what order should you put these things in your letter?

Ask students to work in pairs as they plan what they need and want to say in their letters. This will give each writer an audience. As students move through the prewriting process, it may also be useful to provide them with a sample letter that minimally states the things that must be included.

Such things would include: the purpose of the Celebrity Trash Drive; how the trash will be utilized to raise money for an educational project or a recycling effort; possible deadlines for receipt of the celebrity trash item(s); and a generous, advance thank-you. Working in their teams, students should move through at least two or three drafts of their letters, becoming increasingly concerned about spelling, construction, and grammar.

Students across the nation have had good fortune with celebrity trash drives. Occasionally, favorite soap opera casts autograph a day's script and send it along with a cast photograph to students. Most state and national public officials can be depended upon to send students a copy of the *Congressional Record* or some other item. An athlete may send a worn-out tennis shoe. Singers may forward autographed audio tapes or compact discs.

The Celebrity Trash Drive offers golden opportunities to develop both writing and planning skills. Students can plan and execute the display of the items once they are received; plan an auction of the items; and plan ways to effectively use the proceeds of the auction for a good cause, such as a field trip, purchasing a video on recycling for the library media collection, purchasing trees to plant on the school grounds or in the community on Arbor Day, and a myriad of other possibilities. Of course, a vital and critical ending activity is the writing and mailing of thank-you notes to the celebrities who took the time to make the project work.[2]

Throughout the class participation in the Celebrity Trash Drive, teachers may encourage the development of student planning skills by helping students learn to plan and implement strategies, budget time, meet deadlines, and organize resources. One planning strategy that is highly successful is the use of the backplan. The dynamics are simple. Students brainstorm all the tasks that must be completed in a project in order to realize a successful completion. Next, students assign dates and time periods needed for each task. Once students have identified the work times needed and deadlines, they plan a chronology or timeline for their projects, working backwards from the date of completion to the date of initiating the study. Hence, if Tom is to complete his environmental research study by April 6, he starts his plan with that date, and outlines all the things he must do in the preceding days and months in order to have his project finally and successfully completed by the target date of April 6. Through the use of the backplan, students can closely monitor their own progress. By frequently consulting their backplan schedule, they can continually keep track of whether or not they are progressing satisfactorily or falling behind.[3]

Productive-thinking Talent

Creatively talented students are those who dazzle teachers, their peers, and ultimately, society with their originality or productive thinking. Creatively talented students are able to

1. produce a large number of ideas,

2. originate unusual ideas and products,

3. compose innovative works,

4. invent new products and solutions, and

5. modify and successfully manipulate environments.

One of the most obvious ways students can practice productive-thinking behaviors is through creative thinking exercises and creative writing tasks. The possibilities to tantalize creative young minds are limitless. The ideas listed in figure G.3, pages 80-82, represent beginning points in the wealth of creative prompts that TalentEd teachers may share with students.

(Text continues on page 83.)

Fig. G.3. Creative thinking and writing ideas.

1. How might our city's sanitation department successfully employ an artist-in-residence?

2. How might garbage trucks be made more attractive?

3. What might citizens do to make their trash appear more attractive, and the trash collector's job more pleasant?

4. Write and produce a video commercial about waste management or recycling.

5. How might students solve the problems of waste in the school cafeteria? List ten solutions.

6. Draw before-and-after scenes of an oil spill.

7. Design a pollution-free city. Build a model.

8. Author an "Environmental Ethics Pledge" that every citizen should cite.

9. Compose original responses to these "What if?" questions:

    What if all garbage was launched into outer space?

    What if plastic had never been invented?

    What if each family had to personally dispose of all their trash?

    What if trees could no longer be used to make paper?

    What if taxes were determined by the amount of garbage families generate each year?

    What if automobiles were completely banned tomorrow?

10. Use your imagination! What damage to the environment might you create if you were

    a broken glass bottle?   a discarded candy wrapper?

    automobile exhaust fumes?   a rusty can?

    a rusty nail?   raw sewage?   a bottle cap?

    a partially used can of insect repellent?

11. Imagine that you are a discarded Reebok shoe. Your top is tattered and your sole is worn thin. What adventures have you had? What "trashy" tales can you tell? Write your autobiography.

12. You find yourself in a large waste dump. No food or water in sight. How did you fare so badly? How will you survive?

    Write a seven-day journal of your experiences.

13. You are a reporter interviewing the garbage residing in the local garbage dump. Use the writer's tool of personification. Give some life to the objects in the dump. Make an old tire or battery speak and tell his or her life story. "Whom" or what do you interview? What questions do you ask? What answers do you receive? Write up your interview as a feature story for the Sunday edition of the newspaper.

14. List fifteen new uses for scrap paper.

    List fifteen new uses for empty milk cartons.

    List fifteen new uses for once-used aluminum foil.

15. List the types of containers one might find in a kitchen. These might include coffee cans, egg cartons, salt boxes, soup cans, plastic milk jugs, and spice bottles. Make a chart, according to the example below, listing different types of containers in the first column. In the second column describe how the given container might be altered to put it to a new use. In the third column state the new use.

Container	Alteration	New Use
Egg carton	Paint	Desk tray to hold paper clips, rubber bands, erasers, and so on.

16. Create some "litter-a-ture." Go to the school yard on a nice, sunny day and select an object of refuse or a natural item such as a stone or leaf. Return to the classroom and use personification to tell the life story of the found object. A "vegta-fable" is one such example.[4]

(Figure G.3 continues on page 82.)

Fig. G.3—*Continued*

A Vegta-fable

Alice was a very timid little flower, quite sensitive to the world around her. Often her shyness would envelop her; this usually happened at the big dances, where all the leaves and twigs would blow over for a good time. Alice never had fun at these parties. Everyone was so loud and noisy she would be ignored. Once in a while an old, withered leaf would speak to her, but she did not want an old leaf. She wanted a handsome young twig to notice her.

At one of the get-togethers a dashing young stick had asked her to dance, but she blushed and stammered so much he left. This incident left Alice even more shy than before. Still, she wanted to dance with someone.

The last party before winter was held one brisk night in autumn. Alice was alone, as usual, when an extremely good-looking twig glanced her way and to her surprise approached her. He seemed very timid, yet determined, so Alice did not cringe as she so often did when others came near her. He came up to her and politely asked her name.

"Alice," she quietly answered.

Stuttering slightly, he asked, "Would you, um, well, would you like to dance?"

In a rush of courage, Alice replied, "Certainly," though not feeling half so sure as she sounded.

They danced together all evening, and Alice had never had so much fun. At the end of the evening she had conquered her fears and was having a wonderful time.

After the party the twig was hesitant to leave, afraid he would not see Alice again for a whole winter. Alice asked him to spend the winter with her so they spent a long, cold winter under a warm blanket of snow.

Decision-making Talent

Students talented in the area of decision making are good evaluators. They can examine a problematic situation and make sound judgments about resolving the problem. Students who possess decision-making talent

1. determine the best way to complete a task,

2. assess situations critically,

3. value thoughtful deliberations,

4. compare and contrast alternatives, and

5. weigh the consequences of actions and procedures.

One of the best ways for students to develop and practice decision-making talent is through engagements with problem-solving opportunities. Figure G.4, page 84, provides students with a problem-solving opportunity. It is a problem that was used by students engaged in the international, interscholastic Future Problem Solving Program.[5] Teachers may use the problem in a variety of ways. They may wish to first consult chapter *I* on inventing to become familiar with one popular model of problem solving that may be taught to students. The garbage problem is an excellent hypothetical problem to pose to students while simultaneously teaching the problem-solving method. Other creative teachers may want to use a before-and-after method. That is, they may wish to present the island garbage problem to students for solving both before and after they have been trained to utilize the Isaksen and Treffinger creative problem-solving model described in chapter *I* (see pages 99-102). In this case, students will readily observe that they become more effective in decision making when they employ a systematic approach to problem solving.

Once students have become familiar with the use of a good problem-solving methodology, they can apply the system to additional environmental problems they encounter in their academic pursuits.

Fig. G.4. Solving a garbage problem.

About 1 mile off the coast of South Carolina is Coastal Island, an island community that began as a fishing settlement in the late 1800s. It was not until the 1960s, when the community was discovered by people looking for a vacation area, that the island took on its present character.

Today, in the year 2006, tourism is the main industry of the community. During the summer months people throng to Coastal Island to enjoy its beautiful beaches and warm ocean waters. During the summer, the community's population swells from 50,000 to 80,000. Excellent golf and tennis facilities attract tourists during the spring and fall (as well as in the summer), and the tourists number about 10,000 during those months. During the three winter months there are very few tourists on Coastal Island.

Though tourism is the largest and most profitable industry on Coastal Island, it is not the only source of income for the island's residents. Many of the Coastal Islanders are ocean farmers, raising and harvesting plants and animals from the sea. Several people have jobs at the large food-processing plant, which processes and packages the sea products to be sold in supermarkets all over the world.

The population of Coastal Island has been taking its municipal waste (garbage) to Seaside Landfill on the mainland of South Carolina. Seven other communities on the mainland also use this landfill. Altogether, Seaside provides dumping services for about 400,000 people. Coastal Island has been paying a fee of $27 a ton to dump their garbage at Seaside. It has cost an additional $23 per ton to collect the garbage and to transport it by barge and truck to the landfill. A considerable amount of the funding for this operation comes from a local tax on motel and recreational facilities.

When Seaside Landfill opened in 1990, it met all of the guidelines set forth by the Environmental Protection Agency (EPA) and was considered a model landfill. However, it was confirmed recently that rainwater, which has seeped through the buried garbage, now contains dangerous chemicals and is contaminating the groundwater. The EPA has ordered the immediate closing of Seaside, and it is estimated that it will take at least one year to correct the problem. The next nearest landfill is about 34 miles further inland. To transport the garbage to that landfill will cost the city an additional $18 per ton, a sum that does not currently exist in the city's budget. It has been rumored that similar problems exist at this landfill, and there is a very good chance that it will also have to close.

Like the officials in many communities, the leaders of Coastal Island have not given much thought to the city's garbage, which amounts to about 83,000 tons a year. They are now in a quandary about what to do. Can you use your problem-solving skills to help them (and others who are in similar situations)?

Forecasting Talent

Students talented in the area of forecasting are often visionary youths. They are insightful and are much interested in future possibilities and long-range opportunities and consequences. Talented forecasters are able to

1. extrapolate from the present to project the future,

2. predict alternative futures,

3. perceive cause and effect,

4. excel with if-then reasoning, and

5. anticipate outcomes.

An excellent activity associated with forecasting is scenario writing. Scenarios are described in detail in chapter *H* (see pages 89-95). In a scenario-writing competition where the theme was "Hope + Courage = A Great Future," sixth-grade student Jeremy Johnson caught the intended spirit or theme, the importance of individual contributions and efforts in creating positive futures. His scenario is found in figure G.5, pages 86-87. The hero of Jeremy's scenario is, appropriately, a garbage collector.[6]

Additional forecasting activities within the subject matter of garbage, refuse, and the environment might include the following student prompts:

Propose future methods of recycling.

Design and build a model of a pollution-free city.

Anticipate three problems your state will have in the coming decades with garbage and wastes. Next, propose solutions for each problem identified.

(Text continues on page 88.)

Fig. G.5. An example of a scenario.

<u>Trash Collector</u>

by Jeremy Johnson

The year was 2039. Jack inched the bloated, cumbersome garbage truck up to 157 Zenith Drive. The brakes squealed just as they did on garbage trucks fifty years ago. No one put much effort into improving garbage trucks. Garbage trucks weren't popular. Neither were the people who drove them. Jack swung out of the doorless driver's side and dropped 2 feet to the ground. He stepped around the garbage truck with the haste common to garbage men. To be a successful garbage man, you have to be faster than the dogs, the only other living beings interested in the trash.

Jack heaved the heavy cans and dumped them into the bin of the vehicle. As usual, he swished through the odorous junk looking for usable items. Jack dressed for the occasion in his torn jeans, plaid flannel shirt, heavy gloves, gas mask, and oxygen tank. He tossed the like-new Nintendo, the toy floating remote space vehicle, and a school notebook on disk behind the broad seat of the truck as he jumped in. They clattered against the homework robot and the Eat 'n Burp Baby that could hold its own graham crackers. And that was only the third house on his run. By the end of every week he had enough toys to start his own toy company.

Jack revved the engine of the twelve-cylinder truck. A huge cloud of dark brown carbon monoxide surged out of the tail pipe. Like I said, garbage trucks hadn't improved all that much. Jack patted his pure-white dog, Spotty (Jack had a great imagination).

"Spotty," he said. "I don't favor how wasteful folks are in this society. Especially kids think the only important thing is to buy, buy, buy, buy. The trouble with these toys is that they play with themselves. Kids can just watch and get tired while these toys do the work. The only people having a good time are the guys who think these things up and the people who carry the money to the bank."

Pure-white Spotty barked and gave his master his full attention.

Jack said, "Kids should do something with their brains besides shelve them and count their money." Jack's tannish-brown (Jack called the color "croak") garbage buggy rumbled on through the twelve-hour polluted day. He returned to his lofty (he lived in the attic) dump three times that day to empty his truck of discarded, unwanted toys.

Jack did not sleep well that night. What he said to Spotty had been on his mind for a long time. He dragged himself out of bed feeling like he should pick himself up in his own truck. He looked at himself in the mirror. Suddenly that unique image; the hair that stood up and out with no gel, the unnoticeable-enough-to-be-missing ears, the slightly piggy but refined nose, triggered an equally unique idea.

Three weeks and two days later, Jack opened the "It'll Cost You Toy Exchange." Jack sold his toys for a creative idea and an old toy in exchange. Jack would not give you one of those discarded toys unless you came up with a way to run it without plugging it into the main power source or using batteries. Jack didn't run on promises, either. No toy, unless you arrived with a full, detailed, working drawing of your own unique solution to the energy resources and pollution crisis.

The turnout was amazing. Spotty and Jack served several hundred customers a week. All those unused kids' minds expanded like balloons being filled with helium. Windmills sprang up in backyards everywhere. Kids clustered around waterfalls and fountains with their hydropowered minigenerators in the summer. In the winter, they saved their bath water and sent it down those unused water slides in the garage. In spring they wired high-flying kites to small generators. Power surges were a problem in thunderstorms. They learned to appreciate Ben Franklin and turned to pedal power. Kids learned to pedal and play Nintendo at the same time. Pedal power could be used year-round and was great exercise.

Jack and Spotty were loved by everyone but the toy companies. Business slowly decreased as kids found that Jack's toys were better. They liked using their minds instead of watching their toys. The excitement of the kids made adults more interested in finding a permanent, nonpolluting energy source. At last, toy manufacturers waged an all-out battle against Jack and the It'll Cost You Toy Exchange. They competed with Jack and produced a new line of toys that were more challenging and harder to use than the ones that Jack was trading. Jack couldn't compete. The major toy manufacturers in America celebrated quietly in their offices the day that Jack closed the It'll Cost You Toy Exchange.

They would have been surprised to know what Jack thought.

The year was 2049. Jack inched the stylish garbage truck up to 157 Zenith Drive. The brakes no longer squealed. Garbage trucks had been improved, too, in the creative, curious, careful world that Jack lived in now. He swung out and still moved quickly around the truck. Dogs hadn't changed that much.

Jack lifted the featherweight cans. There wasn't much in them. People didn't throw away much anymore. There was no longer anything to salvage from the trash. Garbage really was garbage. Jack saved, too, on clothes, gloves, and oxygen.

Jack revved the engine of his clean, steam-driven machine. He patted Spotty, who was the same, except older, like Jack.

"Spotty," he said. "I really favor how things have changed since we got this society to think more and throw away less. It's amazing how kids are these days."

Spotty barked and gave his master his full attention. Some things never change and that is good, too.

■ ■ ■

G Is for Garbage

Garbage and related subjects such as the environment and health hazards appear to be vital topics now and for the future, and certainly one of the most promising means for examining these issues in TalentEd classrooms is the curriculum-design model developed by Calvin Taylor. Taylor's model celebrates diversity. Moreover, it provides teachers with a model for articulating and reaching that goal. In an era when heterogeneously populated classrooms are more and more the norm, the Multiple Talents model provides teachers with a tool to greatly individualize and personalize instruction for all students.

Notes

[1] Alain L. Sanders, "Lifting the Lid on Garbage," *Time*, 30 May 1988, 54.

[2] The author wishes to thank Pam Everly for first sharing the idea of the Celebrity Trash Drive with the author. Readers may wish to read another account of a Celebrity Trash Drive: Jan Tanzer, "Treasures in Trash," *English Journal* 70, no. 2 (February 1981): 42-44.

[3] For a further discussion of backplanning, see the author's text *Mystery and Detection: Thinking and Problem Solving with the Sleuths* (Englewood, Colo.: Teacher Ideas Press, 1990), 121-123.

[4] The author wishes to acknowledge and thank Lindsey Thomas for the use of her story. Used with permission.

[5] Reprinted with permission from the Future Problem Solving Program, 315 W. Huron St., Suite 140-B, Ann Arbor, MI 48103-4803. Copyright 1986. All rights reserved.

[6] The author wishes to acknowledge and thank Jeremy Johnson for the use of his scenario. Used with permission.

Teacher Resources

Cherry, Lynne. *A River Ran Wild*. New York: Harcourt Brace Jovanovich, 1992.
  The author-illustrator tells a story, with beautiful illustrations, of how individuals can make a difference in cleaning up the environment.

Isaksen, Scott, and Donald J. Treffinger. *Creative Problem Solving: The Basic Course*. Buffalo, N.Y.: Bearly Limited, 1985.
  A course in creative problem solving utilizing a six-stage model.

Javna, John. *Fifty Simple Things Kids Can Do to Save the Earth*. New York: Andrews and McMeel, 1990.
  Many practical solutions students can implement in their own environment.

Is for Hope

> Hope is the pillar that holds up the world.
> —Pliny the Elder, A.D. 23-79

As a classroom teacher for two decades, the author grew ever more concerned with the growing pessimism about the future each new class of students expressed through their discussions and writings. Believing that it is essential for young people to have the opportunity to contemplate, examine, and explore their own images of the future, he has found the scenario a useful tool in building messages of hope among youth. It is important for youth to imagine the future positively. This is not a new idea. Even in the Old Testament, Solomon warned, "Where there is no vision, the people perish" (Proverbs 29:18).

A scenario is a forecast of future events and conditions. The scenario writer first envisions and then describes life as it *may* be in some future time. The point of view is that of a person living in the future. That is, a scenario written from the time perspective of 2020 is written in the present tense, with all events leading up to 2020 referred to in the past tense. The introduction to a scenario in figure H.1 illustrates this point of view.

Fig. H.1. Introduction to a scenario.

Portland, Oregon   April 6, 2022

Awakening this morning, I glanced out my window at the solar date-clock positioned on the side of Mount Hood. It read: 4-6-22: 6:33. I thought how easily we now take the giant clock for granted. What a battle there had been back in 1998 when it was first proposed. Environmentalists had complained that it would deface the majestic mountain.

89

H Is for Hope

A scenario can paint a broad picture of the future or focus upon the effect of a singular technology, issue, or event. While it is acceptable to display plenty of technological gadgetry in a scenario, the writing should never lose sight of human factors. Technology does not exist in a vacuum. The lives of ordinary people are affected significantly by inventions.

Scenarios differ from science fiction in that they are less concerned with plot and characterization and deal more with the typical and commonplace rather than the fantastic. For example, a scenario in 1940 might have described a typical trip to the supermarket in the 1990s and might have posited such notions as computer price code scanning, payment with credit cards, and the availability of hydroponically grown produce.

Scenarios are typically set no more than twenty to fifty years into the future, and they attempt to portray typical happenings in the lives of ordinary people.

For five years the author worked with a city newspaper in sponsoring an annual scenario-writing project. Students in four grade level divisions, K-3, 4-6, 7-9, and 10-12, wrote scenarios of 1,000 words or less on these and other topics: "Welcome to the Future: It Is Going to Be a Great Place to Be"; "Hope + Courage = A Great Future"; and "Invention: The Heartbeat of the Future."[1]

Students were stimulated to think about their futures imaginatively, constructively, and positively. It has been said that what one person can envision, another can invent. While it may be unrealistic to suppose that today's school-age youth should be about the business of revolutionizing the world with their inventions, it is not too soon to ask young people to be visionaries, to use imagination and creativity to predict the marvels that may be commonplace in the next century. History provides confirmation of this belief. Yes, Einstein, Tesla, Edison, and the Wright Brothers were doers, but they were first dreamers. Only when young people are helped to dream and envision positive futures can such possibilities begin to emerge and take shape as probabilities.

When a scenario theme centered on the use of inventions to forge positive futures, one seven-year-old girl "invented" and described organic shoes. In Amy's future world, no one would ever have to worry about having comfortable, serviceable shoes. Children would be fitted at birth with special shoes made of organic material that would keep pace with each person's growth throughout life. A sixth-grader's winning scenario proposed the MMCI—MicroChip Conscience Insertion—as one way to develop greater harmony among peoples of the Earth. People would be equipped with a microchip that would cause them to develop exceptional caring and compassion for others. Another winning elementary scenario described a "skills machine" that would help people continuously retool and retrain as their current occupations became obsolete in a world where technology changes rapidly.

One of the winning scenarios in the secondary division described a typical day in the life of a future surgeon, who invented and utilized a "lazermold" medical technique that could soften the molecular structure of damaged bones, reshape them, and harden them back to a healthy condition. Young people's inventions were not limited to technological breakthroughs. Some youths proposed educational plans to better educate people of all ages in the future, while others suggested new political techniques and strategies to end conflicts between governments around the globe. The scenarios revealed a genuine desire young people have for playing a role in shaping the world of tomorrow.

Figure H.2 represents a hopeful and positive scenario written by third-grade student Jason Oraker in response to the invention topic.[2] Jason not only wrote the scenario, he even built a prototype model of his hypothesized zero-gravity playground. Jeremy Johnson's scenario "Trash Collector" is in figure G.5 on pages 86-87.

Fig. H.2. Scenario written in response to the invention topic.

<u>Playground of the Future</u>

by Jason Oraker

Rrrrrrring! Recess time for elementary children.

Oh, boy! The new playground equipment has arrived, compliments of myself, the inventor, and the NASA Youth Experiment Sponsorship. My friend Ronnie and I have been chosen to be the first to try the Non-Gravitational Cell, the greatest invention for kids in the last ten years.

It's the year 2002 and this is an excellent way to prepare us kids for the weightlessness of the world before us. Contained in that lightweight, weatherized, insulated, plastic rectangular, boxy shape is a piece of space with the zero gravity that lies above the exosphere. We will practice exercising, playing, eating, and learning in our own little piece of outer space. This playground will help them become excited and "unscared" of new places they will be living in and learn how to survive.

As Ronnie and I crawl through the entry-level tunnel, the feel of Earth gravity becomes less and less. Ronnie goes first. I follow. When we reach the opening, we get out and float around, upward past the big screen flashing instructions for the exercise program. To my surprise, I find myself floating past a bar attached to the solar columns. Ronnie caught the bar and started doing pull-ups. I said, "Why not?" So I tried. At first, I had to get used to it. Back at the school gym, I can only do three to five in a row, but now here, it doesn't stop. Now, there is no pressure. This is easy. "We're going to work to get any exercise." Next, we tried the running circle where only the force of our motion helped us keep our feet on the track. Ten miles in 10 minutes.

"Boy, it's comfortable in here, don't you think, Ronnie?"

"I like this solar heating, Jason."

"Yes," I said. "Let's go to the food cubicle and sample today's special." We had to work our way over by holding onto the crossbar. Ronnie saw a menu. I read it with him. "Seaweed salad and kelp soup. The special is dandelion juice." We saw the salad and soup that was growing continually in the hydroponic disc. We sipped the juice from a pressurized straw attached to the liquid factory. The liquid could not escape or it would just float around us. When we were finished, we took our feet out of the foot clips and grabbed the bar and worked our way to the Satellite Library, where Ronnie floated up to the Game Exchange to play checkers with a Russian boy who appeared on the screen. I sat down and buckled my seat belt and pulled a book down from the shelf to read. Luckily, the rope kept the books from floating around.

(Figure H.2 continues on page 92.)

Fig. H.2—*Continued*

> Next, we took turns playing lunar levers, where we pushed lever No. 1 to go down and lever No. 2 to go up. It was the one thing where we could control our movements. The flashing screen said, "Free lessons on catching the flying saucer." I said to Ronnie, "That's the thing for us. Sounds impossible with no gravity."
>
> "Oh, no, Ronnie. Our time is up." As we left through the tunnel, we felt Earth's gravity more and more. We thought to ourselves what a keen invention to prepare all school kids for the weightless world beyond Earth. Maybe they will be able to improve life in space because they had an experience of playing in my invention: the Non-gravitational Cell, patent No. 8888888. I sure hope so.

■ ■ ■

There are many values of scenario writing regardless of whether students create scenarios collectively or individually. Scenario writing

- encourages students to think positively about the future;

- prompts students to use both creative and critical thinking skills;

- encourages students to utilize prewriting and editing strategies that reinforce composition skills;

- causes students to examine thoughtfully their own future-focused role images;

- accentuates the importance of integrated learning; and

- encourages active family involvement in student learning.

TalentEd teachers can design classroom units and explorations around scenario project themes such as "Invention: The Heartbeat of the Future." Scenario writing can either lead to, or be an extension of, integrated studies. English, science, and social studies are natural subject disciplines that can be combined to provide students with an interdisciplinary and integrated approach to the task of creating future images. Scenario writing provides students with a new writing model or format with which to experiment. When teachers emphasize scenario writing, the focus is not just on the past and the present, but on the future. One young man addressed this point in a testimonial to the benefit of the scenario-writing project. "I am impressed with the effort and enthusiasm which you display every year when scenario season rolls around. You've got a whole city of kids thinking hard about the future rather than watching television, and that's an accomplishment!"

Families can become involved in scenario writing, too. Students of winning scenarios in the project the author created indicated that they often obtained their best ideas from family dinner-table discussions prompted by the scenario themes.

Of course, the greatest benefit of scenario writing is the promotion of hopeful, healthy, and constructive future images among today's youth. That may not be an insignificant gain today. Through the electronic media, in particular, students are almost constantly bombarded with a continuous chronicling of all that is wrong with the world—terrorism, pollution, incurable diseases, homeless families, famine, the everpresent threat of nuclear war, and the threat of global ecological disaster. The cumulative effect of all this nay-saying on youth may be more pernicious than adults realize.

Parents and educators who want to help students maximize their potential for the good of themselves and society must realize that people paralyzed by negative images of the future are unlikely to realize their dreams. The late Norman Cousins perhaps best elucidated this point: "Optimism supplies the basic energy of civilization. Pessimism is a waste of time. The main trouble with despair is that it is self-defeating. People who fear the worst tend to invite it. Heads that are down can't scan the horizon for new openings. Bursts of energy do not spring from a spirit of defeat. Ultimately, hopelessness leads to helplessness."[3]

Yes, it is true that the future will contain challenges, but the wise teacher or mentor conveys to youth the essence of the motto of the Christopher Society: "It is better to light one candle than to curse the darkness."

Youth must be given messages of hope and not messages of despair. Increasingly, educators emphasize the acquisition of problem-solving skills as a vital part of school curricula; but the same educators also need to give young people messages of hope so that they will have reason to believe that they can use such skills constructively in the future. Scenario writing is only one very small pillar of such hope, but it is a beginning. Adults should be conscientious in sharing dreams—not nightmares—with today's youth.

TalentEd teachers help young people find and read stories of hope.

As TalentEd teachers and mentors work with students in the creation of scenarios, they may wish to consider the following tips.

TalentEd Encourage students to think creatively, critically, and encyclopedically about the future. Encourage brainstorming. Students need a wealth of ideas from which to choose images they ultimately incorporate into their writings. One technique that may help young people imagine the future, as well as understand the nature of accelerating change, is to look backward in time. If students plan to set their scenarios twenty years into the future, it may be enlightening to first glance backward twenty years. What significant developments have occurred in society in the past twenty years? Could people twenty years ago have predicted the impact of computer technology, or its pervasiveness in the lives of people today? Would they have predicted the popularity of VCRs and home video games? The microwave oven? As the list grows, students will be amazed at how much daily living changes in a relatively short time span. They should also note that changes in the next twenty years will be likely to occur at an even more rapid pace.

Students should critically analyze projected changes. Is all change good? If humans live in a push-button world in the future where robots do all manual labor, what activities will engage humans? Will new amounts of leisure time be spent productively?

Students should also consider the domino or chain-reaction effect of change. The invention of television provided more than an entertainment source. It has impacted people's buying habits; it has changed the way families interact; it has altered most people's perceptions of the world; it has altered teaching and learning methods. Similarly, the automobile dramatically affected the way people live, far beyond just transporting them from one place to another. When students project inventions and technologies of the future, they should consider the far-reaching effect these developments may have.

TalentEd Encourage students to be creative in the projection of ideas, but to recognize that the futures they imagine must be reality-based. Humans do not possess the anatomical features necessary to transform themselves instantly into birds and fly off into the sky, nor can they fire bullets or laser rays from their fingertips. Students should avoid the comic book and Saturday-morning cartoon super hero syndrome.

TalentEd Urge students to carefully organize their ideas. One good approach is the chronological or sequential method of organization. A student describes a typical day in the future from morning to night. Topical outlines also work well, especially for describing, part by part, how an invention, a system of government, or a medical or learning procedure operates. Organization is crucial. The ideas in a scenario need to be organized into a fluid, cohesive whole.

TalentEd Urge students to seek novel, creative introductions and techniques for transporting readers into their imagined futures. Dreams and time travel are certainly effective ways to convey to readers the forward movement of time, but they tend to be overused. Scenarios should be creative in both content and form.

TalentEd Encourage students to focus upon positive images. Scenarios do not advocate the wearing of rose-colored glasses; they recognize that there will be problems in the future. Scenarios concentrate on how people constructively and creatively solve future problems.

Scenarios are typically written, but many alternative formats exist. Various art media may be used by students who wish to visually display imagined positive futures. The resulting products can be as diverse as watercolors and cartoons. Musically talented students may want to compose music evocative of positive future themes. A group of students might write and produce a one-act play set in the future with a hopeful theme.

There are numerous resources teachers can utilize in helping TalentEd students imagine and write about positive futures. Library media specialists can be especially valuable allies to teachers who want to have their students create scenarios. Library media specialists can secure hard-to-find resources about alternative futures and may also direct youth to references about the most recent advances in science and technology.

Both *Omni* magazine and *The Futurist* are periodicals that contain scenarios written by authors, scientists, and educators. *The Futurist* is a bimonthly magazine published by the World Future Society. This organization also publishes an annual catalog filled with books in fields as diverse as business, medicine, education, the military, and agriculture. To receive the catalog or to subscribe to *The Futurist*, write The World Future Society, 7910 Woodmont Avenue, Suite 450, Bethesda, Maryland 20814. Publication information about *Omni* may be obtained by writing Omni, 1965 Broadway, New York, New York 10023-5965.

E. Paul Torrance, Deborah Weiner, Jack Presbury, and Morgan Henderson edited *Save Tomorrow for the Children*, a collection of scenarios written by children and youth from around the world. Although Gerard K. O'Neill's scenarios were written more than a decade past, *2081: A Hopeful View of the Human Future* contains positive and exciting images of the astonishing possibilities that lie in front of humanity through the next century.

Space studies are natural extensions of any discussions of positive futures. Two agencies are especially geared to help educators make students aware of the positive potential space study and exploration may have for the future. The United States Space Foundation (1525 Vapor Trail, Colorado Springs, Colorado 80916-2780) has an extensive library of print and visual materials teachers may access. Similarly, NASA (Lyndon B. Johnson Space Center, Houston, Texas 77058) publishes significant learning materials for teacher-student use. The national distribution center for NASA teaching materials is NASA CORE, 15181 Route 58 South, Oberlin, Ohio 44074.

As Thomas Jefferson said, "I like the dreams of the future better than the history of the past." TalentEd teachers and mentors concur with Jefferson's sensibility. They acknowledge the importance of hopeful futures and positive tomorrows. They resist the temptation to be pessimists, or to let their students be paralyzed by fear of the future. They recognize that students who are encouraged to dream about and imagine positive tomorrows are well on their way to making such dreams come true. Finally, they encourage their students to believe in their own talents and abilities to make their dreams come true. They share the wisdom of a great and talented teacher, Margaret Mead, who said, "Never doubt that a small group of thoughtful, committed citizens can change the world; indeed, it's the only thing that ever has."

Notes

[1] A complete description of the scenario program, with further student examples, may be found in the author's book *Inventing, Inventions, and Inventors: A Teaching Resource Book* (Englewood, Colo.: Teacher Ideas Press, 1989), 112-115. See also Jerry D. Flack, "Inventing the Future," *Writing Teacher* 1, no. 4 (February/March 1988): 6-9.

[2] The author wishes to acknowledge and thank Jason Oraker for the use of his scenario.

[3] Norman Cousins, "The Case for Optimism," *Outward Bound*, premier issue (Summer 1985): 11.

Teacher Resources

O'Neill, Gerard K. *2081: A Hopeful View of the Human Future*. New York: Simon & Schuster, 1981.

Scenarios for the twenty-first century by an eminent futurist and physicist. The author explores the scientific fact and conjecture that led him to the predictions found in the scenarios.

Torrance, E. Paul, Deborah Weiner, Jack Presbury, and Morgan Henderson, eds. *Save Tomorrow for the Children*. Buffalo, N.Y.: Bearly Limited Press, 1987.

Youths from around the world share their positive images of the future.

# Is for Invention

> The most powerful forces that change the way we live are the applied sparks of insight that we call invention.
>
> —Robert Jarvik, M.D.

A chorus of voices is heard today advocating much more intellectual vigor in American public school education. Much of the impetus for this concern may be traced back to the now famous report of the National Commission on Excellence in Education, which began with this warning:

> Our nation is at risk. Our once unchallenged preeminence in commerce, industry, science, and technological innovation is being overtaken by competitors throughout the world.[1]

The concern expressed in *A Nation at Risk*, and in similar reports that have followed, is not unfounded, and the problems it addressed have not been solved. One example: For the past decade, foreign countries and individuals have accounted for 47 percent or more of all patents issued by the United States Patent Office.[2]

The study of inventing, inventions, and inventors offers educators an exceptionally fine curricular framework for facilitating the intellectual growth of students. Inventing provides a vehicle teachers can use in TalentEd classrooms to substantially increase the knowledge base of students, while simultaneously developing and challenging their thinking and problem-solving skills.[3]

Invention is one of the great themes of civilization. Indeed, probably no human endeavor is more commonly associated with genius than the original act of invention. When people think of intellectual brilliance and accomplishment, inventors and discoverers such as Marie Curie, Thomas Edison, and Robert Jarvik immediately come to mind. The creation of a new theory to explain the origins of the universe, the discovery of penicillin, or the invention of the CAT-scan are creative acts universally applauded. When students examine the act of inventing, they are well on their way to becoming expert problem solvers.

Another current national educational movement is the push for the teaching of thinking skills and problem solving for all students, at all grade levels, and in all disciplines. However, the teaching of process skills in isolation and unrelated to content is of questionable merit. A focus on inventing and innovation allows for a meaningful synthesis of both content and process. The study of invention and inventors provides creative students with countless avenues for gaining new and meaningful data. The study of inventing as problem solving provides students with significant skill development in a meaningful context. Inventing also provides fertile ground for the application and further development of student knowledge of physics, chemistry, and mathematics. Careers in engineering and other related fields (e.g., patent law) may be explored. Investigations about the lives of inventors, current and past, shed light on the behaviors and commitment to excellence inventors and innovators need to possess. Investigations of current inventing within the fields of semiconductors and supercomputers are of undeniable value to students who will spend the bulk of their lives using these inventions as their twenty-first-century work tools.

What Is Innovation?

A beneficial, and logical, beginning point for the study of inventing and innovation in TalentEd classrooms is the clarification of terminology. Ask students to define such terms as *invention*, *imagination*, *evolution*, *engineering*, *discovery*, and *creativity*. If students are spending a significant amount of time exploring inventing and innovation, it benefits all to share common ground with respect to their understanding of these terms, and the often subtle semantic differences between them. Students should realize the broad and incredibly rich variation to be found in the world of inventing. Inventions may be classified as new products (Eli Whitney's cotton gin), or as improvements of existing products (a better mousetrap). Inventors may also receive patents for new designs (e.g., a new silverware pattern or A. Bertholdi's Statue of Liberty) and processes (e.g., a new method of silver plating). Inventors have received patents for plant variants, such as a new variety of poinsettia. Even animals have been patented. A few years ago a patent was awarded to Harvard University for a genetically engineered mouse.

During an initial discussion of inventing as problem solving, students will profit from reading some of the more provocative statements that have been made about inventing and creativity. What messages are conveyed through the following quotations?

> I invent nothing. I rediscover.
> —Auguste Rodin

> Imagination is more important than knowledge.
> —Albert Einstein

> Genius is one percent inspiration and ninety-nine percent perspiration.
> —Thomas A. Edison

An equally relevant early discussion with students may center upon these metacognitive questions: Where do ideas come from? What are our minds doing when we engage in the act of inventing? A favorite activity utilized by the author to help students pursue this discussion involves the use of the now ubiquitous paper airplane contest. Divide students into cooperative groups. Ask each group to create a paper airplane that will soar farther, and remain aloft longer, than the products designed and constructed by their counterpoint groups. Ask the teams to pay particular attention to all of the mental processes they use as they proceed through the task. How are they thinking as they design and construct a glider? Ask each group to choose a recorder who will note all the many and varied thinking skills and mental processes utilized by the group throughout the entire inventing process in conceiving, building, and trying out their product. For example, where does memory fit into the process of inventing? How about trial and error? Intuition? Observation? Imitation? Comparison? Evaluation? Generalization? Imagination? If students need to be familiarized with the terminology of thinking, one excellent source is *The Care and Feeding of Ideas* by James L. Adams. This author has also found it useful to ask recorders to additionally note the positive and negative comments made by participants. Then, during the debriefing discussion students may examine how criticism and encouragement affect the inventing process. A fine resource that explores how inventors think and work is *Inventors at Work: Interviews with 16 Notable American Inventors* by Kenneth A. Brown.

TalentEd students can also gain a perspective of the inventive process of problem solving through the exploration and study of how things work. If students are going to be inventors, they need to have at least a rudimentary knowledge of tools and machines. The ages of students will most likely determine how basic or how sophisticated lessons in this direction will be. Students should become familiar with how basic appliances and machines that affect their daily lives operate. Ask each student to choose a modern invention, research its development and operation, and report back to the class how it works. The list of possible inventions is limited only by teacher and student imagination. The following may suggest ideas to students: VCR, television, radio, tape recorder, microwave oven, telephone, computer, fluorescent lighting, camera, and watch.

Students may also examine the breakthrough inventions that have dramatically changed the way people live, the means via which they get new information about both Planet Earth and space, and the tools they use to communicate and solve problems. What, for example, are lasers? How do they work? How have they changed everyday living? Equally fitting questions may be asked about microprocessors, satellites for weather forecasting and communications, telescopes, computer-aided design and manufacturing, the CAT-scan, and fiber-optic communications. In each case, teachers should ask students to note the problems solved with the creation of each invention.

While it is considerably more whimsical, a fun and provocative activity in invention problem solving is to ask each student to use all of the six simple machines (the lever, the inclined plane, pulley, screw, wedge, and wheel and axle) to build a Rube Goldberg-style "Thingamabob" or "Whatchamacallit." Many excellent resources exist that both the teacher and the students can utilize in learning how things work. Two especially fine resources are *The Way Things Work* by David Macaulay, and the National Geographic Society publication *How Things Work*.

Linking Inventing and Problem Solving

Many of the tools and processes utilized in creative problem solving (CPS) have direct application to the process of inventing. There are a great many models of CPS utilized by professionals in government and the private business sector. A few of these models have been adopted by educators for classroom use with their students. Perhaps the most widely utilized CPS model in education today is one created by Scott G. Isaksen and Donald J. Treffinger. Isaksen and Treffinger invented a six-stage model for problem solving that will be used here as the reference point for discussing the role of inventing as problem solving.[4]

MESS FINDING

The first stage of the CPS model is mess finding. In this first stage of creative problem solving, participants recognize that there is a problem and accept the challenge to attempt solutions. Inventors as problem solvers are aware of the vital importance of keeping open minds, and keeping their eyes wide open for problem-solving opportunities. Indeed, inventors as problem solvers actually look for problems. The following example illustrates this predisposition or orientation toward problem finding that astute inventors adopt. For many years, motorists were plagued by the heat buildup in locked, parked cars exposed to the sun. Most people just endured the heat and complained. An enterprising inventor saw this "mess" as an opportunity for problem solving, and invented the widely used folding auto windshield sunscreen. Encourage TalentEd students to go beyond being good problem solvers; challenge them to become good problem finders, too.

DATA FINDING

The second step in the six-step CPS model is data finding. Before smart inventors begin building better mousetraps, they engage in some vital data finding to determine if there is really a need for new mousetraps, the cost of building new mousetraps, and whether others have already patented the mousetraps they have in mind. The phrase "Why reinvent the wheel?" merits considerable attention in this phase of the CPS process. The presidential report of the American Library Association on literacy in the United States offers dramatic evidence of the need to teach students the critical importance of this part of the process:

> A manufacturing company had a research team of three scientists and four technicians working on a project, and at the end of a year the team felt it had a patentable invention in addition to a new product. Prior to filing the patent application, the company's patent attorney requested a literature search. While doing the search, the librarian found that the proposed application duplicated some of the work claimed in a patent that had been issued about a year before the team had begun its work. During the course of the project, the company had spent almost $500,000 on the project, an outlay that could have been avoided if it had spent the approximately $300 required to have a review of the literature completed before beginning the project.[5]

One of the most effective ways of collecting data is to ask the reporter's five W + H questions: Who? Where? What? When? Why? How? When students can satisfactorily provide answers for these questions, relative to the invention problem that they have chosen, they are well on the way to becoming excellent thinkers and successful inventors and problem solvers.

PROBLEM FINDING

Once the inventors as problem solvers have a solid understanding of all the dynamics associated with a problem area, they are ready to address the problem finding stage of the CPS process. From a wide array of possible problem foci, they select the key problem. It takes little talent to spot wrong answers, but it takes a creative mind to spot wrong questions. Charles Wales and Robert Stager, inventors of the Guided Design teaching model, share a story that illustrates a critically important lesson about problem finding. Early in the development of the space shuttle program, NASA engineers posed this problem: "Find a material that will withstand a temperature of 14,000°F for five minutes." The problem was related to the enormous amount of heat generated during the space capsule's reentry into the Earth's atmosphere. Of course, the engineers were confronted with a problem that was impossible to solve, as there is no known material capable of withstanding the required temperature. An astute thinker and good problem finder restated the problem as follows: "Find a way to protect a capsule and the person inside during reentry." The newly focused problem was solved with the ablation system now in use.[6]

The point is that inventive problem finders and problem solvers may not ask the question: How can we build a better mousetrap? Instead, they may focus on the more appropriate problem: What's the best way to get rid of mice?

IDEA FINDING

Once the key problem has been identified, problem solvers move to the next phase of CPS: idea finding. Here, problem solvers generate many ideas. So-called wild ideas are welcome. The sky is the limit. After all, who would have ever believed that hula hoops, pet rocks, and teenage mutant ninja turtles would have mass audience appeal? In the idea finding stage of inventing, the problem solver keeps an open mind and looks for new ways of combining and altering tools of the known world. The SCAMPER technique invented by Robert Eberle is a particularly effective tool for students to utilize in the idea finding stage of CPS. SCAMPER is a handy acronym that reminds student problem solvers to:

> **S**ubstitute
>
> **C**ombine
>
> **A**dapt/Adjust
>
> **M**odify, Minify, Magnify
>
> **P**ut to other uses
>
> **E**liminate, Elaborate
>
> **R**everse, Rearrange[7]

In looking at present-day inventions, one can easily think of many examples of SCAMPER at work. The bicycle industry has been dramatically revitalized by adapting the standard bicycle to perform on rough terrain. Millions of mountain bikes are now sold each year. Enterprising inventors and entrepreneurs have seized the concept of minification and have given consumers countless variations of light foods and beverages. One ski resort has put to new uses the pedestrian garbage bag. A ski resort in the Pacific Northwest prints its logo on plastic garbage bags, precut with openings for the head and arms, for skiers to use on wet, drizzly days.

SOLUTION FINDING

Solution finding is a convergent and evaluative phase of the creative problem-solving process. No matter how much fun the inventors are having by generating creative ideas, sooner or later they must choose the *best* idea and begin the process of implementation. Typically, in the CPS model, a grid is utilized to compare the most promising ideas generated in the previous step. Criteria are selected and are utilized to make critical judgments about the advantages and disadvantages of the best ideas generated. Typical criteria include cost factors, feasibility data, ethical considerations, and environmental impact. Obviously, each invention problem identified will dictate the number and types of criteria selected to utilize in this phase. Good inventor problem solvers would rarely limit themselves to consideration of only one criterion. True, inventors are primarily interested in finding the answer to the question: Which solution will work best? But, what happens then when they find out that the solution chosen will be so costly to produce that no one will be able to afford its purchase? Just as students should very carefully and deliberately choose the best problem finding statement, they should also be highly selective in choosing criteria to use in the evaluation of their ideas.

ACCEPTANCE FINDING

The final phase of the CPS model applied to inventing is acceptance finding. One problem that surfaces all too frequently in CPS training in schools is the failure to give students concrete and meaningful problems to which they can apply this final step in creative problem solving. Students have fun exercising their creative thinking skills in identifying problems and creating innovative solutions to problems. Existing conditions, however, are not such that they are able to really dig in and implement their proposed solutions. One of the special advantages of inventing as problem solving is the opportunity afforded to students in the acceptance finding and implementation phase. With inventing as their focus, students can identify real-world problems, consider viable alternatives, select the most workable ideas from many alternatives, and proceed to physically invent and implement their best solutions. Teachers who wish to present models of such behavior to students may want to consult *Breakthroughs* by P. Ranganath Nayak and John M. Ketteringham. The authors share many stories of how products such as the microwave oven, Nautilus equipment, and the Walkman made it from an idea in an inventor's mind all the way to the marketplace.

What to Invent?

Inventors, not surprisingly, invent solutions to problems that are found in their primary environments. Inventors create tools and processes to improve environments where they live and work. Familiar environments for students include their homes and classrooms. Factors such as age, geography, program goals, and classrooms objectives may determine what TalentEd teachers and library media specialists ask students to invent.

Students may be especially innovative in creating new educational toys and games. They may also be interested in improving the existing tools and products they use in their classroom work or for completing homework. Innovations in their bedrooms at home offer students possible challenges, too. Perhaps they can create new designs for more effective reading lamps. Possibly, they can invent procedures or tools to help them better organize and readily display their clothing. Regardless, invention foci should take into account the needs, interests, and environments with which students can identify and problem solve.

Civilization marches onward in a grand and panoramic parade. The cadence of that march is invention, and the drummers have been, and no doubt will continue to be, inventors and discoverers. There is much wisdom in Walt Disney's observation, "Our greatest national resource is the minds of our children." It is fitting that the nation's young people in TalentEd classrooms should use their great potential for creative and innovative thinking to build a better world for the future. A vital part of their education should be the acquisition of problem-solving skills that will assist them in not only learning about past inventions, but also will orient them toward the cultivation and development of skills to invent and build more creative tomorrows for everyone.

Notes

[1] National Commission on Education, *A Nation at Risk: The Imperative for Educational Reform* (Washington, D.C.: Superintendent of Documents, 1983), 5.

[2] U.S. Department of Commerce, Bureau of the Census, *Statistical Abstracts of the United States 1988* (Washington, D.C.: Superintendent of Documents, 1988), 518.

[3] Material in this chapter first appeared in the author's book *Inventing, Inventions, and Inventors: A Teaching Resource Book* (Englewood, Colo.: Teacher Ideas Press, 1989); and in Jerry D. Flack, "Inventing as Problem Solving," *THINK* 2, no. 1 (October 1991): 14-20.

[4] For a complete discussion of this CPS model, see Scott G. Isaksen and Donald J. Treffinger, *Creative Problem Solving: The Basic Course* (Buffalo, N.Y.: Bearly Limited Press, 1985).

[5]American Library Association Presidential Committee, *Final Report: Presidential Committee on Information Literacy* (Chicago: American Library Association, 1989), 3.

[6]Charles Wales and Robert Stager, *Guided Design* (Morgantown, W.Va.: University of West Virginia Department of Engineering, 1977), 14.

[7]Robert Eberle, *Visual Thinking: A SCAMPER Tool for Useful Imagining* (East Aurora, N.Y.: D.O.K., 1982).

Teacher Resources

Aaseng, Nathan. *The Unsung Heroes: Unheralded People Who Invented Famous Products*. Minneapolis, Minn.: Lerner Publications, 1989.

    The creators and inventors of Dunlop tires, Coca-Cola, and Hummel figures are among those profiled.

Adams, James L. *The Care and Feeding of Ideas: A Guide to Encouraging Creativity*. Reading, Mass.: Addison-Wesley, 1986.

    Adams offers both insightful and practical tips for being more creative.

Brown, Kenneth A. *Inventors at Work: Interviews with 16 Notable American Inventors*. Redmond, Wash.: Tempus Books, 1988.

    Inventors of pacemakers, lasers, and microprocessors talk about how they invent new technology.

Caney, Steven. *Steven Caney's Invention Book*. New York: Workman, 1985.

    Caney provides information on all aspects of the invention process. He also provides readers with entertaining stories about the invention of such things as the zipper, roller skates, and Life Savers candy.

Haskins, Jim. *Outward Dreams: Black Inventors and Their Inventions*. New York: Bantam Books, 1992.

    Elijah McCoy and Benjamin Banneker are among the inventors described in this book. A special feature is an appendix listing several hundred Black inventors and their inventions.

Hooper, Meredith. *Everyday Inventions*. New York: Taplinger, 1976.

    Short, easily read stories about a wide variety of inventions such as nails, canned food, the sewing machine, and barbed wire.

Macaulay, David. *The Way Things Work*. Boston: Houghton Mifflin, 1988.

    A delightful book that both entertains and instructs readers about how machines operate.

National Geographic. *How Things Work*. Washington, D.C.: National Geographic Society, 1983.

    From vending machines to traffic signals, this book tells how everyday inventions work.

Nayak, P. R., and J. M. Ketteringham. *Breakthroughs!* New York: Rawson Associates, 1986.

    Fascinating stories of modern inventing and marketing, including the stories behind the invention of VCRs, microwave ovens, and Toyota automobiles.

Reid, Struan. *Invention and Discovery*. London: Usborne, 1986.

> Although this book was first published in Great Britain, it is widely available in the United States and provides students with a wealth of information about inventing.

Shlesinger, B. Edward, Jr. *How to Invent: A Text for Teachers and Students*. New York: Plenum Press, 1987.

> A patent attorney who is also an inventor describes how to become an inventor. Many fine visuals complement the clear and concise directions.

Vare, Ethlie Ann, and Greg Ptacek. *Mothers of Invention: From the Bra to the Bomb, Forgotten Women and Their Unforgettable Ideas*. New York: William Morrow, 1988.

> Beginning with Hypatia, born in Alexandria in A.D. 370, the authors work forward through time to tell the stories of remarkable, inventive women and their inventions.

Is for Journals

Journals are the notebooks of the mind. Journals are places for experimenting, ideating, reflecting, observing, problem solving, communing with one's self, and filing random thoughts, ideas, and data for possible later use. Journal writing should receive daily attention in the TalentEd classroom.

Journals typically feature informal writing in the first-person voice. Noted journal-writing expert Toby Fulwiler writes that the journal is found somewhere between the highly personal and private diary and the more public class notebook: "The journal is somewhere between the two. Like the diary, the journal is written in the first person about ideas important to the writer; like the class notebook, the journal may focus on academic subjects the writer wishes to examine."[1]

Journal keeping has a distinguished history. Leonardo da Vinci conceived the helicopter and the military tank in his notebooks. The young naturalist Charles Darwin kept vital journals of the plant and animal life he observed while a passenger on the *Beagle* in the 1830s. Nathaniel Hawthorne purportedly planned and developed *The Scarlet Letter* in his journals. Benjamin Franklin, John Quincy Adams, Herman Melville, Marie Curie, Albert Einstein, John Steinbeck, Eleanor Roosevelt, Thomas Edison, and many, many more creative and talented individuals kept journals.[2]

Creative people recognize the valuable role journals can play in the creative process. Creativity doesn't just happen. Creativity is realized through a series of steps taken that include inquiry, observation, reflection, incubation, hypothesis formulation, experimentation, confirmation, and reexamination. Journal keeping is a powerful tool when utilized to activate and articulate these steps.

It is unfortunate that journal writing has become the target of some interest groups critical of public school educational practices. Journals need not and should not be invasions of student privacy. Students should keep journals to develop thinking and writing skills. Journals should also be recognized for their pedagogical benefits. Teachers nervous about the use of journals may wisely consult and share the statement of guidelines for using journals in school settings from the National Council of Teachers of English (NCTE). The NCTE position statement cites sound educational research in support of the use of journals in classrooms. Writing about the connections between new knowledge and existing knowledge improves student learning. In the learning process, it is vital for students to use all language modes, including writing. When students write about new knowledge and information as well as read, talk, and listen about it, they learn better.[3]

Students in TalentEd classrooms should write in their journals on a daily basis to improve their writing fluency skills. Journal writing also helps young writers recognize and trust their own writing voice.

Journals should also be recognized for the positive role they play in the conservation of ideas. Infant ideas are endangered; fledgling ideas that are not noted in journals for later consideration and elaboration are most likely lost forever. The journal is to the writer and inventor what the sketch pad is to the artist.

Journal writing is exceptionally useful and habit forming. The modes of writing found in journals and the uses of journals are extremely varied. Journals may be utilized to initiate new topics. Teachers can introduce a new topic at the beginning of a class period and ask students to write their prior knowledge and perceptions about the topic for five minutes in their journals. Teachers beginning a new unit on inventions might begin a class with these questions or prompts: What do you think an invention is? Who is/was the greatest inventor of all time? Name the greatest invention ever created. Make a list of all the things in the classroom that had to be invented. Such writing helps students begin to focus on the topic at hand and to pull together the thoughts and ideas they have about the subject. This technique facilitates student engagement, the first prerequisite of learning. Another benefit to starting class with such a journal-writing assignment is that this practice allows and requires each student in the class to be the master of his or her own thinking. Students must first think and then write for themselves. The thoughts of students are not contaminated by the first or second or third oral response offered by most outspoken students in the class.

In a similar fashion, journals may be utilized to bring closure to a lesson. The final five to ten minutes of a class period may be reserved for students to summarize in their journals what they have learned during the class hour. What new information and knowledge do they possess? How can they relate what they have learned to their prior knowledge? What kind of "fit" can they make? What questions do they have that they didn't have at the beginning of the period? The latter question illustrates the cyclical use journals may achieve in the classroom. Questions posed in students' journals at the end of one class period may be the questions utilized for discussion at the beginning of the next class meeting.

A creative middle school science teacher uses journals in a unit on the environment. Students use their journals on field trips to make many kinds of observations about the wilderness. They both draw and write about what they see. On another day the students are asked to describe the most vivid memory they have that is associated with trees. On yet another occasion, they are asked to imagine that they have just been named as employees of the Environmental Protection Agency (EPA). As EPA officials, what are the first five things they will do to improve the environment?

A TalentEd junior high school teacher in Colorado Springs, Colorado, has his students maintain learning journals (fig. J.1) when the class is studying Shakespeare and reading *Hamlet*. Jim Keating instructs his students to divide the pages of their journals into two columns. Students use the left column to summarize his lecture notes about sixteenth-century England and Shakespeare and to summarize what happens in each act of *Hamlet*.

Fig. J.1. Learning Journal.

Class notes, film notes, chapter summaries	My ideas, understandings, and reflections

■ ■ ■

The journal note keeping encourages active participation and a higher level of learning for students. The right side of the page is saved for student responses to the notes they make. Completion of the right column of each journal page provides students with opportunities to evaluate, synthesize, analyze, and apply knowledge as it is received. At one point in their study of *Hamlet*, Mr. Keating also asks his students to keep a procrastination journal, once again utilizing the split-page format. Students write about times when they have procrastinated in the left column of their journal pages. "With this self-history students should include a response section; this allows students an avenue to explore the reasons for their own procrastination. It also provides an opportunity for the students to examine just how universal procrastination is, and to examine some of the reasons that prevented Hamlet from acting immediately."[4]

Creative English teacher Dennis McCloskey of Castle Rock, Colorado, has his ninth-grade English students create and keep reaction journals as they read *Romeo and Juliet*. On some occasions, he asks students to analyze aspects of the play such as the importance and meaning of Mercutio's Queen Mab speech in Act I, scene IV. At still another time, he asks students to write simulated journal entries that Romeo or Juliet might pen about themselves.

Journals can be employed for problem solving. Mathematical operations, scientific methods, critical-thinking models, and creative problem-solving strategies may be practiced in student journals. One example: TalentEd teachers may introduce a procedure such as the creative problem-solving model found in chapter *I*, perhaps sharing one step of the procedure each day. Students make notes in their journals about each step of the process and then select individual or class-generated problems for practice. Their journals become the repositories for all their ideas, notes, data, problem statements, criteria lists, evaluation grids, and final plans of action. Teachers can check student journals to note how well students are grasping the problem-solving methods and procedures.

Journals may definitely serve as friendly sounding boards where students can safely try out ideas and alternatives, sort priorities, and engage in personal problem solving, such as, What are all the benefits of having my own paper route? What problems might such a new job create? What will be the best use of my earnings? and Will having a paper route cause me to better manage my time? In years to come, such recorded memories may prove invaluable. An adult writing his or her personal history is immeasurably glad to have documentation of this kind.

Journals can function as observation logs. For example, when students are to be absent from school for family trips, makeup work can take the form of journal entries. Encourage students to describe the sights, sounds, smells, and impressions of the places they visit. What unusual people do they observe? What is the most creative product or souvenir they notice? What new things do they learn? How does this new information expand their existing knowledge base or their perceptions about the world? Similar journal questions and prompts may be used for class and school field trips.

Journals make terrific file folders. TalentEd teachers encourage students to fill their journals with character sketches, new words, pieces of dialogue overheard or imagined, and small gems of verbal imagery that ultimately may be incorporated into poems, essays, and short stories. Journals provide a great place for students to keep laundry lists of things to do: good books to read, assignments to complete, wish lists, daydreams (see chapter *D*), letters to write, and the like.

Journals can serve as laboratories where talented students brainstorm possible experiments to be conducted for future science fair projects or independent study modules. Journals should contain more than words. Sketches and doodles are most appropriate. In past patent disputes, an inventor's dated journal or notebook has been the authoritative proof needed to prove prior ownership of an invention or idea. A primary teacher in Indiana uses a unique approach to both writing and drawing in the prompt she gives her students when inventions are being studied: "Describe your ideal bicycle. On another, separate page in your journal make a drawing of your bicycle. I want to read your description first so I can imagine the bicycle as you have described it before I look at your drawing."

Some TalentEd teachers require that their students draw concept maps for the chapters assigned and covered in their class textbooks. In science and social studies classes, for example, students may achieve deeper and broader understandings of the course content and of how diverse pieces of information are connected and interrelated, if they are required to visually summarize and demonstrate what they have learned from their reading. A student in a social studies class might summarize a chapter on the operation of the federal government with an illustration that would reveal the three branches of the federal government, and visually represent the checks and balances that exist among and between the executive, judicial, and legislative branches of the government. The aforementioned NCTE guidelines for journal use in the classroom state that "when people think and figure things out, they do so in symbol systems commonly called languages, most often verbal but also *mathematical*, *musical*, *visual*, and so on."[5]

Journals are not just for students. Just as parents and teachers should be seen reading in order to be effective models of literacy, they should also be observed in the process of keeping journals.

Parents and teachers may also initiate journal dialogues with youth. The procedure is simple. The student periodically offers his or her journal to the teacher or parent for reading, always noting in the margins passages that are private and should not be read. The reader responds to the writer with comments, suggestions, answers, and questions about the topics the student has raised or addressed. Young people enjoy the personal touch two-way journal communication provides, and often realize for the first time that the teacher is paying attention to their work and behavior and is genuinely interested in their ideas and their progress in the class.

The shared-journal concept is taken to positive new dimensions by an award-winning teacher in Boulder, Colorado's Whittier Elementary School. Craig Yager's fifth-grade students exchange journals with senior citizens in Project Wise. Each child is matched with a senior interested in journal keeping. The seniors write about the times through which they have lived: the Great Depression, World War II, the Eisenhower years, and the 1960s. The younger generation students write about what it is like to grow up in contemporary society. One student, a baseball fan, had the good fortune to share journals with a man who had been a groundskeeper when Babe Ruth was playing baseball. Parent volunteers transport the journals back and forth between the seniors and the students.[6]

Journals become personal time capsules. Years from today young people can observe their personal evolution and development documented in their journals. As hard as it may be to imagine, today's fifteen-year-olds will be parents one day. If they keep journals, preserve them, and have the wisdom to consult them years hence, their memories will be yet green, and they may have greater appreciation and empathy for the struggles their own children will face.

Perhaps the greatest benefit of the journal in a TalentEd classroom is that it can become a good friend and constant companion of gifted, creative, and talented students. One of the most frequent complaints such students voice is that they finish with their assigned work much earlier than other students do and are required to sit, bored, and with nothing further to do as they wait for the rest of the students in the class to finish their work so the class can move on to the next task. Students should never be placed in such a position. Giving these students more of the same work is not a satisfactory solution. The chances are that the students did not need to do as many practice problems, grammar exercises, and the like as assigned in the first place to demonstrate mastery of the material. Students should always have their journals with them. When their assigned work is completed, they should know that they are invited to open their journals and begin writing or sketching. They can work on independent projects, free writing, personal explorations, visual mapping of the concepts in a text chapter assigned for a future date, or use any of the other journal options mentioned in this chapter. Once students have acquired the journal-writing habit, they never again need to be bored or engaged in unproductive behaviors in classrooms.

The numerous broad suggestions for journal uses outlined in this chapter should provide TalentEd teachers with many journal-writing ideas. Even so, the journal-writing topics or prompts in figure J.2 may be shared with students when, if ever, they run out of things to write about.

Fig. J.2. Journal topics.

Describe the latest book you have read. What is the single most important thing you learned about or noted from reading the book?

Select a daydream you listed when your teacher asked you to complete the *D Is for Daydreams* assignment. Plan a trip or adventure that you might take to realize the dream. Tell a banker why he or she should finance your adventure.

What is the most important lesson about life that you have learned this year?

Which of your senses (e.g., sight, touch, etc.) do you most value? Why?

(Figure J.2 continues on page 110.)

Fig. J.2—*Continued*

List ten things you would do if you won a million dollars in a lottery.

Name your favorite charity or service organization. What makes this organization special? What new action or behavior might you take to help this organization better perform its work?

Pick a topic, profession, or interest area about which you know relatively nothing. Go to the library media center and find a book chapter, vertical file, or encyclopedia article about the topic. Read the chapter or article and list five things you know now that you did not know before today.

Draw a picture or concept map of five things you learned this past week that you didn't know or understand before. Include in your drawing any connections between your new information and prior knowledge. For example, you might draw a square and place in it the names of three inventions that Thomas Edison created. You knew that Edison invented these three things before you read an article about his work. Then, you might draw an outline of a light bulb and place in it the names of three inventions Edison created that you had not known about before reading the article. On your journal map, you might draw an arrow from the square to the light bulb to indicate the flow of information from known to newly acquired facts.

Put yourself in someone else's shoes for a time. Try writing journal articles for famous people from history, current events, or even fairy-tale or fictional characters. Who might have written this journal entry about an eventful evening?

> Wow! What an awesome time I had last night. My ugly stepsisters never even knew I was at the prince's bash. They stood there all night watching me jam with the prince. He is totally cool and a wonderful dancer! I wish I hadn't lost my slipper, though, 'cause I cut my foot running down those stairs barefooted. Bummer!

Can you write journal entries for George Washington at Valley Forge? Neil Armstrong on 20 July 1969? Brian Robeson after the crash of the Cessna 406 in Gary Paulsen's novel *Hatchet* (New York: Puffin Books, 1988)? Create a journal entry that a favorite person or character might compose.

■ ■ ■

From *TalentEd: Strategies for Developing the Talent in Every Learner*, © 1993 Teacher Ideas Press, P.O. Box 6633, Englewood, CO 80155-6633

Notes

[1] Toby Fulwiler, *Teaching with Writing* (Portsmouth, N.H.: Heinemann Educational Books, 1987), 16.

[2] Teachers may wish to share with students a sample page from Thomas Edison's diary found in Jerry D. Flack, *Inventing, Inventions, and Inventors: A Teaching Resource Book* (Englewood, Colo.: Teacher Ideas Press, 1989), 42-43.

[3] National Council of Teachers of English, "Guidelines for Using Journals in School Settings," in Toby Fulwiler, ed., *The Journal Book* (Portsmouth, N.H.: Heinemann Educational Books, 1987), 5-8.

[4] Jim Keating, unpublished paper, University of Colorado, 5 May 1992.

[5] See National Council of Teachers of English, *The Journal Book*, 5.

[6] Janet Bingham, "Innovative Boulder Teacher Wins Reader's Digest Award," *Denver Post*, 9 April 1992, B-2.

Teacher Resources

JOURNALS AND DIARIES

Darwin, Charles. *The Voyage of the Beagle*. Ed. by Millicent E. Selsam. New York: Harper and Brothers, 1959.

> A young Charles Darwin began a sea voyage around the world in 1831 that was to change his life and the face of modern science. His personal journals tell the story of his odyssey.

Edison, Thomas A. *The Diary of Thomas A. Edison*. Old Greenwich, Conn.: Chatham Press, n.d.

> A facsimile edition of the diary the great inventor kept in July 1885 during the first vacation he had taken from his work in more than twenty-five years.

Frank, Anne. *The Diary of a Young Girl*. New York: Washington Square Press, 1963.

> This classic diary describes a life spent in hiding in Amsterdam during the Nazi occupation of the Netherlands during World War II.

Holden, Edith. *The Country Diary of an Edwardian Lady*. New York: Holt, Rinehart & Winston, 1977.

> Beautiful illustrations and comments on nature make this an especially lovely journal.

L'Engle, Madeleine. *A Circle of Quiet*. New York: Farrar, Straus & Giroux, 1972.

> A popular author of both adult and young adult fiction chronicles her thoughts on faith, family, and writing.

Lewis, Meriwether. *The Journals of the Expedition Under the Command of Captains Lewis and Clark*. Ed. by Nicholas Biddle. New York: Heritage Press, 1962.

> The exciting exploration of the Louisiana Purchase from the Missouri River to the Pacific Ocean, 1804-1806.

BOOKS ABOUT JOURNAL WRITING

Teachers who wish to begin journal writing may enjoy these volumes about adult and student journal keeping.

Baldwin, Christina. *Life's Companion: Journal Writing as a Spiritual Quest*. New York: Bantam Books, 1991.

The use of writing as a self-transformational tool to personal fulfillment.

Capacchione, Lucia. *The Creative Journal: The Art of Finding Yourself*. North Hollywood, Calif.: Newcastle, 1989.

A guide to realizing personal potential through journaling.

Chapman, Joyce. *Journaling for Joy: Writing Your Way to Personal Growth and Freedom*. North Hollywood, Calif.: Newcastle, 1991.

Two hundred strategies to achieve positive journal experiences.

Dahlstrom, Lorraine M. *Writing Down the Days: 365 Creative Journaling Ideas for Young People*. Minneapolis, Minn.: Free Spirit, 1990.

Creative journal-writing ideas for each day of the calendar year are shared in this fine teaching guide.

Fulwiler, Toby, ed. *The Journal Book*. Portsmouth, N.H.: Heinemann Educational Books, 1987.

A compendium of forty-two excellent articles about the use of journals.

Steiner, Barbara, and Kathleen Phillips. *Journal Keeping with Young People*. Englewood, Colo.: Teacher Ideas Press, 1991.

Many creative ideas for journal writing explorations are shared in this fine resource book.

Walsh, Jill Patton. *The Green Book*. New York: Farrar, Straus & Giroux, 1982.

A highly readable science fiction account, especially for teachers of younger students, of the exodus of a group of families from Earth and how they find a place known as Shine. Journal keeping plays a pivotal role in how the history of the exodus is known and shared.

# Is for Kingdoms

One of the favorite activities of gifted, creative, and talented youth is the creation of chimerical kingdoms, utopias, and other imaginary worlds. It is intriguing to note how frequently such kingdoms appear, often described in great detail, in the early writings of highly gifted children and adolescents whose eminence as adults is widely recognized. The young Wolfgang Amadeus Mozart fashioned the kingdom of Rucken where the king was kind and all citizens were virtuous. Charlotte and Branwell Brontë first created the Glass Town Confederacy and later the kingdom of Angria. Their younger sisters, Emily and Anne, invented Gondal, another mythical kingdom. Wars, political intrigue, murder, exploration, and great love affairs figured prominently in each of the sagas the young Brontë children created. A youthful C. S. Lewis occupied countless childhood hours creating the world of Boxen, complete with maps, histories, and stories of adventures. His early images of Boxen provided rich source material for *The Chronicles of Narnia*.[1]

Of course, adults are not immune to this favored creative activity of inventing imagined places and societies, both realistic and fantastic. A dictionary of imagined places might include Sherwood Anderson's Winesburg, Ohio, for example. A more fantastic gazetteer might list such places as Camazotz, Middle Earth, Earthsea, and Asteroid B-612. The contemporary popularity of Garrison Keillor's Lake Wobegon, Minnesota, and George Lucas's phenomenally popular *Star Wars* series are proof that the fascination with creating mythical societies is still very much in evidence.

Recognizing the characteristic predisposition many gifted, talented, and creative youth have toward the creation of imagined societies and communities, the author has sought ways to capitalize on this interest in the classroom. One caveat in the education of talented youth seems to be that, although such students should be engaged in creative, challenging, and meaningful scholastic work, they should not miss exposure to content or products essential for all students in their school system.

A few years ago, the author was faced with the problem of assuring that gifted and talented students enrolled in an honors English class were familiarized with the basic content of American folklore, a unit of study prescribed for all eighth-grade students in a large midwestern school system, while significantly differentiating the content and accompanying assignments in order to match their particular interests and skills. Obviously, simply reading stories about the exploits of Paul Bunyan and John Henry, and preparing a folklore notebook cataloging classic American folklore figures, were not appropriate activities for gifted students. Still, the students needed exposure to American folklore as a prerequisite for later high school studies of American literature. Thus, students did explore the pantheon of American folklore figures through varied readings, but went beyond introductory materials to consider folklore and mythology as universal phenomena. Further, they examined the work done by folklorists, oral historians, and ethnographers, and the methodologies employed by such scholars.[2]

To utilize fully what they had learned as well as to capitalize upon their creative, productive talents, students were required to create imaginary kingdoms and to provide their kingdoms with a representative folklore or mythology. Specifically, student directions read:

Create your own imaginary society and fashion a folklore appropriate for its people. You may discover a lost society (e.g., Atlantis), create a contemporary society, or describe a contemporary community anew. You may reveal your society's folklore through some grand adventure (story form), through the writings of an anthropologist (quasi-scientific report), or invent another presentation format.

Your presentation should include references to and explanations of your community's heroes, architecture, music, entertainment, sports, superstitions and beliefs, unique vocabulary, totems and amulets, tools and products, class structure, literature and art.

Your final product should include at least one original myth or folktale, one hero or heroine, a history of the people, diagrams and drawings of structures found in the society, maps, and a glossary of vocabulary unique to the citizenry.

A crucial part of the assignment was the creation of a unique delivery system involving an explanation of how contemporary society might learn about the imagined culture, and the packaging of the completed project.

Completed projects revealed excellent transfers of knowledge about the patterns and traditions of cultures, and provided striking examples of individual creativity both in descriptions of societies and in the delivery systems employed. The complexities of one student's society, the Tribbots of the Middle Moon, were revealed through a top secret NASA document. Another student chronicled the lives, adventures, and folklore of the Glaciens, a highly advanced but doomed people who lived and died under glacial formations in Boothis Bay in the Arctic. A renowned anthropologist had discovered the Glaciens and had recorded their history and folklore. Tragically, he had perished along with the Glaciens when their environment collapsed, but not before wrapping his journals in heavy oilcloth and setting them adrift on an ice floe. The student, posing as a contemporary anthropologist studying the Netsilik Eskimos, miraculously discovers the journals and reveals them to a fascinated world.

Closer to home, another student revealed how the residents of a sleepy small town were radicalized by a hip, Black minister. Black pride became the predominant theme in the student's culture. Another contemporary societal issue was given play in one particularly liberated young lady's explanation of the Bermuda Triangle mystery. The Greek demigoddess, Hera, became disgusted with the attention her husband, Zeus, paid to Athena. In a huff, she created the undersea continent of Atlantic Bermuda where a superior race of women could live without men. But, down through time, one problem remains: Men are still needed to perpetuate the race. Using their incredible powers, the beautiful and brilliant women of Atlantic Bermuda are able to detect when a boat or plane carrying especially good specimens of the male species is positioned directly above them. Presto! The plane or ship disappears without a trace, and the problem of procreation is solved. Alas (for the men), the victims are never freed.

A creative outgrowth of students' studies of history, economics, geography, anthropology, government, science, and language arts can be the creation of imaginary kingdoms and cultures. This activity can be a group activity, planned and executed in the classroom, or it can be an individual project completed chiefly by a gifted child or adolescent working at home.

K Is for Kingdoms

TalentEd students should create kingdoms with clearly identified and articulated cultures. Students are explorers who "discover" previously unknown civilizations. The culture of each student's kingdom may be revealed through some grand adventure tale (e.g., *The Hobbit* or *Star Wars*), or through a quasi-scientific paper that an anthropologist might author for a scholarly ethnography journal. The projected kingdoms should be represented by many of the following traits found in a civilization.

Heroes and Heroines	Architecture	Classes of Society
Music	Sports and Leisure	Recreation
Tools	Products	Economics
Work	Symbols	Art
History	Traditions	Holidays or Festivals
Family Life	Language	Government
Education	Religion	

TalentEd students may proceed to create their kingdoms in the following manner:

1. Give the kingdom a name.

2. Create a map of the land inhabited by the society.

3. Create names for the cities, rivers, and mountains.

4. Describe the people of the kingdom and tell how they were "discovered."

5. Explain how the society functions. What are the major forms of work? How is the kingdom governed? Is there more than one class of people?

6. Describe at least one holiday, religious festival, or feast.

7. Replicate the most stunning pieces of the kingdom's art and architecture.

8. Retell one of the legends of the kingdom's heroes, or recount one of the kingdom's greatest literary masterpieces.

9. Describe how children in the kingdom are educated.

10. Create a unique delivery system to communicate all of the above information about the existence of this civilization to the rest of the known world.

Advise students that each of the component parts must be congruent with other traits or artifacts. For example, the artwork ascribed to the imaginary kingdom must be able to be fashioned with the tools the people of the kingdom are said to possess.

Once all the TalentEd students have created their civilizations, a United Nations forum should be held, and each person or group should *creatively* reveal the civilization to the other students. Countless spinoffs then become creative classroom options. All of the kingdoms are going to be affected by the depletion of the ozone. How might the many civilization leaders rectify this alarming situation? In an open forum, a travel agent from each civilization could entice vacationers to visit their utopias. Ask students to imagine that one of the kingdoms has a history of war and aggression. How can the remaining kingdoms protect themselves without risking the start of a brand new war? How might conflict resolution techniques be utilized?

The creation of kingdoms in TalentEd classrooms is an exciting and creative venture for both teachers and students.

Notes

[1] See *Amadeus Mozart* by Ibi Lepscky (New York: Barron's Educational Series, 1982); *Unquiet Soul: A Biography of Charlotte Brontë* by Margot Peters (New York: Doubleday, 1975); *Boxen: The Imaginary World of C. S. Lewis*, edited by Walter Hooper (New York: Harcourt Brace Jovanovich, 1985); and the *Chronicles of Narnia* by C. S. Lewis, illustrated by Pauline Baynes (New York: Macmillan, 1950).

[2] For a more detailed account of this student project, please see Jerry D. Flack, "Is There a Gifted Program in Lake Wobegon," *Gifted Child Today (G/C/T)* 37 (March/April 1985): 13-14.

Teacher Resources

Manguel, Alberto, and Gianni Guadalupi. *Dictionary of Imaginary Places*. Illus. by Graham Greenfield. New York: Macmillan, 1980.

Maps and illustrations highlight famed imaginary places born of literature, including Tolkien's "Middle Earth," C. S. Lewis's "Narnia," Baum's "Oz," and Barrie's "Never-Never Land."

Tolkien, J. R. R. *The Hobbit: or There and Back Again*. Illus. by Michael Hague. Boston: Houghton Mifflin, 1984.

The mythic battle between good and evil is found in the classic adventures of hobbit Bilbo Baggins.

# Is for Literature

> Literature is a transmission of power. Textbooks and treatises, dictionaries and encyclopedias, manuals and books of instruction—they are communications; but literature is a power line, and the motor, mark you, is the reader.
>
> —Charles P. Curtis

> The whole reason for going to school is to get the impression fixed for life that there is a book side to everything.
>
> —Robert Frost

Literature is lasting power. The finest kind of power: the power of the intellect. Teachers and parents who want to give young people a great gift teach them to love literature. In a TalentEd classroom books are everywhere. Literature is everywhere. Students quickly come to appreciate the import of Robert Frost's wisdom. The teacher may begin or end a class with an oral reading of a poem or an outstanding passage from a biography or work of fiction, regardless of the age of the students. Good teachers know that oral reading is as vital to stimulate and challenge high school seniors as it is for first-grade students. There are also periods of quietude when every person in the room, including the teacher, is reading silently. Shelves and book carts containing a wide sampling and range of literary genres are present. Dust jackets of notable new books adorn bulletin boards. Quotations about the power and value of literature are found on posters that decorate classroom walls. A reading center may also be a part of the environment in the TalentEd classroom.

TalentEd teachers are concerned about developing the reading of gifted, talented, and creative youth in at least three ways. They want their students to read widely, critically, and creatively.[1] First, good teachers want students to experience and savor a comprehensive reading program. Teachers and library media specialists need to expose students to the choice authors of literature for children and adolescents. Student awareness of who is writing, what is being written, and common literary themes and styles should be developed. Youth should read often enough and widely enough to become author-conscious. That is, after a time, they should recognize a prose passage by Katherine Paterson or Gary Paulsen as easily as they can recognize and attribute a poem to Robert Frost or e. e. cummings. Young people do not automatically select good literature to read. Library media specialists, parents, and teachers need to share great books with students through oral reading and through the provision of reading lists of good books for students.[2] Many titles of excellent works of literature are suggested in this chapter, and readers are also guided to agencies such as the American Library Association for titles of other fine literary works. As good as fiction for young people is, it is also important that young people, who will invest so much of their lives in nonfiction books, move beyond fiction to read choice examples of literature from history, poetry, natural science, and biography.

Students also need to learn to read critically. They need to develop the ability to discriminate between good literature and trivial and poorly written works. Library media specialists, with their training, resources, and love of literature, can be especially helpful in recommending quality literature to talented youth. Literary criticism, with its emphasis on the analysis and evaluation levels of Bloom's Taxonomy, is one component of critical reading. Another critical reading skill is the ability to discern an author's purpose. Teach students to develop appropriate criteria to judge literature and to apply it to what they read. Good critical readers, for example, are able to read two or more biographies of a subject's life, critically examine both works, and determine which biographer has done the better job of sharing the subject's life with readers. Critical readers come to know that themes such as death, the nature of evil, racism, and coming of age are found in literature, and they can appraise multiple works with similar themes and determine which authors handle themes truthfully and with grace, and which authors miss the mark.

Students ultimately need to read creatively. That is, they need to use good literature as the grist for their own thinking about important ideas and themes, and as the catalyst for finding and using their own voices to write about things that matter to them. Critical reading is chiefly a convergent process, even when practiced with high-level text material. Creative reading is a divergent process. Creative readers go beyond the text page; they do get off the subject. Students may begin with a discussion of a work they have read, but they vault beyond the printed page to discussions of life itself. In 1980, the author taught a seventh-grade girl who wanted to read *Hamlet* as an extension of the class reading of Shakespeare's *The Taming of the Shrew*. This was the time of America's anguish when Iran held Americans as captives. Her creative response to a reading of Shakespeare's great piece of literature was to rewrite Hamlet's famed "To be or not to be" soliloquy as if President Jimmy Carter were Hamlet deliberating in anguish over what best course of action to take. She found meaning in what she read and she responded creatively.

It is impossible to suggest in one brief chapter all the great literature young people should read. Rather, readers are invited here to look at ten outstanding novels for young people that feature gifted, creative, and talented central characters. Next, recommended literature for college-bound youth as suggested by the American Library Association is noted, and ten outstanding works drawn from poetry, fiction, biography, and nonfiction are described. Finally, book-sharing ideas that may encourage creative responses to literature from young people are listed.

> Truly each new book is as a ship
> that bears us away into the
> movement and splendor
> of life's infinite ocean.
> —Helen Keller

Fiction with Gifted Characters

Characters depicted in fiction for youth display a panoply of traits and characteristics associated with gifted, creative, and talented students. Some characters are skillful problem solvers. Others are precocious, budding scientists. There are creative, insightful writers, artists, and musicians. Some of these youthful characters are supremely confident and handle their giftedness with aplomb and admirable poise. Others are deeply troubled and confused. Some are lonely and isolated, while others have an admiring throng. Some abuse their talents; others are themselves abused. Some characters receive encouragement and applause; others suffer censure and indignity. In short, literature for youth provides a literary microcosm of the world of gifted youth that young readers can explore and at least for a time, inhabit vicariously.[3]

The tapestry of literature about talented and creative youth is complex and diverse. There are deep, troubling novels by skillful authors like Virginia Hamilton and Katherine Paterson that provide readers with rich, fully developed characters involved in complex human relationships that require young readers to engage in critical thinking involving moral reasoning and evaluation. Whether young readers are reticent or comfortable in discussing their own creativity or giftedness, the world of fiction offers a reasonably safe arena in which they can explore, discuss, and evaluate the behaviors of gifted characters who may reflect their own interests, problems, ambitions, and concerns. Literature about gifted youth may provide the grist for the gifted youth's thinking about his or her own giftedness. It may provide answers or at least provoke thoughtful questioning.

A special kind of friendship forged between two lonely, gifted children is the subject of Katherine Paterson's hauntingly beautiful *Bridge to Terabithia*. Jesse Oliver Aarons, Jr., is a talented young artist whose cultural, geographic, and socioeconomic isolation threaten to extinguish his giftedness. Only the music teacher at Lark Creek recognizes Jesse as unusually talented. His father disdains his talent for art as being unmanly.

In the summer of his fifth-grade year, Leslie Burke enters Jesse's world. The precocious Leslie inhabits a world of culture and ideas foreign to Jesse and the other children of Lark Creek. Her parents are authors; she reads *Moby Dick* and *Hamlet* and listens to classical music. The isolation both children feel serves as a catalyst to cement a rare and beautiful friendship, perhaps one so rare that it was meant only for their magical kingdom of Terabithia. It is in the special wooded retreat of Terabithia where they are totally free to be gifted, to be themselves, without apology.

Jesse teaches Leslie the survival skills, the mores of rural culture. Leslie, in turn, provides Jesse with an emotional mirror in which to see and appreciate his giftedness. She opens worlds to him he never knew existed. Her tragic death awakens within Jesse the knowledge that he can be comfortable with his gifts, that he can cope with the world, and that he can find meaning in life.

This Newbery Medal-winning novel provides a very special window through which gifted children can view some of the special problems gifted children may face in growing up, and the special, unique friendships they can forge to cope with their loneliness and lack of acceptance.

Katherine Paterson won her second Newbery Medal for the beautifully written *Jacob Have I Loved*, a modern retelling of the story of Jacob and Esau. As World War II rages in the background, a private war rages within Sara Louise Bradshaw. Her twin sister Caroline is the favored, the gifted, the adored one with the magical voice. "She was so sure, so present, so easy, so light and gold, while I was all grey and shadow." Paterson's novel offers a rare glimpse of what life may be like for the sibling of a gifted youth who feels less gifted. While she is gifted in her own right, the radiance that accompanies Caroline's triumphs blinds Louise to her own value. Only with healing, time, and maturity does she come to accept herself and her own worth.

Virginia Hamilton further explores familial relationships in *Arilla Sundown*. Arilla Adams is a gifted adolescent searching for her own identity. She is both loving and ashamed of her family and its roots. "This is the queerist, dumbest family that ever there was," she laments. Her mother is Black, has been a ballet dancer, and now teaches dance. Her father is part Black, part Native American, and not wholly content nor accepted in the non-Indian world. Her brother Jack Sun Run is a rebellious youth who drowns his own uncertainty about his racial heritage in an orgy of Amerind pride. Arilla is bright and excels in both language arts and math. Her brother suggests her solitary search for her identity is misunderstood by her peers. "The signal they get from you is one of thinking. Of the smarts. You get good grades and they understand being alone when it's a smart girl with an arty mom." Arilla's coming to terms with her father, her deeper understanding of her brother, and her gradual acceptance of herself add up to a thoroughly satisfying novel about a gifted youth growing up.

The terrible price society and individuals pay when talent is expected to coexist with the despair of emotional, social, and economic deprivation is dramatized in Virginia Hamilton's *The Planet of Junior Brown*. Junior Brown is prodigious both in girth and in his talent for music. He desperately tries to cling to sanity in a world he finds oppressive and peopled by an overly possessive mother who waits for a father who never comes, and a music teacher who never allows him to make music. Buddy, himself an abandoned child who is bright in math and science, attempts to create a refuge, a planet where Junior will be safe, offering him the only real understanding he has ever received. The starkness of the novel should provoke thoughts and discussions about the peril that exists when talent is expected to thrive in dysfunctional environments, and of how such talent might be saved before it is irretrievably lost.

Elizabeth Borton de Trevino's *I, Juan de Pareja* is steeped in history. Juan de Pareja is born into slavery in seventeenth-century Spain. When his late mother's mistress dies, he is "inherited" along with his mistress's other "possessions" by her nephew, the artist Velazquez. Juan's growth to manhood is paralleled by the artist's growing stature as a painter. Juan travels with his master to the Spanish court of King Philip IV and to the Vatican of Pope Innocent X. His travels are exciting and his master is kind, but Juan yearns to be a free man and an artist, a profession forbidden to slaves. This Newbery Medal-winning novel offers readers a central character who personifies the extreme obstacles gifted and creative individuals in the past have often had to overcome. It reminds readers that giftedness is not something newly invented for the space age, nor is it bound by race, nationality, or station in life. Giftedness is talent realized through courage and determination.

Natalie Field is one of two talented high school seniors in Ursula K. Le Guin's *Very Far Away from Anywhere Else*. Natalie is a gifted musician who wants to attend the Eastman School of Music to study composition. She is not a starry-eyed dreamer; she questions both the depth of her talent and the struggles she will have as a female in a profession where, traditionally, men dominate. The novel explores her relationship with Owen Thomas Griffith, a young man with talents for science and mathematics, and tells of the special friendship and understanding these two talented young adults forge through the fragile and difficult process of growing up. Le Guin wisely recognizes that while talented adolescents face some unique problems and circumstances in developing their gifts, they share common problems with all teenagers, particularly the search for sexual identity. The novel deals sensitively with the growing feelings of sexuality in its characters in an honest and caring manner.

Sixteen-year-old Sibilance T. Spooner, the protagonist of Bruce Brooks's *Midnight Hour Encores*, is one of the world's most promising cellists, and the winner of three world competitions. She has been raised in Washington, D.C., by her unconventional father, Cabot Spooner, whom she affectionately calls "Taxi." She has never seen her mother who gave her up willingly the day she was born. In her sixteenth summer, Sib decides it is time to meet her mother and she and her dad begin an odyssey to San Francisco in a 1960s Volkswagen bus. The journey is not just geographical. Taxi amplifies the cross-country drive with music and stories from the 1960s. He knows he may be on his final journey with his daughter, and he wants her to know the person he was when he chose to raise her alone. Music lovers will enjoy the everpresent references to classical music and the musicianship Sib exhibits. While her incredible talent places her in rarified air, musically, Sib personally faces the same problems many adolescents face in leaving childhood behind and learning to make the lasting decisions of adulthood.

No discussion of precocity in characters from fiction would be complete without mention of Charles Wallace, Meg's "dumb baby brother" in Madeleine L'Engle's *A Wrinkle in Time*, winner of the 1963 Newbery Medal. Charles Wallace does not even talk at four, but by the age of five speaks in complex sentences, learns new words like *exhaustive* daily, and can quote verbatim definitions of words such as *compulsion* from the *Oxford Concise Dictionary*. Like their parents who are gifted scientists, Meg and Charles Wallace Murry are exceptionally gifted intellectually. The siblings' search for their missing father involves richly portrayed fantasy, but is equally a search for identity and self. Early in the novel, Meg complains to her mother, "I have been an oddball." Their companion, Calvin O'Keef, is another gifted young man whose talent and ability cause him to be seen as different and out of sync. Happily, readers can follow further adventures of Meg and Charles Wallace Murry in *A Wind in the Door* and *A Swiftly Tilting Planet*.

The Westing Game by Ellen Raskin also won the Newbery Medal and features four gifted, creative, and talented youths. The novel is both a mystery and a puzzle game for readers to unravel. Sixteen heirs to the Westing fortune, valued at over $200 million, engage in a game to determine the murderer and beneficiary of Samuel W. Westing. Doug Hoo, eighteen, is one of the heirs. He is also a gifted high school athlete who can outrun college milers. He later wins gold medals in the Olympic Games. Chris Theodoraskis, fifteen, is confined to a wheelchair and speech is difficult for him. He is an exceptionally bright youth and he is a gifted ornithologist. His older brother, Theo, is a talented writer. The prime sleuth in *The Westing Game*, however, is Tabitha Ruth Wexler, thirteen, better known as "Turtle." She is not only a good detective, she is also an accomplished stock-market player. Raskin provides readers with an exceptionally fine mystery plot and with characters whom she wisely follows into adulthood. The gifted characters in their adult lives are refreshingly free of sex-role stereotyping. Turtle, for example, is an enormously successful corporation executive.

A sensitive, older artist helps Carrie Stokes find meaning in her life in Zibby Oneal's *The Language of Goldfish*. Carrie, thirteen, who is gifted both in art and mathematics, finds growing up in an affluent suburb of Chicago too difficult. She retreats into the memories of childhood and her idealization of a childhood goldfish pool with its safe, secure island haven. A failed suicide attempt places her in the hands of a psychologist, Dr. Ross, who along with her caring art teacher, Mrs. Ramsay, helps her through the process of growing up and leaving her island and childhood behind.

Reading Lists

Reading lists of literature for both children and young adults may be secured from most local libraries and school library media centers. The American Library Association publishes pamphlets on Outstanding Books for College Bound students in several categories that include fiction, biography, nonfiction, fine arts, and drama. To secure copies, teachers and library media specialists may write the American Library Association, 50 East Huron Street, Chicago, Illinois 60611.

> **Without books God is silent, justice dormant, science at a stand, philosophy lame, letters dumb, and all things involved in a Cimmerian darkness.**
> —Anonymous

Ten Fine Books

The ten books described below represent a somewhat eclectic grouping of outstanding literature for children and young adults. Works of fiction, biography, poetry, and nonfiction are included. The choices represent only a few of the many, many significant books of the latter half of the twentieth century that young people today should read.

Russell Baker's autobiography *Growing Up* won the Pulitzer Prize for biography in 1982. It is a wonderful story about youth and about growing up in America during the Great Depression. Like all the writers in this list, Baker is masterful. His portrayals of family, friends, and teachers are wonderful.

Richard Bradford uses the vast and awesome New Mexico landscape as a backdrop for his coming-of-age novel *Red Sky at Morning*. His finely written novel explores the lives of three high school students in a small New Mexico mountain town during World War II. Bradford manages to portray all the tensions and emotions of growing up with hilarity, poignancy, and compassion.

No list of fine books for young readers would be complete without a reference to at least one picture book. Illustrators such as Leo and Diane Dillon, Chris Van Allsburg, Maurice Sendak, Tomie dePaola, and Thomas Locker have made the picture book one of the finest art forms of the last two or three decades. Lynne Cherry is one of the newer illustrators to grace the picture book genre. In *A River Ran Wild*, Cherry's words and rich illustrations tell the story of the Nashua River in Massachusetts over the past 600 years. The book chronicles the human impact on the environment from the time when the pebbled river bottom shone clearly to Native Americans to a point in the 1960s when the river was declared environmentally dead, and then on through the restoration of the river as a clear, clean waterway achieved by the concerted efforts of environmentally conscious citizens.

Michael Hart writes 100 excellent short essays in *The 100: A Ranking of the Most Influential Persons in History*. Hart's essays on such men and women as Muhammad, Jesus, Queen Elizabeth I, and Picasso provide fascinating insight into how and why given individuals have such lasting and great impact on the history of the world.

Kenneth Koch and Kate Farrell beautifully combine ancient and modern poetry and art in *Talking to the Sun: An Anthology of Poems for Young People*. Poetry as diverse as Hopi and Navajo Indian chants, the words of William Shakespeare, and the verse of Emily Dickinson, Langston Hughes, and Christina Rossetti takes on new meaning when imaginatively combined with great art treasures from the collection of the Metropolitan Museum of Art. This visually and verbally splendid book is organized around themes such as dreams, babies and children, feelings, animals, and love.

Number the Stars by Lois Lowry is a Newbery Medal novel for younger readers that deserves to be read by people of all ages. The novel portrays the story of two girls, one Christian and one Jewish, in Copenhagen in 1943. In telling the individual story of Annemarie Johansen and Ellen Rosen, Lowry effectively tells the real-life story of the heroic Danish Resistance that saved the lives of at least 7,000 Jews who were taken to freedom in Sweden during some of the darkest hours the world has ever known. The novel makes a superb reading companion to *Anne Frank: The Diary of a Young Girl*.

Illustrator David Macaulay helps readers fathom the secrets of modern technology in his insightful and user-friendly book *The Way Things Work*. The workings of 300 or more machines such as the fire extinguisher, the toilet tank, robots, flight simulators, parking meters, can openers, laser printers, microcomputers, hovercraft, and grand pianos are explained in both words and pictures that even those readers who believe themselves to be technologically illiterate will find accessible. Macaulay explains the scientific concepts that govern the working of machines, and reveals to readers important linkages between such diverse machines as windmills and dentist's drills and zippers and plows. This book proves that nonfiction reference books can be every bit as entertaining, exciting, and enjoyable as works of fiction.

Photographs play a pivotal role in Patricia MacLachlan's deeply moving short novel *Journey*. The author sensitively and skillfully explores a sadly relevant contemporary topic: dysfunctional families. She also, however, reveals the warmth and hope and courage often found in nontraditional family structures as the young protagonist and his grandfather bond with one another. Even though the protagonist, Journey, is only eleven years old, high school students love this novel as much as younger readers do.

Ernest Hemingway said that Beryl Markham's writing in *West with the Night* was so fine that, by comparison, he was ashamed to call himself a writer.[4] Markham's memoirs tell of a remarkable childhood spent in Kenya, and of an even more incredible adulthood that included work as a mail carrier and racehorse trainer, and a difficult solo flight across the Atlantic Ocean the hard way, west to east.

Every list of good books for young people should contain at least one survival book, and one of the best is Gary Paulsen's *Hatchet*. Thirteen-year-old Brian Robeson is on a bush plane headed for the wilderness of northern Canada when the pilot dies suddenly. The youthful protagonist must not only land the plane, but survive in the wilderness with nothing more than the clothes on his back and a hatchet. Readers who at an earlier age fell in love with Jean Craighead George's *My Side of the Mountain* will greatly enjoy *Hatchet*.

Book Sharing Ideas

The scene of the crime. It is almost closing time at the local library in Anytown, U.S.A. A young man enters the doors and stealthily moves to the section marked Young Adult Fiction. Hurriedly, almost feverishly, he stalks the shelves. A book encased in an electric blue dust jacket emblazoned with red stripes and lettering catches his eye. "I'll do that one," he says to no one in particular. Book in hand, he sits at a nearby table, opens a notebook to blank pages, and glances furtively first left, and then right. "Good," he thinks, "no one is watching." Nervously, he handles the book, turning it over in his hands, opening the cover. Quickly, he begins to copy down the words a publicist has written for the inside flaps of the dust jacket. The pages of the novel remain virginal, unexplored territory. As the last words are hurriedly copied, the youth is already in motion: chair pulled back, notebook closing, footsteps heading toward the exit. A cynical, twisted smile begins to emerge on his face. He has pulled off another successful heist. The book report due the next morning is done.

The crime committed in this scene is surely repeated a thousandfold in towns and cities all across the nation. Perhaps it can be argued that the young man would not have read any book no matter how stimulating the book report assignment, but it can also be asserted that the traditional book report assignment is about as imaginative and exciting as the "What I Did Last Summer" essay, and invites responses that are similarly boring, bogus, or both.

The book sharing ideas listed in figure L.1 constitute an effort to halt the kind of criminal activity described above. The figure may be duplicated and given to TalentEd students at the beginning of the school year. Students can then refer to it periodically as book sharing assignments and opportunities occur throughout the school year.

Fig. L.1. Book sharing ideas.

1. Design a teaching guide for a novel or biography. Include vocabulary activities, discussion questions, a word search or crossword puzzle, suggested extending activities, and additional items that will assist other students who may read the book. Contribute the completed study module or book kit to the classroom learning center or the school library media center.

2. Make a list of the major locations such as houses, stores, streets, parks, and rivers mentioned in a novel. Draw a map showing a birds-eye view of the area. Number each locale on the map. At the bottom of the map list each locale and describe what happens there in the novel. Example: 1. Essex Park. Colonel Moran's body is discovered here.

3. Plan a Chinese dinner for the characters in a novel you have read. Prepare a fortune cookie for each of the main characters. The fortunes should relate to the respective personalities of the characters and the events that involve them in the book.

4. Create a special-edition newspaper related to the characters, plot, and setting of a novel you have read. News stories, features, classified ads, advice columns, cartoons, horoscopes, and sports may be created to highlight the characters and events in the novel.

5. Assume that you are a world-famous psychologist. Write a case study profile of the main character in a novel you have read. Where appropriate, recommend a specific course of therapy for the character.

6. Create a poster that bookstores might utilize for autographing parties featuring the author of the book you have just read.

7. From the Yellow Pages of the phone book, select five businesses in which the main character of a mystery novel might be interested. Explain the connections.

8. Create a spring kite. Paint images of favorite characters, settings, or episodes from a favorite novel on the face of the kite. Save your kite for the spring kite festival day when all students share their books and then fly their kites.

(Figure L.1 continues on page 126.)

Fig. L.1 — *Continued*

9. A very impatient man who is definitely a curmudgeon asks you to describe the main character in the novel you have read in *exactly* sixty-four words. Can you do it?

10. Compile a scrapbook suggested by information in a book you have read. The contents might include references to the character's likes and dislikes, origins, needs, and travels.

11. Write a letter to the chairperson of a content area in your school. Urge the chairperson to consider using a book you have just read as required or recommended reading for his or her department. For example, you might try to convince the head of the science department that Jean C. George's *My Side of the Mountain*, Gary Paulsen's *Hatchet*, or Lynne Cherry's *A River Ran Wild* would make first-rate reading for students in environmental science classes.

12. Create an old-fashioned patchwork quilt. Such quilts were fashioned from scraps of fabrics assembled into a block. Using the image of a block quilt, plus the collage technique, make a block quilt that represents a single character, many characters, actions, scenes, and events from a favorite book. The "scraps" may be drawings, magazine pictures, newsprint, commercial packaging, wallpaper samples, or other unique media.

13. Create a board game based on the plot or subject of a book. Movement around the playing board may be determined by the ability of participants to answer questions about the contents of the book.

14. Assume the position of the main character or subject in a book. Based upon what has been learned about this character or person, write a series of poems, journal entries, or letters reflecting how the character views life.

15. Create a passport for the main character or subject of a book. Include a photo or drawing of the person, and reference all travel the character or person experiences. Include probable future destinations as well.

■ ■ ■

> The world of books is the most remarkable creation of man.
> Nothing else that he builds ever lasts. Monuments fall.
> Nations perish. Civilizations grow old and die out.
> After an era of darkness new races build others,
> but in the world of books are volumes that live on
> still young and fresh as the day they were written.
> Still telling men's hearts of the hearts of men centuries dead.
>
> —Clarence Day

Notes

[1] Robert L. Tresize first used these three descriptors in "Teaching Reading to the Gifted," *Language Arts* 54, no. 8 (November/December 1977): 920-924.

[2] Readers who wish to investigate further connections between the school library media specialist and gifted students may consult Jerry D. Flack, "A New Look at a Valued Partnership: The Library Media Specialist and the Gifted Student," *School Library Media Quarterly* 14, no. 3 (Summer 1986): 174-179.

[3] Readers who wish a more detailed analysis of fictional gifted characters may consult Jerry D. Flack and Pose Lamb, "Making Use of Gifted Characters in Literature," *Gifted Child Today (G/C/T)* (September/October 1984): 3-11.

[4] Ernest Hemingway, letter to Maxwell Perkins, in Mary S. Lovell, *Straight on Till Morning: The Biography of Beryl Markham* (New York: St. Martin's Press, 1987), 326.

Teacher Resources

Baker, Russell. *Growing Up*. New York: New American Library, 1982.

Bradford, Richard. *Red Sky at Morning*. New York: Harper & Row, 1968.

Brooks, Bruce. *Midnight Hour Encores*. New York: HarperCollins, 1986.

Cherry, Lynne. *A River Ran Wild*. New York: Harcourt Brace Jovanovich, 1992.

de Trevino, Elizabeth Borton. *I, Juan de Pareja*. Farrar, Straus & Giroux, 1965.

Frank, Anne. *Anne Frank: The Diary of a Young Girl*. New York: Washington Square, 1967.

George, Jean C. *My Side of the Mountain*. New York: E. P. Dutton, 1959.

Hamilton, Virginia. *Arilla Sundown*. New York: Greenwillow Books, 1976.

———. *The Planet of Junior Brown*. New York: Macmillan, 1971.

Hart, Michael H. *The 100: A Ranking of the Most Influential Persons in History*. New York: Galahad Books, 1978.

Koch, Kenneth, and Kate Farrell, eds. *Talking to the Sun: An Illustrated Anthology of Poems for Young People*. New York: Holt, Rinehart & Winston, 1985.

Le Guin, Ursula K. *Very Far Away from Anywhere Else*. New York: Atheneum, 1976.

L'Engle, Madeleine. *A Swiftly Tilting Planet*. New York: Farrar, Straus & Giroux, 1978.

_____. *A Wind in the Door*. New York: Farrar, Straus & Giroux, 1973.

_____. *A Wrinkle in Time*. New York: Farrar, Straus & Giroux, 1962.

Lowry, Lois. *Number the Stars*. Boston: Houghton Mifflin, 1989.

Macaulay, David. *The Way Things Work*. Boston: Houghton Mifflin, 1988.

MacLachlan, Patricia. *Journey*. New York: Delacorte Press, 1991.

Markham, Beryl. *West with the Night*. San Francisco, Calif.: North Point Press, 1983.

Oneal, Zibby. *The Language of Goldfish*. New York: Viking Press, 1980.

Paterson, Katherine. *Bridge to Terabithia*. New York: Thomas Y. Crowell, 1977.

_____. *Jacob Have I Loved*. New York: Thomas Y. Crowell, 1980.

Paulsen, Gary. *Hatchet*. New York: Bradbury Press, 1988.

Raskin, Ellen. *The Westing Game*. New York: Dutton Children's Books, 1978.

M Is for Mystery

Imagine a time and place a century past. It is London, circa 1890. The foggy atmosphere invokes mystery and intrigue. The sounds of horses' hooves reverberate on cobblestone streets. The hansom cab is occupied by a distinguished-looking couple. The driver halts the progress of the hansom and announces that the destination of 221 B Baker Street has been reached. The couple climb the front steps of a brick row house, and ring the door chime. A kindly lady, Mrs. Hudson, meets them and surmises their purpose. "This way," she beckons and ushers them up a winding staircase and into the sitting room occupied by the world's greatest consulting detective, Sherlock Holmes. A tall, angular man greets them. "Pray tell, what brings you to seek out Dr. Watson and myself?"

"Mr. Holmes, we are teachers and we need to find some fresh and imaginative ways to teach critical-thinking and problem-solving skills to our students."

"It's elementary! Absolutely elementary," Holmes replies. "Use mystery and intrigue."

Once again, Holmes solves a mystery. Critical-thinking and problem-solving skills can be taught effectively by TalentEd teachers who add a dash of mystery and intrigue to the curriculum.[1]

Presently, great national attention is being paid to the importance of teaching critical-thinking and problem-solving skills in all areas of the curriculum. Teachers are not content with knowledge-based acquisition as the sole aim of education in the classroom. In every discipline across the school curriculum, greater emphasis is being placed upon rigorous thinking and the development of problem-solving skills on the part of students. As teachers search for methods, materials, and ideas to help them teach these vital life skills to their students, they would do well to examine the rich possibilities offered through student encounters with the mystery literature genre. Like its cousin, science fiction, mystery literature has been kept in the educational closet too long. The use of mystery literature needs no apology. Freud and Jung are but two intellectual giants who enjoyed mystery literature. Presidents Abraham Lincoln and Franklin D. Roosevelt joined Nobel Prize-winning authors Pearl Buck, T. S. Eliot, Rudyard Kipling, George Bernard Shaw, John Steinbeck, and William Faulkner as writers of mysteries. Mystery literature is highly motivating. More than a few reluctant readers have been successfully engaged in reading and research when introduced to the thrilling adventures of Sherlock Holmes and Doctor Watson, Miss Jane Marple, Hercule Poirot, and a host of other sleuths.

Mystery literature addresses critical values essential to a stable society, and may be the most moral of all forms of literature young readers experience. The cardinal rule of all mystery writing is that the guilty are caught and punished. Virtue triumphs over evil; goodness reigns. Moreover, in these modern morality tales, goodness prevails because clever and skillful detectives use reason and brainpower to uncover wrong and vanquish wickedness and corruption. Unlike so many contemporary television and movie heroes offered up to young people, classic literary detectives such as Jane Marple and Sherlock Holmes bring culprits to justice and right wrongs with mind power, not gun power.

Fortunately, classic literature in the mystery genre is widely accessible. The stories of Poe, Conan Doyle, Christie, and others may be easily found for older and more gifted readers. Even at the primary level, many excellent mysteries are available. Mystery authors such as David Adler, Harry Allard and James Marshall, and Eve Bunting have provided splendid mysteries for the youngest mystery readers. The bibliography of mystery literature beginning on page 141 offers a sampling of recommended mysteries.

Classic sleuths offer students splendid role models as problem solvers. The preeminent example is, of course, the primary resident of 221 B Baker Street: Sherlock Holmes. In all of literature it is hard to find a hero or protagonist who better exemplifies the intellectual traits and behaviors teachers want their students to acquire. Holmes was a student of all disciplines. He recognized the need to study science and mathematics as well as history, art, and languages, and to integrate all he learned. He believed education to be a lifelong pursuit. He believed unswervingly in the power of reason, and he was a rigorous and indefatigable problem solver. Witness this description of Holmes as a problem solver offered up by Doctor Watson in "The Man with the Twisted Lip":

> Sherlock Holmes was a man who when he had an unsolved problem upon his mind would go for days, and even for a week without rest, turning it over, rearranging his facts, looking at it from every point of view until he had either fathomed it or convinced himself that his data were insufficient.[2]

Is this not the same kind of intellectual tenacity TalentEd teachers want to develop in young critical thinkers and problem solvers? Any observation of the intellectual behavior of Holmes reminds educators of the similarity between the good critical thinker and the skillful sleuth, and how parallel the steps are that they take in solving their respective problems or cases. Over the years, the author has observed first-grade students, science fair prize-winners, graduate students, and fellow colleagues approach, tackle, and solve all manner of problems. The similarity between their behaviors and those of master detectives has not escaped his attention. Sherlock Holmes and the fourth-grade inventor share certain common stages or steps in problem solving. First, there is a motivational step. The motivation may be extra credit, acclaim, or just the joy of pursuing the truth. Good problem solvers and detectives are bloodhounds for facts and clues. They are systematic in their search for data. Next, they sort and analyze data with open minds. They seek to prove or disprove their hunches or hypotheses with data and expert reasoning. They dislike messy, untidy situations; they like things tidied up. They seek closure and resolution so they can move on to the next mystery and pursue new avenues of research. Figure M.1 graphically represents the parallelism found in good problem solving and sleuthing. Students may want to gauge their own problem-solving and sleuthing skills, or analyze those of their favorite detectives, using these models.

The infusion of mystery into the classroom may begin with the creation of a web of intrigue similar to the one found in figure M.2, page 132. Ascertain what students already know about mystery and detection. How many fictional sleuths can they name (Jessica Fletcher, Nancy Drew, Encyclopedia Brown)? What are some of the common behaviors they associate with sleuths and sleuthing? Why are detective stories so popular? Who are their favorite mystery writers? Both teachers and students should quickly perceive that a study of mystery and detection can quickly move beyond the scope of detective fiction. What careers, for example, are characterized by the use of good detection skills [medical research, archaeology, space exploration]? *Mystery* and *detection* are code words with multiple layers of meaning. A unit about mystery and detection can originate with an examination of good detective fiction, but it can also be the springboard for examinations of real-life mysteries, conundrums, and enigmas wherein critical-thinking and problem-solving skills are essential just as sleuthing skills are the prerequisites for Sherlock Holmes and Doctor Watson.

Fig. M.1. Models for problem solving and sleuthing.

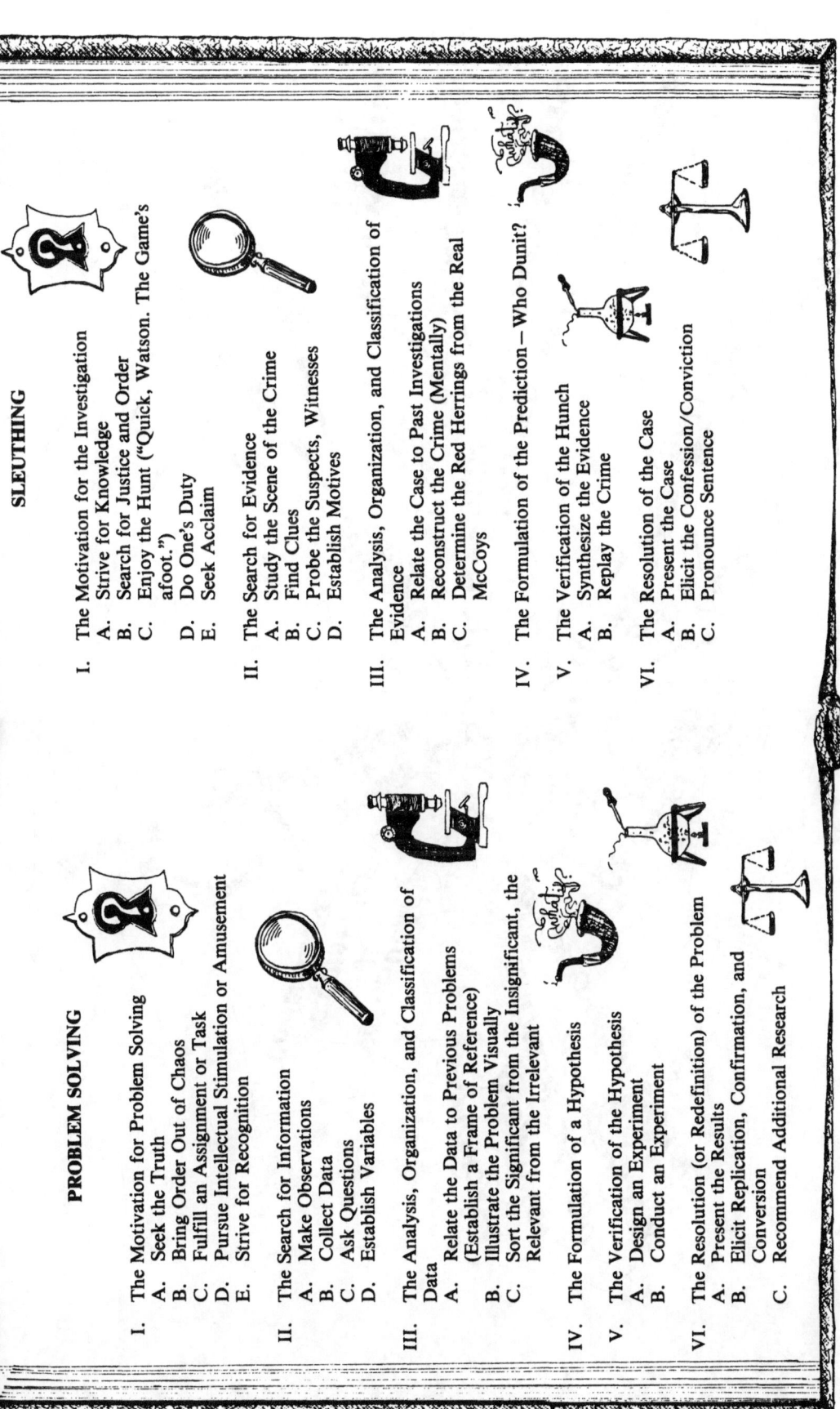

PROBLEM SOLVING

I. The Motivation for Problem Solving
   A. Seek the Truth
   B. Bring Order Out of Chaos
   C. Fulfill an Assignment or Task
   D. Pursue Intellectual Stimulation or Amusement
   E. Strive for Recognition

II. The Search for Information
   A. Make Observations
   B. Collect Data
   C. Ask Questions
   D. Establish Variables

III. The Analysis, Organization, and Classification of Data
   A. Relate the Data to Previous Problems (Establish a Frame of Reference)
   B. Illustrate the Problem Visually
   C. Sort the Significant from the Insignificant, the Relevant from the Irrelevant

IV. The Formulation of a Hypothesis

V. The Verification of the Hypothesis
   A. Design an Experiment
   B. Conduct an Experiment

VI. The Resolution (or Redefinition) of the Problem
   A. Present the Results
   B. Elicit Replication, Confirmation, and Conversion
   C. Recommend Additional Research

SLEUTHING

I. The Motivation for the Investigation
   A. Strive for Knowledge
   B. Search for Justice and Order
   C. Enjoy the Hunt ("Quick, Watson. The Game's afoot.")
   D. Do One's Duty
   E. Seek Acclaim

II. The Search for Evidence
   A. Study the Scene of the Crime
   B. Find Clues
   C. Probe the Suspects, Witnesses
   D. Establish Motives

III. The Analysis, Organization, and Classification of Evidence
   A. Relate the Case to Past Investigations
   B. Reconstruct the Crime (Mentally)
   C. Determine the Red Herrings from the Real McCoys

IV. The Formulation of the Prediction—Who Dunit?

V. The Verification of the Hunch
   A. Synthesize the Evidence
   B. Replay the Crime

VI. The Resolution of the Case
   A. Present the Case
   B. Elicit the Confession/Conviction
   C. Pronounce Sentence

From *Mystery and Detection: Thinking and Problem Solving with the Sleuths* by Jerry D. Flack. Illustrated by Gay Miller. (Englewood, Colo.: Teacher Ideas Press, 1990.)

132 **M** Is for Mystery

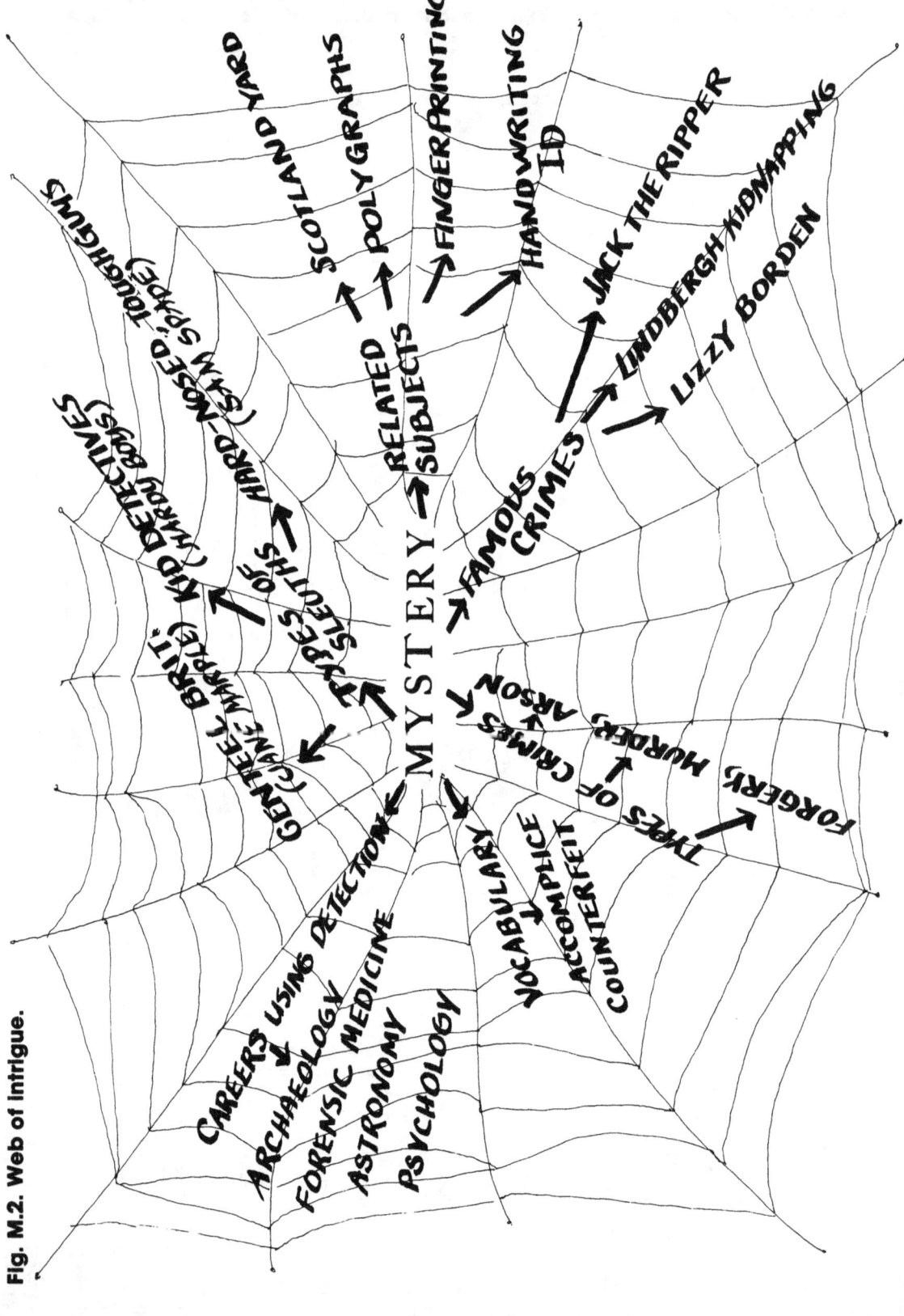

Fig. M.2. Web of Intrigue.

From *Mystery and Detection: Thinking and Problem Solving with the Sleuths* by Jerry D. Flack. Illustrated by Gay Miller. (Englewood, Colo.: Teacher Ideas Press, 1990.)

There are no limits to the possibilities for stimulating classroom and independent-inquiry activities that exist across the whole spectrum of the curriculum. Indeed, one additional attraction of a mystery unit is the interdisciplinary and integrative nature of the learning experiences it suggests. A brief sampling of these multidisciplinary activities follows. TalentEd teachers, like good sleuths in search of clues, will be on the lookout for still newer and fresher ideas.

Encourage even the youngest detectives to begin a mystery notebook or a sleuth's journal. The journal serves as the repository for reactions to mystery literature they read, critical-thinking behaviors noted in the sleuths they encounter, original ideas for their own mystery stories, information acquired about fingerprinting or bloodtyping, questions they want to ask, and searches they want to conduct. Encourage students to emulate the behaviors of the best sleuths: Always record evidence.

Combine the reading enjoyment students experience with the development of their problem-solving skills. Orally, read a good mystery selection halfway through. At the outset, encourage students to practice good sleuthing skills. Instruct students to listen carefully and take notes in their detective journals about the crime, the characters, complete with their motives and alibis. At the halfway point in the story, stop reading and ask students individually or in cooperative learning groups to solve the mystery using reasoning and the evidence they have. Students will be motivated to complete the story and to compare their solutions with the one provided by the mystery writer.

After students have sampled a few good mysteries, ask them to construct a list of critical-reading questions that may be employed by all readers of mystery stories. Help students move beyond knowledge-level questions to questions that require analysis and evaluation. A set of good critical-reading questions will assist students in becoming more sophisticated readers. The list of questions will also assist them later in constructing their own mystery stories. Sample questions students may produce may include examples like these: What kind of reasoning did the sleuth use to solve the case? What kinds of questions did the sleuth ask that proved to be valuable in solving the case? What kinds of observations did the sleuth make that proved to be of value in solving the case? What techniques did the author use to create suspense? What characteristics or traits made the sleuth seem interesting?

Encourage students to use their thinking and reading skills to deduce the structure of mystery stories. Ask them to brainstorm all the elements common to mystery stories. [A crime is planned. The crime is discovered. The sleuth enters the scene....] Next, direct students to categorize, chronologically, the elements according to when each occurs in a classic mystery format. The list of mystery story elements students create will serve them both in the evaluation of their further reading as well as in the construction of their own mysteries.

The study of vocabulary can be one of the strongest benefits of a mystery and detection unit. The vocabulary of mystery is rigorous and sprinkled with Latin phrases (e.g., *corpus delicti*, *habeas corpus*). Encourage students to bring to class new words they encounter in reading mysteries and to enter all new words in their mystery journals. A classroom bulletin board can be devoted to new vocabulary found and learned in the mystery unit. Mystery-fare vocabulary may include *accomplice*, *alibi*, *disguise*, *surveillance*, *perpetrate*, *malice*, *forgery*, *felony*, *larceny*, *misdemeanor*, and *villain*.

Poetry need not be left behind in a mystery unit. T. S. Eliot tipped his hat to Conan Doyle in his poem "Macavity: The Mystery Cat" from *Old Possum's Book of Practical Cats*, when he referred to Macavity as the "Napoleon of crime," the same descriptor Doyle used to describe Professor Moriarty, Sherlock Holmes's arch villain. What poetic forms can students creatively employ to celebrate the exploits of Sherlock Holmes, Nancy Drew, or the Hardy Boys?

One of the most popular formats ever employed in mystery literature was the medium of radio. Some of the most popular radio dramas of the 1930s and 1940s were radio mysteries such as "The Shadow" and "The Green Hornet." Many examples of these old-time radio programs are readily available in audio cassette format and can be used in the classroom. Once students have sampled a radio mystery program, place them in small groups and assign them the task of creating their own audiotapes that simulate the "golden age" of radio. Perhaps they can adapt one of James Howe's delightful tales, such as *The Celery Stalks at Midnight*, for audio dramatization. Much creativity and problem solving occur as students translate the narrative to a broadcast script, create sound effects, and rehearse and deliver their final broadcast.

There are possible art connections that may be made when students are studying mysteries. They can read about great art robberies such as the theft of Leonardo da Vinci's *Mona Lisa* in 1911. They can examine the illustrations of Sidney Paget that accompanied the original Sherlock Holmes stories in the *Strand* magazine, as well as create their own illustrations for their favorite mystery stories. Students can create their own conundrums for their classmates to solve. Ask students to create picture mysteries. First, have students name current, historical, or fictional heroes. Then ask them to imagine what might be found in the desks or workplaces belonging to their heroes by enterprising sleuths. From fictional or biographical data, what predictions can they make about what might be found in the desk of Trixie Belden or the office where Helen Keller worked? Once students have determined all the items that they might find in the desk or work place of their subject or character, they can artistically represent such scenes just as the illustrator of this book has done in figures M.3 and M.4, pages 135 and 136. Can students use their observation and critical-thinking skills to determine to whom these work spaces belonged? (The answers appear at the end of the chapter, pages 144 and 145.)

Fingerprints are central to many, many mysteries, so why not include them in an arts approach to mystery? The only tools students need are their fingers, pencils, paper, inked rubber stamp pads, and their own creative and critical-thinking skills. Students ink a finger or thumb, make a fingerprint anywhere on a clean sheet of paper, and then complete their drawings by adding necessary lines to complete a figure, object, or scene. Single drawings of crooks and detectives may be completed, or the student may choose to tell an entire mystery using only fingerprint art. While students are completing their fingerprint drawings, teachers can share some fascinating information about fingerprints, such as the fact that fingerprints have been used for purposes of identification since A.D. 782 in China; or, the fact that no two people have the same fingerprints, including identical twins.

An examination of fingerprints is a natural introduction to the whole world of forensic science and the science side of mystery and detection. Modern police detection methods are fascinating. A forensic specialist from the local police department will be a most impressive resource speaker to bring into the classroom. Students can read, research, and learn about how to investigate crime using a microscope, and how to analyze fingerprints, strands of hair, blood samples, and clothing fibers. A TalentEd teacher in Great Britain uses the following forensic science activity with middle school students. He collects from each student a packet of clues including strands of hair, broken fingernails, threads of clothing, and even blood samples. By secret drawing, a culprit and victim are chosen and a crime is announced. The crime may be the theft of a book or a piece of clothing. The victim reveals his or her identity. Only the teacher and the culprit know of the latter's identity. The class is faced with the task of solving the crime. They now have great motivation to learn the basics of forensic science in order to catch the culprit. Incidentally, once the culprit is identified, the students next conduct a mock trial. The final verdict is not necessarily a foregone conclusion. The culprit, like his or her classmates, has learned much about the nature of evidence. The culprit may be able to convincingly point out major flaws in the evidence brought forth by the prosecution.[3]

Any investigation of forensic science would be incomplete without an examination of how other scientists, such as archaeologists, use evidence to solve mysteries and riddles of the past, or how astronomers work to unlock the secrets of the cosmos in order to foretell the future.

Mathematics need not be forgotten or ignored in the development of a mystery and detection unit of study. For younger students, creative teachers can write story problems with a mystery accent and with Nancy Drew, Detective Pin, the Penguin, or Encyclopedia Brown as characters. The statistics of crime also offer fertile areas for student exploration. Students can utilize mathematics and research skills through a study of various aspects of the statistics of criminality in our nation. Many school library media centers will have the *Statistical Abstracts of the United States* in the reference section. Published annually by the Department of Commerce and available from the U.S. Government Printing Office (Washington, D.C. 20402), this informative resource provides statistical data on a wide range of topics including arrests, burglary, costs of criminal behaviors to society, crime prevention measures, juvenile

Fig. M.3. Picture mystery no. 1.

Fig. M.4. Picture mystery no. 2.

crime, and robbery. From this resource students can determine the incidence of various types of crime in each region of the nation, how much their own state spends on law enforcement, the costs of keeping prisoners, and much more interesting information. Students may consult the *Historical Statistics of the United States* to determine the growth patterns in various types of crime, and to make predictions about the growth of future types of crimes and criminals.[4] Police departments currently feed such data into computers which then draw geographical areas that require extra patrols to curb rising crime.

Social studies lessons within the mystery and detection unit can be oriented toward studying geography by following the footsteps of Sherlock Holmes and Doctor Watson through the streets of London and beyond into the English countryside. A grand economics lesson may also be had as students cooperatively determine the financial side of creating their own detective agency. How does one obtain a private investigator's license? How much does the detective need to budget for office space, secretarial services, insurance, and other expenses? How much should the detective charge clients in order to cover expenses and make a profit?

Of course, students may also become historical detectives and investigate mysteries that continue to baffle historians. What became of the Anasazi people who were the cliff dwellers of Mesa Verde? Was explorer Meriwether Lewis murdered? What made Aaron Burr tick? Biographical detectives may wish to study famous criminals such as Jesse James and Belle Starr, or famous crimebusters that may include Eliot Ness, Allan Pinkerton, and Sheriff Pat Garrett.

There is really no end to the rich possibilities for individual, whole class, and cooperative group learning that can take place as part of mystery studies to develop and enhance students' critical-thinking and problem-solving skills. The recommended culminating activity, however, is the creation of original mysteries written by students, individually or collectively. The creation of original mystery stories gives students the opportunity to employ all the facts, information, and processes they have learned throughout their study.

Even though the story may be the culminating project, it should be assigned early on to ensure that students will have plenty of time to write and edit several drafts. Considerable time should be expended in prewriting efforts: creating the sleuth, plotting the crime, exploring character motivations, practicing the writing of dialogue, and devising an original resolution. Indeed, one of the virtues of the mystery story writing assignment is that it forces students to organize their thinking and tighten their writing. A well-crafted mystery has a very tight organizational structure with details given to readers in a highly systematic fashion. Writers are very alert to the clues they provide and the ordering of the clues given. For students who have never exercised much control in their written work, crafting a mystery story is both a highly motivating challenge and an opportunity to hone and sharpen their composition skills.

There are many writing strategies students may want to consider in authoring their own mysteries. Writing sequels to existing mystery stories and employing existing famous detectives may offer a safer route for some timid and unsure younger authors. Countless authors have written further adventures for Conan Doyle's classic hero, Sherlock Holmes. Excellent mystery stories can find their plot structure in classic fairy tales, mythological tales, or nursery rhymes. Agatha Christie based a number of her mysteries on such literary allusions.

Contemporary news events such as hostage crises or examples of government duplicity may suggest further ideas for stories. A forced association technique may also serve as a prompt for student writers. The teacher may simply suggest five or six random words (e.g., blue, scream, woods, perfume, knife, darkness) and ask students to build a mystery around the given words. Similarly, the teacher can describe a fictional event created at random and ask students to build a mystery story upon the brief description provided. The following are examples:

> The school mascot, Opie, had disappeared. Where on earth could he be? There just didn't seem to be any reasonable explanation.

> John wandered aimlessly in the school parking lot at 2 A.M.

M Is for Mystery

Most creative and talented students will easily generate their own ideas for mystery stories. For those few students who develop a writing block, the story starters in figure M.5 may serve as the catalysts needed.

Fig. M.5. Mystery story starters.

- You are Madison High's whiz kid detective. The school bully knows it. He bumps into you in a crowded hallway during the passing of classes and whispers to you, "If you know what is good for you, you'll forget about Mrs. Andre's missing grade book." What mystery lurks behind this provocative incident?

- "Why did I do it? Why did I do it?" Try as he might, he could not erase those five simple words from his conscious mind. What did the person do, and why did he do it?

- There has been a fire at the home of famed British mystery writer Dudley Smythe-Finkel. His entire study-library burned and his whodunit works-in-progress were destroyed. All that remain are a few charred fragments of paper. Can you come to poor Dudley's rescue? Help him reconstruct first-rate mystery stories from these singed remains:

    "... no weapon, no clues, no body, yet he knew a crime had been committed."

    "The shards of pottery on the floor told the whole sad story of ..."

    "The light of the moon silhouetted the burglar as he ..."

- Thomas Alva Edison was totally baffled. He was used to solving the mysteries of electricity, not the wily ways of criminals. But he had no choice but to apply his brilliant mind to what would be a new kind of detection for him. If the theft and vandalism in his laboratory were not soon halted, his entire new project would have to be jettisoned. What are the specifics in the Edison mystery? Who is the criminal? What is the motive? How does Thomas Edison solve the mystery?

- Your favorite rock group is in big trouble. The police have issued a warrant for the arrest of the group's leader. Your skills in sleuthing are urgently needed. What is the crime? What evidence do the police have? How can you prove the innocence of your hero? Tell the dramatic story.

From *TalentEd: Strategies for Developing the Talent in Every Learner*, © 1993 Teacher Ideas Press, P.O. Box 6633, Englewood, CO 80155-6633

Students as Mystery Writers

One of the highlights of any school year can be the sharing of the final products young mystery writers create. The author's students greatly enjoyed and profited from sharing their mysteries with their peers. Further, he placed students in groups of five to six students and asked each group to choose one of their mysteries to serve as the basis for a final mystery problem-solving activity. Each group dramatized key opening scenes from their mystery for the rest of the class. Prior to the dramatization, each group secreted vital clues to the mystery throughout the classroom and the school. After each dramatization, the rest of the class had the task of solving the given mystery in the following twenty-four hours.

Sleuthing can be great fun and highly motivating. It also provides students with splendid opportunities to discover and develop their critical-thinking and problem-solving skills (figure M.6, page 140, will provide students an opportunity to exercise such skills).

A great deal of satisfaction comes from solving the problems that confront people, whether they are fictional mysteries or real-life conundrums. In the safety of the TalentEd classroom, students can hone and sharpen their critical-thinking and problem-solving skills and become skillful sleuths and adept problem solvers.

(Notes follow on page 141.)

Fig. M.6. Race of mystery participants.

Read the following clues to solve the mystery of what animals are participating in the race. The footprints will guide you through the mystery.

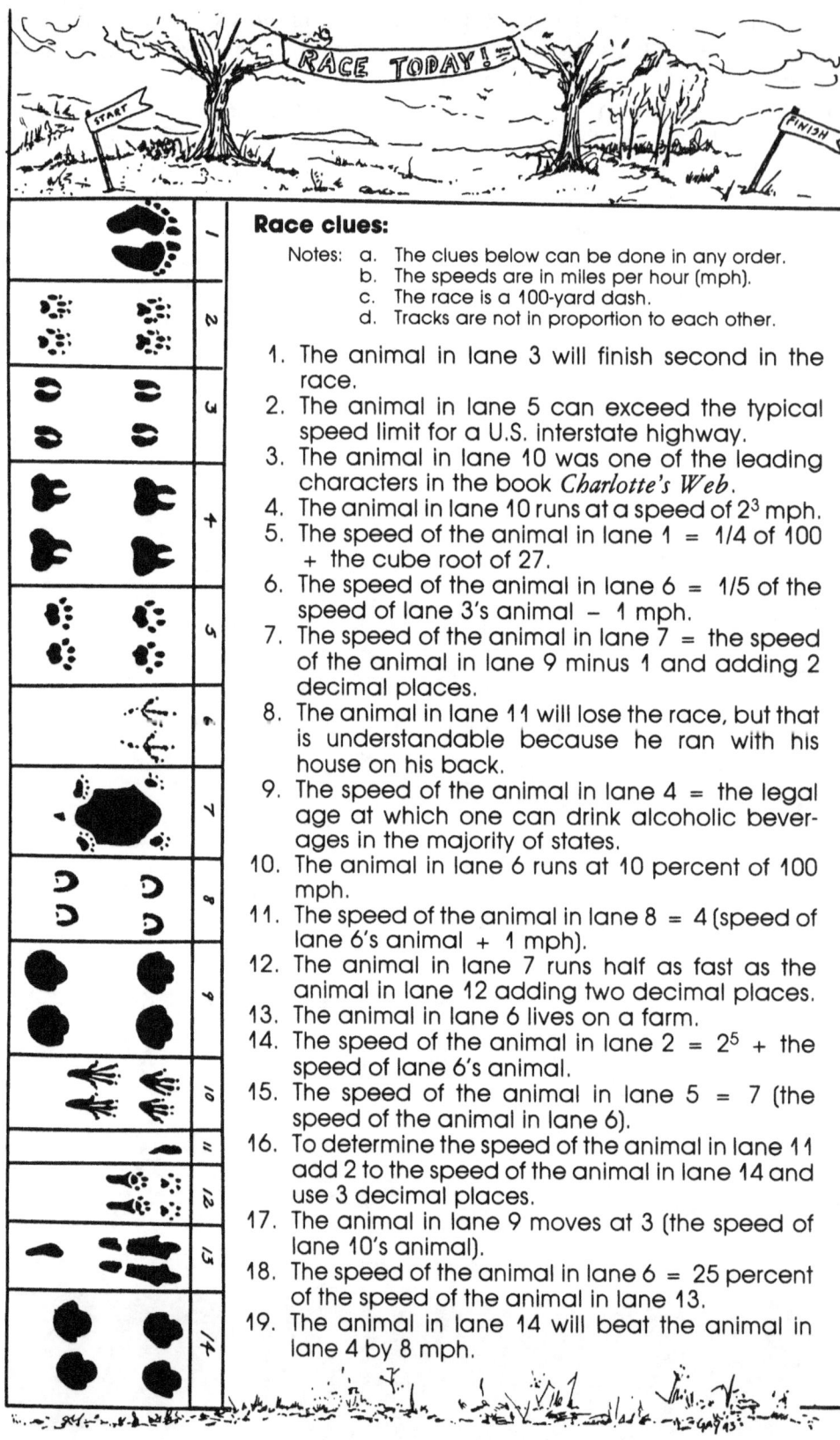

Race clues:

Notes:
a. The clues below can be done in any order.
b. The speeds are in miles per hour (mph).
c. The race is a 100-yard dash.
d. Tracks are not in proportion to each other.

1. The animal in lane 3 will finish second in the race.
2. The animal in lane 5 can exceed the typical speed limit for a U.S. interstate highway.
3. The animal in lane 10 was one of the leading characters in the book *Charlotte's Web*.
4. The animal in lane 10 runs at a speed of 2^3 mph.
5. The speed of the animal in lane 1 = 1/4 of 100 + the cube root of 27.
6. The speed of the animal in lane 6 = 1/5 of the speed of lane 3's animal − 1 mph.
7. The speed of the animal in lane 7 = the speed of the animal in lane 9 minus 1 and adding 2 decimal places.
8. The animal in lane 11 will lose the race, but that is understandable because he ran with his house on his back.
9. The speed of the animal in lane 4 = the legal age at which one can drink alcoholic beverages in the majority of states.
10. The animal in lane 6 runs at 10 percent of 100 mph.
11. The speed of the animal in lane 8 = 4 (speed of lane 6's animal + 1 mph).
12. The animal in lane 7 runs half as fast as the animal in lane 12 adding two decimal places.
13. The animal in lane 6 lives on a farm.
14. The speed of the animal in lane 2 = 2^5 + the speed of lane 6's animal.
15. The speed of the animal in lane 5 = 7 (the speed of the animal in lane 6).
16. To determine the speed of the animal in lane 11 add 2 to the speed of the animal in lane 14 and use 3 decimal places.
17. The animal in lane 9 moves at 3 (the speed of lane 10's animal).
18. The speed of the animal in lane 6 = 25 percent of the speed of the animal in lane 13.
19. The animal in lane 14 will beat the animal in lane 4 by 8 mph.

Notes

[1] Some of the material in this chapter originally appeared in the author's book *Mystery and Detection: Thinking and Problem Solving with the Sleuths* (Englewood, Colo.: Teacher Ideas Press, 1990), and in three journal articles: Jerry Flack, "In Search of Serendipity," *Understanding Our Gifted* 1, no. 5 (May 1989): 16-17; Jerry Flack, "Mystery and Intrigue in the Composition Classroom," *Writing Teacher* 4, no. 2 (November 1990): 7-11; Jerry Flack, "Put Some Mystery in Your Classroom," *Teaching Pre-K-8* 21, no. 3 (November 1991): 62-66.

[2] Arthur Conan Doyle, "The Man with the Twisted Lip," *Adventures of Sherlock Holmes* (New York: Ballantine Books, 1975), 133.

[3] David George, Nene College, Northampton, England. He employs this simulation with gifted middle school students.

[4] United States Department of Commerce, Bureau of the Census, *Historical Statistics of the United States: Colonial Times to 1970*, vol. I (Washington, D.C.: U.S. Government Printing Office, 1975), 414. Also, *Statistical Abstracts of the United States*, 108th ed. (1987), 160.

Suggested Bibliography of Mystery Literature

PRIMARY READERS

Adler, David. *Cam Jansen and the Mystery of the Monster Movie*. New York: Dell, 1984.

   A reel of the movie Cam and friends are watching suddenly disappears and Cam Jansen uses her detection skills to find it. This is but one of many entries in the Cam Jansen series by Adler.

———. *My Dog and the Green Sock Mystery*. New York: Holiday House, 1986.

   Adler proves that mysteries may be written for even the youngest readers with this entry in A First Mystery Book series.

Allard, Harry, and James Marshall. *Miss Nelson Is Missing!* Boston: Houghton Mifflin, 1977.

   Allard and Marshall have created one of the most delightful, endearing, and popular children's books to be found. Miss Nelson reappears in *Miss Nelson Is Back* (Houghton Mifflin, 1982) and *Miss Nelson Has a Field Day* (Houghton Mifflin, 1985).

Bunting, Eve. *Jane Martin, Dog Detective*. New York: Harcourt Brace Jovanovich, 1984.

   Jane Martin follows all clues, including paw prints, to locate missing canines in this delightful introduction to mysteries and sleuthing for younger readers.

Kellogg, Steven. *The Mystery of the Flying Orange Pumpkin*. New York: Dial Books for Young Readers, 1980.

   A delightful tale of mystery at Halloween time.

Quackenbush, Robert. *Sherlock Chick's First Case*. New York: Gruner & Jahr, 1986.

A case in need of a solution awaits Sherlock Chick as soon as Emma Hen and Harvey Rooster's new son pops out of his shell wearing a deerstalker cap.

Razzi, Jim, and Mary Razzi. *The Sherluck Bones Mystery-Detective, Book 1*. New York: Bantam Books, 1981.

Sherluck Bones lives in Kennelwood, U.S.A. No mystery escapes the notice of this delightful and brilliant canine sleuth.

INTERMEDIATE READERS

Bellairs, John. *The Curse of the Blue Figurine*. New York: Bantam Books, 1983.

Bellairs's books are extremely popular with middle school readers. This book skillfully combines mystery and fantasy.

Howe, James. *The Celery Stalks at Midnight*. New York: Avon Books, 1983.

Howe's books share a popularity as great as the *Miss Nelson* books with young readers. In this adventure, Bunnicula, the vampire bunny, is missing and it is up to the other animals in the Monroe household to find him.

Kastner, Erich. *Emil and the Detectives*. Trans. by May Massee. Garden City, N.Y.: Doubleday, 1930.

A band of child sleuths help Emil recover the money stolen from him in this children's German literature classic.

Monsel, Mary Elise. *The Mysterious Cases of Mr. Pin*. New York: Pocket Books, 1989.

Mr. Pin, a penguin with a love of chocolate and a knack for solving mysteries, solves three baffling cases.

Raskin, Ellen. *The Westing Game*. New York: Avon Books, 1978.

This is a modern classic in children's literature that won the Newbery Medal. A host of insightful young characters are found in this book, which offers not only a good mystery, but a puzzle to solve as well.

Roos, Kelly, and Stephen Roos. *The Incredible Cat Caper*. New York: Dell, 1985.

Three children, a Siamese cat, Simba, and a cat burglar all become involved in this delightful mystery penned by Edgar Award-winning authors.

Snyder, Zilpha Keatley. *The Egypt Game*. New York: Dell, 1967.

This is an excellent book that defies categorization. There is mystery here, however, as modern-day children connect with ancient Egypt. Readers will be enthralled and entertained.

Treat, Lawrence. *You're the Detective!* Boston: David R. Godine, 1983.

Following his success with *Crime and Puzzlement* (David R. Godine, 1982) for adult readership, Lawrence Treat created a similar puzzle book of picture and word mysteries for children.

Twain, Mark. *Tom Sawyer, Detective*. New York: New American Library, 1985.

Twain's most famous characters, Tom Sawyer and Huck Finn, unravel a case of murder and theft.

Wilson, Eric. *The Green Gables Detectives*. Toronto: Collins, 1988.

This excellent Canadian mystery is set in the very farmhouse on Prince Edward Island where Lucy Maud Montgomery wrote *Anne of Green Gables*. Wilson has penned an entire series of mysteries that take place in prominent Canadian locales.

ADVANCED READERS

Christie, Agatha. *The Mysterious Affair at Styles*. New York: Bantam Books, 1983.

Christie's first mystery. She is probably the best puzzle conjurer ever to write mysteries. Happily, most of her mysteries are entirely suitable for classroom use.

Collins, Wilkie. *The Moonstone*. New York: Dodd, Mead, 1951.

Collins was the father of the English detective novel, and this is his best work.

Doyle, Arthur Conan. *Adventures of Sherlock Holmes*. New York: Ballantine Books, 1975.

Doyle created the most famous fictional sleuth ever.

Dvorkin, David. *Time for Sherlock Holmes*. New York: Dodd, Mead, 1983.

This is an ingenious mystery in which the evil Moriarty has stolen H. G. Wells's time machine, and Sherlock Holmes must go into the future to foil him.

Milne, A. A. *The Red House Mystery*. New York: Dell, 1984.

Secondary readers who loved Winnie-the-Pooh will be delighted that his creator also wrote a very fine mystery.

Sayers, Dorothy L. *The Five Red Herrings*. New York: Harper & Row, 1986.

Lord Peter Wimsey, Sayers's aristocratic sleuth, solves the mystery.

144 *M Is for Mystery*

Key to figure M.3, mystery picture no. 1, the Wright Brothers' desk.

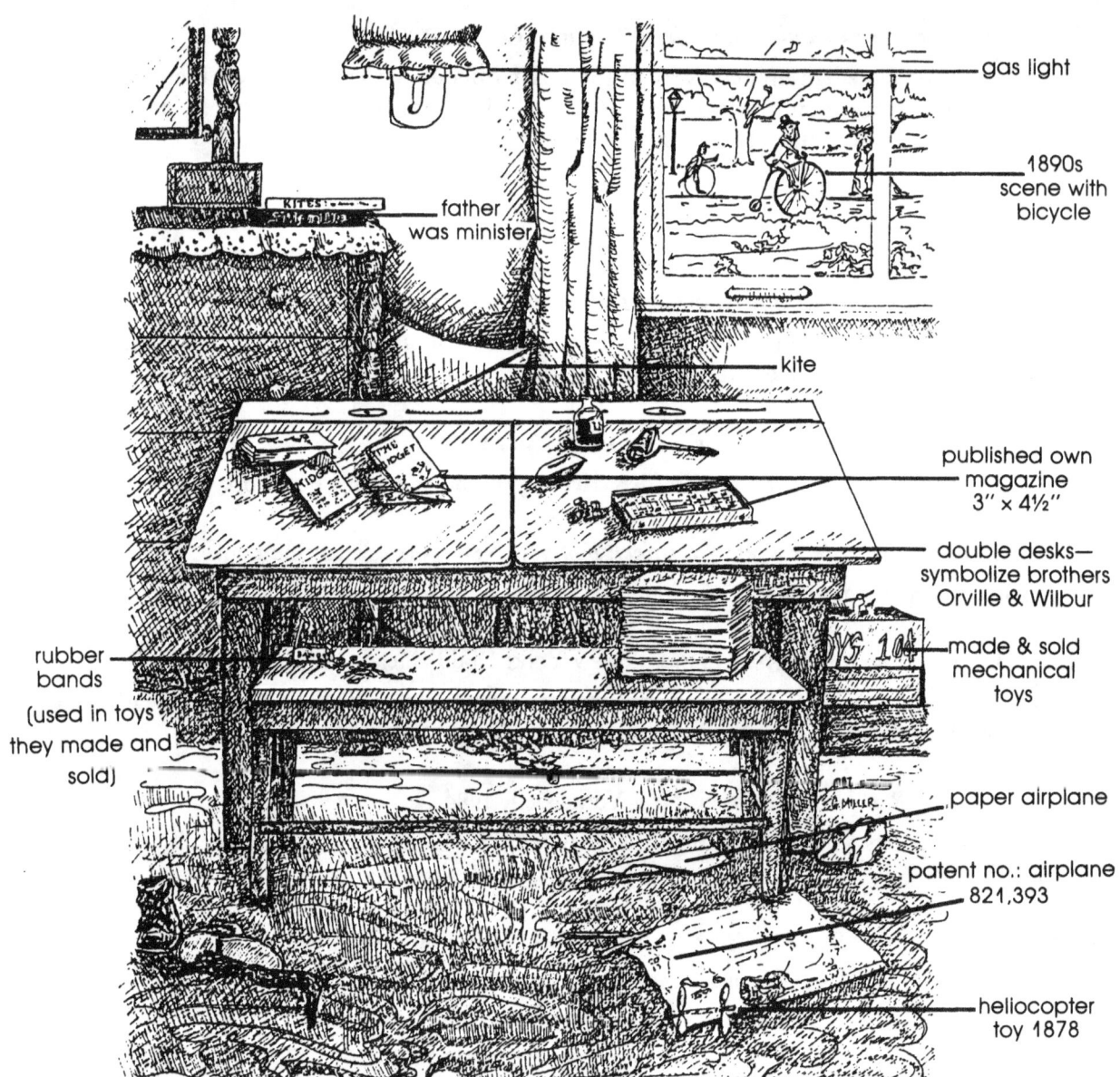

M Is for Mystery 145

Key to figure M.4, mystery picture no. 2, Albert Einstein's desk.

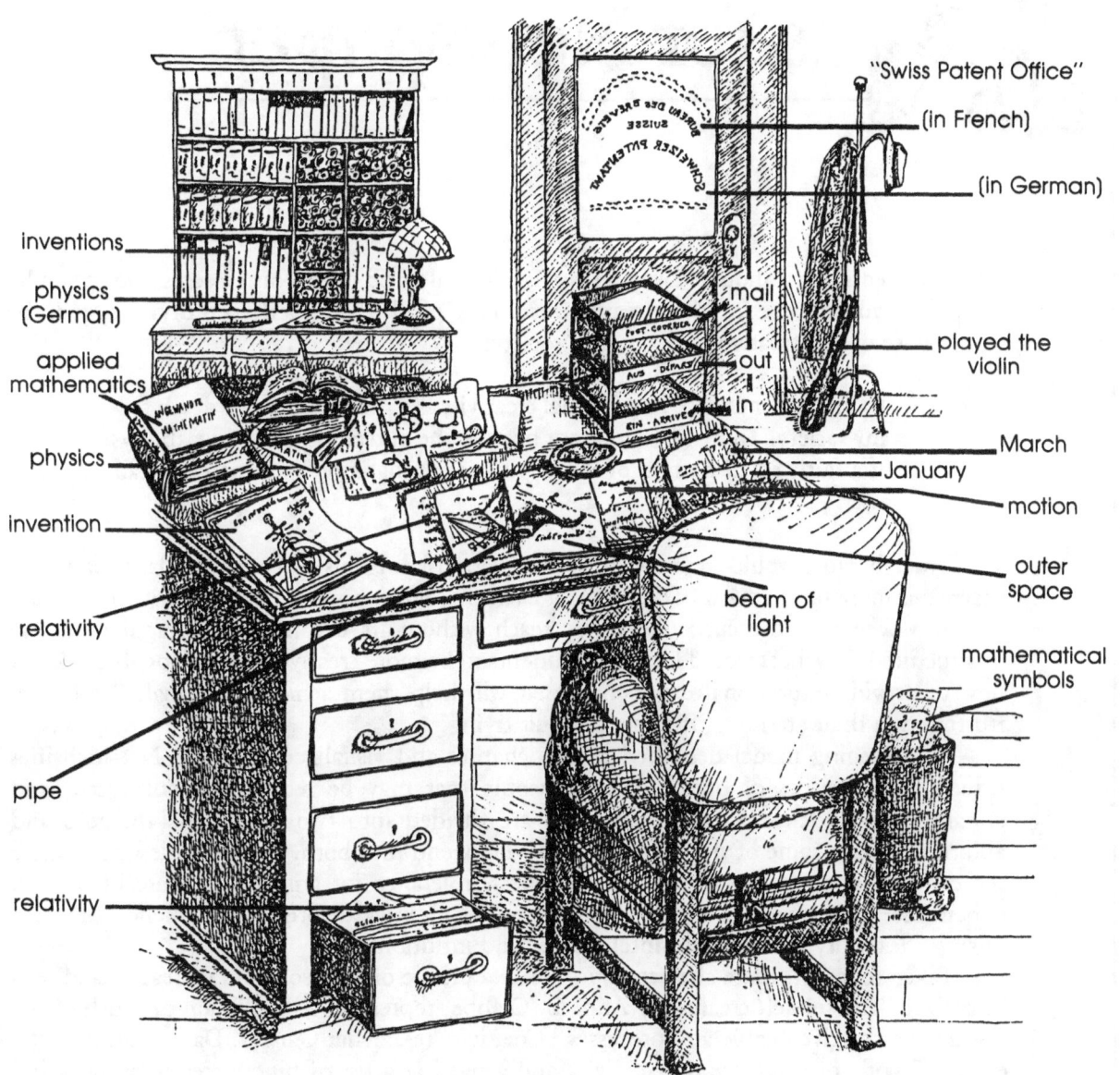

Answers to the race:

Lane	Animal	Place	Speed
1	Human	8	28 mph
2	Dog	4	42 mph
3	Deer	2	55 mph
4	Camel	10	21 mph
5	Cheetah	1	70 mph
6	Chicken	11	10 mph
7	Turtle	13	.23 mph
8	Horse	5	41 mph
9	Elephant	9	24 mph
10	Rat	12	8 mph
11	Snail	14	.031 mph
12	Rabbit	3	46 mph
13	Kangaroo	6	40 mph
14	Rhinoceros	7	29 mph

# N Is for Newspaper

That educators should foster creativity in TalentEd classrooms seems indisputable. Arnold Toynbee, one of the greatest historians of the twentieth century, stressed the importance of the creative individual to society:

> To give a fair chance to potential creativity is a matter of life or death for any society. This is all-important because the outstanding creative ability of a fairly small portion of the population is mankind's ultimate capital asset.[1]

Though most would agree with Toynbee, translating his dictum into daily classroom practice is more problematic. Teachers, for example, often wonder how creativity instruction can be woven into the curriculum they teach without its becoming too fragmented and unstructured. Teachers would like their students to be more creative, but do not always know how to provide educational experiences that will help them achieve that goal. Sometimes frustrated in their attempts, they simply quit trying.

The teaching model described in this chapter and visualized in figure N.1 identifies fifteen characteristics of highly creative people that may be recognized, cultivated, and enhanced in students. The characteristics are divided into two categories, attitudes and abilities, though some of the characteristics will extend into both. The attitudes are positive self-concept, openness to ideas, perceptiveness, tolerance for ambiguity, sense of humor, persistence, expressiveness, and independence. The abilities are originality, fluency, problem solving, flexibility, elaboration, intelligence, and intuition.

Taken together, these characteristics create a profile of a person who is creative and self-actualized. The model, created by Anne B. Crabbe, represents a distillation of much of the research on creative people and processes.[2] Creativity researcher Gary A. Davis examined the extensive body of literature on creativity and arrived at a list of ninety creativity traits and characteristics.[3] Obviously, such a list is not easily manageable when educators start converting theory and research into practice.

Anne Crabbe's model provides a perspective of creativity that breaks the psychological construct of creativity into manageable, teachable components. Much as a basketball coach subdivides the game into teachable skills—dribbling, shooting, blocking, and guarding—so, too, can teachers work on the individual aspects of creativity with their students. By enhancing the parts, the whole will be strengthened.

Fig. N.1.

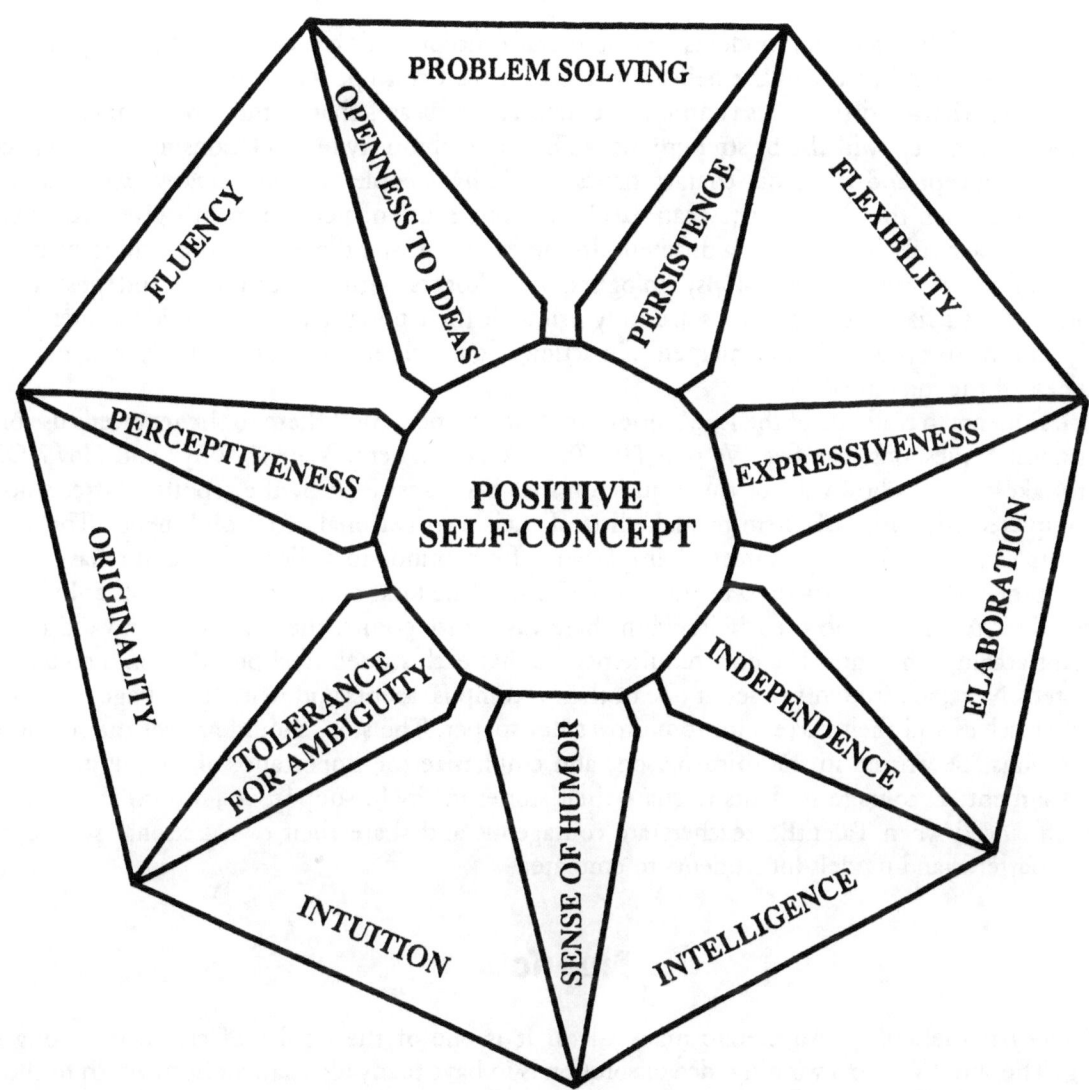

The newspaper as a teaching tool is the frame of reference in this chapter for exploring the fifteen creative dimensions outlined in the Crabbe creativity model. Two factors dictate this choice. First, the newspaper is a great teaching resource for bright, talented, and eager students of all ages. Second, the information and data found in newspapers are fresh and current. With the dramatic changes that have occurred in the immediate past, textbook publishers find it nearly impossible to keep up with continuously shifting world events.

There is also a professional preference here for using concrete examples when discussing creativity. It seems more beneficial "to do" creativity rather than to talk about it only in the abstract. Students learn best from this perspective as well. Therefore, as each attitude and ability of this model is described, a newspaper-based activity designed to strengthen the creativity trait will be shared. The newspaper provides a generic format similar to that found with the ABC books described in chapter *A*. Students are encouraged to be creative, but they are given parameters and structures as guides.[4]

Positive Self-concept

The heart of this creativity model is a positive self-concept. This creativity attribute appears at the center of the diagram because of the belief that a positive self-concept is crucial to the maximization of all of the other characteristics. This central placement also indicates that as the other characteristics are developed, self-concept will also be strengthened. Thus, a symbiotic type of relationship exists between a positive self-concept and the other characteristics. Typically, people are most creative when they feel confident and when they believe they can excel. A strong sense of personal worth gives students the confidence to take risks, to march to a different drummer, to withstand peer pressure, and to be unique.

One of the century's foremost psychologists, Carl Rogers, equated creativity and positive self-concept. Self-actualized human beings are fully using all their potential in a creative manner. Rogers wrote, "The creative process is the emergence in action of a novel relational product, growing out of the uniqueness of the individual."[5]

Ask students to read one of the lead stories in the newspaper. Alert them to the reporter's use of the six journalistic questions, the five Ws plus H: Who? What? Where? When? Why? and How? Direct them to take notes on how each of these questions has been answered by the reporter. After students have completed this task, ask them to make lists of their own personal accomplishments. The accomplishments can be of varying degrees of importance from minor to major. If students have trouble beginning the task, instruct them to begin with such mundane tasks and accomplishments as being able to brush their teeth or comb their hair. From these easy entry points, they can move onward to more significant accomplishments. The only requirement is that each student feel proud of each accomplishment listed. Next, ask students to select one of their accomplishments and write front-page news stories about themselves and their success for tomorrow's newspaper. The story should answer the six journalistic questions, be written in the third person, and emphasize the importance of the subject and the accomplishment. Encourage students to share their stories in small, supportive groups. This activity is greatly enhanced when TalentEd teachers are courageous and share their own personal success news stories as patterns and models for students to emulate.

Fluency

Fluency is the ability to generate many ideas. It is one of the staples of creativity testing and training. The surest way to a winning idea or solution is to have many alternatives from which to choose. Philosopher Emile Chartier observed, "Nothing is more dangerous than an idea when it is the only one you have."[6] Too often in schools, educators look for one right answer. In their haste to get on to the next lesson and master the information on achievement tests, teachers may fail to help students realize that there may be many different correct answers. Students become addicted to the right-answer syndrome, and after a while, they fail to look beyond one answer for every question. In the real world, almost every question has several different answers, and every problem, many solutions.

Ask students to turn to the sports pages of the newspaper. Working in pairs, they should review articles about athletic competitions and contests and find as many different terms as they can that mean "to defeat," as in the headline: "Michigan defeats New Mexico." After students have compiled a considerable list of verbs and verb phrases from newspapers, ask them to search their own memories and imaginations to add to their lists. When imaginations and memories have been exhausted, allow students to use dictionaries and thesauri. When the lists have been completed, write all the terms on one large piece of butcher paper. Prepare to be amazed at how many ways one team can defeat another. Consider how dull the sports pages would be if *defeated* was the only verb available to describe the outcome of athletic events.

Another fluency activity involves the use of the classified advertisements found in the newspaper. Ask students to locate "pets for sale," and select an advertisement for a specific animal. Tell students that the owner has had no luck in finding a home for the pet. The owner is leaving the country and cannot take the pet with him. Ask each team to think of as many ways as they can to find a new owner for this great pet.

Tolerance for Ambiguity

Creative people tend to be comfortable with uncertainty. Psychologist Abraham Maslow noted that creative people are able to tolerate inconsistencies and contradictions. He notes that highly creative people are able to resolve seeming inconsistencies and dichotomies such as work and play, duty and pleasure, and selfishness and altruism into unities. Great artists, inventors, teachers, philosophers, and leaders are able to bring together separate, divergent, and even opposite integrators, and unify them.[7]

This capacity of the creative person to assume different, even quite opposite, roles is elaborated upon further by Roger von Oech who believes that creative individuals actually have four different roles they must play during the creative process. Those roles are: explorer, artist, judge, and warrior. The explorer looks for new ways to do things. The artist creates the product or develops the idea. The judge evaluates the effectiveness of the product or idea, and the warrior fights for acceptance from the public for the product or idea.[8]

Write one word (*explorer*, *artist*, *judge*, or *warrior*) on each of several slips of paper and distribute the slips of paper randomly to students. Give the students copies of the newspaper and ask them to find one example of a person acting out the role specified on their slips of paper. An explorer might be a person who has searched for unusual places or a cure for a disease. An artist might be someone who has created a new fashion look. A judge might be someone who has studied and evaluated the effectiveness of a new piece of atheltic equipment. A warrior might be a person who is leading a cause, such as helping disaster victims or abused children.

After people in the news have been identified, ask students to pretend that the people in the articles they have chosen are highly creative and move easily from one role to another. Ask students to write articles in which they describe the activities of their chosen person in the other three roles, as well as the one they first noted. An extension of this activity is to divide the class into four-person groups where each group contains students representing all four roles. Ask the students to role-play their selected persons and react, as that person would react, to current-events issues. Issues might include these:

All students should remain in public education until they are qualified for a job.

Summer vacations should be eliminated; students should attend school twelve months of the year.

To stretch their tolerance for ambiguity still further, teachers can randomly assign two members of each group to the affirmative side and two members to the negative side of a debatable issue. Participation in debate, which asks students to support positions with evidence and logic, is a valuable tool for strengthening tolerance for ambiguity.

Flexibility

Flexibility and a tolerance for ambiguity complement one another. People who keep their thinking limber are able to find new and unexpected connections, redefine the known world, and make transformations. Flexible people are able to be both adaptable and spontaneous. Both teachers and students need to guard against the rigidity that sometimes accompanies the aging process. It has been said that "as people get older, they tend to get hardening of the categories."

Flexibility requires that people escape from ruts and try new things. Flexible thinkers are able to shift gears easily. They look for new ideas everywhere. They are not afraid of change.

Students can have some fun being food editors in this exercise. Ask them to pretend that they are the food editors of a major city newspaper such as the *Denver Post*. Their boss, the wealthy and powerful publisher of the newspaper, calls on them and says, "I need to entertain some guests from China this weekend, and I want you to plan a wonderful, typically American meal for six people." Ask students to begin planning.

After about two minutes, interrupt the students and tell them the publisher has just called. She forgot to mention that two of the guests are vegetarians, so meat should not be included in the meal. Ask students to adjust their planning and proceed.

After another minute or two, interrupt again to tell the students that the publisher's secretary just called to say that one of the guests has recently undergone oral surgery, so all the food needs to be soft. Instruct students to continue their planning.

Another few minutes go by. Interrupt the students and tell them that the publisher's security guard has called to say that the publisher's home has been robbed, and the thieves have made off with all of the silverware, so there are no spoons, forks, or knives. Instruct the students to adjust their menus accordingly.

After a few more minutes, ask student to share the menus they have compiled. Also ask them to share their reactions to being interrupted so often and having to change the direction of their thinking.

To provide students with another crack at flexibility, invite them to be flexible in their reading. Ask them to read a section of the newspaper they usually ignore or read the newspaper in a different sequence than normal. Students who always begin reading with the sports pages should try reading the stock market pages first. Students who never read the business section of the paper should read that section. After students have read a section of the newspaper that is new to them, ask them to make a list of five new things they learned. What things from their reading can they apply to their lives? In *A Kick in the Seat of the Pants*, Roger von Oech encourages people to become versatile in their behaviors and use what he calls their "explorer personality" to search for new ideas from a wide variety of sources. He tells readers that "anyone can look for fashion in a boutique or history in a museum. The creative explorer looks for history in a hardware store and fashion in an airport."[9] Von Oech cites such examples as legendary Notre Dame football coach Knute Rockne, who found the idea for his famed "four horseman" backfield shift while watching the performance of a chorus line. Cubist artists Picasso and Braque were sources for World War I military designers who borrowed their art ideas in order to create more effective camouflage patterns for tanks and guns.[10]

Persistence

> Nothing in the world can take the place of persistence. Talent will not; nothing is more common than unsuccessful men of talent. Genius will not ... the world is full of educated derelicts. Persistence and determination alone are omnipotent. The slogan "press on" has solved and always will solve the problems of the human race.
>
> — Calvin Coolidge

Persistence is endurance. It is tenacity. It is never giving up. Madeleine L'Engle won the prestigious Newbery Medal for her children's classic *A Wrinkle in Time*, but relates in her published journal, *A Circle of Quiet*, that she suffered through a decade of rejections of the *Wrinkle* manuscript before finding a publisher willing to take a chance on her highly imaginative novel.[11] Glenn Miller flunked his music class in harmony at the University of Colorado, but he remained undaunted and became one of the most successful popular music composers ever. Dancer Agnes DeMille received a D in dance class at the University of California, but persisted and became one of the greatest names in American dance.

Walt Disney was once fired from a newspaper staff because he had "no good ideas."[12] That loss of a job did not halt the creator of Mickey Mouse from pursuing his dreams.

The stories of Abraham Lincoln's persistence have become legendary and inspirational. Lincoln experienced a steady stream of failures in business and politics before he finally succeeded, winning the presidential election in 1860. How different the lives of Americans would be today were it not for the persistence of Abraham Lincoln.

Ask students to read the newspaper with an eye toward finding stories about individuals who have persisted in some way. The stories may be found in any section of the newspaper to include news, sports, business, editorials, features, and even the comics. Ask students to summarize their stories and report on them to the rest of the class. As an extension of this activity, teachers may desire to establish a persistence bulletin board and ask students to bring in news stories of courage, tenacity, and persistence of motive. This is a good time to share with students outstanding biographies of heroes and heroines such as Rick Hansen, Terry Fox, and Mary McLeod Bethune.[13] It is also a fine opportunity to share with students important quotations about hope, courage, and persistence such as this one from Terry Fox, the marvelous Canadian hero: "I just wish people would realize that anything is possible if you try. Dreams are made if people try."

An examination of persistence that is more financial can be had when students experiment with stock market activities. Give students copies of the business section of the newspaper and direct them to the pages reporting the activities of the New York Stock Exchange (NYSE). Explain how to read the information in each column for each of the stocks. Ask each student to choose a stock and pretend to have 100 shares. Then, ask students to record and chart the daily progress of their investments for the next thirty days. At the end of thirty days, students can compute the gains and losses of their investments. This long-term assignment requires persistence and conscientiousness on the part of students.

Openness to Ideas

People who are open to ideas search for and accept ideas from a wide variety of sources that include other people, the environment, new experiences, and their intuition. A hallmark of people who evidence openness to ideas is that they like to gather as much information as possible before making decisions, and they generally resist rapid closure, much to the frustration of those who like quick decisions. These people, according to creativity researcher E. Paul Torrance, are reluctant to judge and limit ideas, preferring to play with many ideas and making new connections and associations.[14]

Form groups of four or five students and ask the groups to create new and more imaginative headlines for five to ten stories that appear in the pages of the daily newspaper. In order to develop new headlines, ask them to all work together on each headline and brainstorm lots of possibilities for each story. Remind students of the rules of brainstorming: (1) Defer criticism; (2) Think of many ideas; (3) Encourage wild ideas; (4) Elaborate or build on previously mentioned ideas. It is critical that all members of each group contribute to this activity, and even more important that all members of the group listen to and encourage the ideas of others.

In a second round of brainstorming, ask the same students to create original newspaper headlines for classic nursery rhymes. For example, "Noted Citizen Killed in Fall" might be a headline describing the demise of Humpty Dumpty. What headlines can students create for Little Jack Horner, Jack and Jill, and Old Mother Hubbard?

Human-interest stories are often told from only one point of view. Ask students to find an unusual human-interest story in the newspaper. After reading the story, the students should think about other points of view that may exist. Ask them to rewrite the story from a fresh perspective. For example, a recent newspaper story told of a man who hired a bulldozer and had his former home destroyed rather than comply with a judge's ruling to turn the home over to his recently divorced wife. How might this story be presented from the judge's point of view? The wife's point of view? The bulldozer-operator's point of view?

A delightful example of events viewed from a new and fresh perspective is in Jon Scieszka's *The True Story of the 3 Little Pigs by A. Wolf*. Here, A. Wolf tells his side of the story in a front-page feature of the *Daily Wolf* newspaper.[15]

Intuition

Intuition is knowing something without making a conscious effort at reasoning. Hunches are classic examples of intuitive thinking. Intuition may involve metaphorical thinking, fantasizing, and dreaming (both day and night). Highly creative people often rely heavily on their intuitive powers in their creative endeavors. Artists have often recounted experiences in which they felt their creative production was guided by forces other than their own immediate consciousness. Samuel Taylor Coleridge's description of the creation of his poem "Kubla Khan" is one famous example.[16]

Give students copies of the newspaper and invite each to find an article of interest to read. After they have read their articles, ask them to close their eyes and imagine what will happen next to the individuals or groups about whom the article was written. Urge students to write newspaper articles about their predictions. Students can also make horoscope predictions for famous people, either living or dead. Fictional characters also make good subjects for this activity, too. For example, what type of day will Scarlett O'Hara have tomorrow? Before writing their horoscopes, students need to read several examples from the paper and understand the elements that typically make up horoscope predictions.

Independence

In his study of creative architects, Donald MacKinnon found that a sense of independence fostered in childhood was of enormous importance in the development of these people.[17] In their study of highly creative youths, Jacob Getzels and Philip W. Jackson discovered that one of the common qualities in the child-rearing practices of their subjects' parents was the high degree of independence allowed. Parents of these highly creative youths encouraged their children to be very independent.[18]

Independence involves the traits of self-reliance and autonomy. Independent children and adults may more frequently question the rules of society and of disciplines. They may challenge those rules that seem illogical or unfair to them. Creative people choose to follow paths other than the safe and established ones. Pablo Picasso comes to mind as one example. The great Spanish artist broke with European traditions to become one of the creators of cubism, and he seemed never to be content to work in just one style. His prodigious output of 20,000 pieces of art represents an unprecedented variety of styles and media.

Independent people tend to be motivated more by internal needs than by external pressures. The activities of creative people are frequently guided by what they deem to be important. They set very high goals for themselves.

Though human relationships are important to all, so, too, is solitude. Highly creative people often enjoy working alone for long periods of time with only their vivid imaginations for company.

Ask students to use both classified and display advertisements in the newspaper to design and furnish their ideal "getaway" places. Have them develop a very personalized den, playhouse, library, or sanctum sanctorum where they can be their creative best.

Another idea: Have students create their own newspapers. Divide the class into two or three teams and ask each team to divide the activities according to the talents and interests of those on the team. Each paper will need editors, reporters, artists, layout specialists, and proofreaders. Assign deadlines for the final products. Having responsibilities and deadlines positively fosters the growth of independence.

Originality

Originality is the ability to generate novel ideas and new solutions to problems. An important distinction regarding originality should be stated here. It is important when working with children to modify the concept of originality by stating that the novelty of an idea or solution need only be new to the learner. Creativity researcher Don Fabun states one salient reason: "We can never establish newness because our knowledge of history is so incomplete. History is full of instances of simultaneous invention."[19] Thomas Edison reputedly gave one of his colleagues this sage advice: "Make it a practice to keep on the lookout for novel and interesting ideas that others have used successfully. Your idea has to be original only in its adaptation to the problem you are working on."[20]

The field of invention is a fertile ground for looking at the dynamics of originality. Paper was invented through the original work of Ts'ai Lun in China in the year A.D. 105 and became widely used in China in the second century. It was not until A.D. 750, however, that the secret of paper making was learned westward from China. Arabs captured some Chinese, learned this secret, and began producing paper in Baghdad. Europeans did not learn to make paper until the twelfth century. It was not until A.D. 1454 that the second revolution in communications occurred, when Johannes Gutenberg made printing an integral part of the communications process. In the centuries that followed, many, many variations were added to the basic tools of paper making, printing, and communication.

With an eye toward invention, H. D. Lasswell defined creativity as "the disposition to make and recognize valuable innovations."[21] Probably more than any of the other attitudes and abilities in this model, originality is the one most closely associated with creativity. When asked to identify someone creative, the chances are great that most people will mention an individual who has developed a new idea, a new solution, a unique approach to art or music or dance, or technology. Thomas Jefferson, Thomas Edison, Isadora Duncan, Leonardo da Vinci, Albert Einstein, Pablo Picasso, and Galileo might be mentioned. These people are known for the breakthroughs they made in the way people do things and view the world. They were truly original thinkers.

Ask students to review the newspaper and find examples of originality. Advertising is one good place to look for original ideas. The comic section of the newspaper is another place where the products of original thinking can be observed. After cutting out examples of originality from the pages of the newspaper, students should create an originality bulletin board, or better still, conceive of a different way to display their found examples of originality.

Newspapers often carry stories about subjects of huge proportions such as the national debt, stock exchange transactions, the distances of Earth to various celestial bodies, and the salaries of professional sports stars. Ask students to search the newspaper for a reference to a big number. Next, ask them to depict that number in the most original manner possible. With the exception of numbers, anything may be used in the way the figure is represented. Encourage students to stretch their minds and present their figures in ways that are truly unique. Although it helps to have a variety of supplies such as clay, yarn, rice, crayons, glitter, and glue available, encourage students to supplement the classroom supplies with items from their homes.

Expressiveness

Donald MacKinnon, E. Paul Torrance, and Gary Davis are just a few of the many creativity researchers who have noted the kind of electric atmosphere that surrounds creative people.[22] These people seem to be highly charged, and to exude unbounded energy. Many, though certainly not all, are physically demonstrative in the way they express themselves. Their ideas may be conveyed through a variety of means that include music, dance, drama, the visual arts, storytelling, writing, or speech. They find new and unique ways to express themselves through their dress, through presentations, and in their communication with others.

Expressive people know the newspaper has many uses. Tell students that they are going to use the newspaper to fashion creative and expressive hats for themselves. First, ask them to brainstorm a variety of events for which the wearing of a hat would be appropriate. List the events on the board. Ask students to select one of the events they might like to attend and make an appropriate hat to wear to the event. This activity strengthens their visual expressiveness and challenges their originality. Be sure to have markers, tape, scissors, crayons, and other materials on hand.

An alternative idea is to assign students to two-member teams. Give each team a newspaper and a box of toothpicks. One member of the team becomes the creative and expressive designer and the second student serves as the model. The designer must use only the newspaper and the toothpicks to dress the partner in the most expressive manner possible.

Place students in groups of three to five members. Instruct the groups to find a situation described in the newspaper that lends itself to dramatization or recreation. Hint: The letters to advice columnists such as Ann Landers and Dear Abby are generally episodic and lend themselves well to dramatization. Ask the students to act out their stories for their classmates. This activity helps to develop the whole child, the drama in the child as well as the intellect. Students can pantomime a story from the sports pages or improvise a conflict portrayed in a front-page photograph.

Still another expressive activity to engage students is to ask them to convert news stories to poetry. Can they write an exciting sports poem about a last-minute touchdown, or an ode to a hero whose picture is on page one?

Elaboration

Elaboration is the capacity to take a seed of an idea and nurture it to full bloom. As long ago as 1926, Graham Wallas identified elaboration as an important component of the fourth step of the creative process that he called "verification."[23] During the elaboration phase, the creative person adds detail, discards extraneous aspects, reevaluates the product or concept, and continues to refine and modify. Elaboration shows careful planning and thought. It can involve painstaking work. Indeed, the word *elaboration* comes from *laborare*, which means "to labor" or "do work." This is the time-consuming phase of creative thinking, as artists nurture and mold their ideas into fully mature and presentable forms.

Frank Williams and E. Paul Torrance are two gifted education leaders who have made elaboration a component of both testing and teaching creativity.[24] Initially, people may see elaboration as being in conflict with fluency, and on a timed or power test this may be so. However, in real-life situations, the two components of creativity complement each other. Fluency is critical in the initial ideation phase of creative thinking, while elaboration is more important during the final step of a creative-thinking cycle.

Invite students to review the classified advertisements until they find examples that evoke images for a story. Then, ask them to create stories based on those images. For example, the following classified advertisement appeared in a South Carolina newspaper: "Lost: large, tame vulture. Does not fly. Cannot feed itself. If found, please call 689-4921." What kind of story can students create about the elements of this advertisement? What kind of person keeps a vulture for a pet? How did the vulture get loose? Where has the vulture been keeping itself? The possibilities for great story writing are endless.

Tell students that L'eggs, Hanes, and other giants of the panty-hose industry have found a surprising new market for their product: men. Panty-hose provide leg support without bulk for men who are athletes or whose job responsibilities find them on their feet much of the day. The only problem is that men are still hesitant and shy about going into stores and buying panty-hose for themselves. Arrange students into small groups and provide them with newspapers. Ask them to review the display advertisements found in the newspaper, especially in the sports pages, and then create an advertisement for panty-hose that will convince men to buy the product. Provide materials such as poster board and markers so the teams can fully develop their newspaper advertisements.

Using people, events, and numbers found in the newspaper, students can also create original story problems for mathematics classes.

Intelligence

Some people believe that creative acts and products magically and mysteriously appear out of the blue—that a composer leaps from his bed in the middle of the night and pens a masterpiece, or that a novelist or sculptor creates a masterpiece of words or clay with no real effort. They think the muses dictate the words or chisel the marble.

It just does not happen that way. Creativity is hard work. It is often a trial-and-error process. The creative geniuses of the recent past—Marie Curie, Georgia O'Keeffe, Thomas Edison, Pablo Picasso, to name but a few—were hard workers. They used their intelligence and they had a solid and substantial knowledge base as the foundation from which to launch their creative endeavors.

Jacob Getzels and Philip W. Jackson support the belief that there are differences between high levels of intelligence (as measured by intelligence tests) and high levels of creativity (as measured by creativity tests and products).[25] Howard Gardner explores the difference between creativity and intelligence as he discusses the seven intelligences he believes all people possess.

> I define giftedness as property of individuals who are "at promise" in an intellectual domain. A person is more gifted than other people in a specific domain (e.g., musical, understanding people, logical-mathematical) if he can advance more quickly in competence given the same amount of exposure to the domain. Giftedness is therefore a function of rapidity of development. Giftedness is domain- and intelligence-specific. Giftedness is also unrelated to creativity. A person may advance very quickly in competence but lack originality. Creativity is doing something in a new way.[26]

While there may be differences in the two modes of thinking, the main point to be made is that while intelligence and creativity may be distinct from one another, intelligence is the foundation from which creativity springs. Know-how or intelligence is a vital ingredient in the creative equation.

Have students select and read news articles in the newspaper. The news stories do not have to be national or international news. Students may find news stories in the business, sports, regional, and family sections of the newspaper. Instruct students to circle all statements and words they find that are opinion rather than fact. Next, instruct students to reread the circled words and to label each opinion as either expert or lay opinion. Have the students read aloud the passages they have circled and express their reasons for labeling the text as opinion, either lay or expert. The sharing and resulting discussions will reveal that even hard-news stories are filled with a great deal of opinion. Students become more discriminating readers and better critical thinkers when they learn to note such differences.

Sense of Humor

Laughter is generally heard wherever creative people are found. Many researchers have found humor to be a trademark of creative people. Perhaps it is because of their innate or well-developed tolerance for ambiguity that they find humor in life's quirks and twists. Witness, for example, the popularity of cartoonist Gary Larson among creative people.

Roger von Oech shares a story of a research study in which two talented groups of students were compared on their results in a creativity test. The treatment group listened to tapes of comedy routines prior to taking the test, whereas the control group had no such preparation. The result was that the treatment group performed significantly higher on the test.[27]

Humor may be linked to the first trait, that of positive self-concept. People who are being creative generally feel good about themselves. Smiles are frequent during creative experiences, and smiles are often followed by laughter. It feels good and joyous and even humorous to be creative. People laugh at their own wild ideas and those of others. Plus, laughter is infectious. It spreads.

Place students into threesomes. Ask them to examine their favorite comic strips of a humorous nature such as Jim Davis's "Garfield." Have them select one strip and outline the events that are occurring in the lives of the central characters. Next, tell them that the illustrator/creator needs to be on vacation for a week and has requested that they take over the strip. Ask the students to develop the situations for the next seven days. Encourage the students to draw their ideas in comic-strip form. While the quality of the drawings may inadvertently evoke laughter, be sure to emphasize that drawing talent is not a prerequisite. The focus should be on the story line and events that take place. Of course, teachers are free to "stack the deck" by including one artistically competent student in each threesome.

Perceptiveness

Perceptiveness is the ability to take in stimuli from various sources, retain those impressions, and then be able to call upon them for later use. A high degree of intensity of each of the senses is needed to reach a high level of perceptiveness. Highly creative people do not just look at an image; they take in all of the visual aspects from the very obvious to the extremely subtle. When they listen, they hear everything. And so on with all of the senses. Erich Fromm said, "Creativity is the ability to see (or be aware) and to respond."[28] Creative and perceptive people are capable of looking both inward and beyond themselves to see other people and the needs other people have. One synonym for perceptiveness could be sensitivity. Creative people can be highly sensitive themselves as well as sensitive to the needs of others.

Curiosity is one natural extension of perceptiveness. Ask students to push themselves, mentally, into the far future. They become aliens visiting Earth in the year 2999. They discover a well-preserved, thousand-year-old newspaper that is an important artifact of late twentieth-century humans. What important things does the artifact reveal about these ancient beings? What kind of lives did they have? Where did they eat? What did they do for entertainment? Did they have heroes and heroines? Tell students that they are on a fact-finding mission to Earth and they must use the artifact they have found to write a report to their government about the ancient civilization that used the artifact. Be sure to remind students to remain in character as aliens when writing their reports. They will have to be perceptive and imagine how the ancients used many of the items, words, and symbols found in the artifact. For example, the aliens may confuse the sports pages with world news and incorrectly hypothesize that a story about a contest between two professional football teams is a news report of a battle between two nations at war. The resulting student reports should be both insightful and entertaining.

Students may also examine the lyrics of popular songs or poetry that explore human emotion, problems of youth, or contemporary social issues. Ask students to then write a letter to Ann Landers or Dear Abby about the problem or issue that is the core of the chosen song or poem.

Problem Solving

Creative people love to solve problems. Generally speaking, the more complex the problem, the greater the appeal. The process of solving a problem is often more rewarding than is reaching a solution.

Problem solving is a very positive and constructive act. While some individuals are apt to see a problem in a negative light, creative people tend to view problems as opportunities. They see problems as challenges and view their solutions as opportunities for improving the status quo.

Ask students to use newspapers to create the tallest, largest, or sturdiest geodesic dome possible. How many can fit under the dome? Can they build a dome strong enough to support the weight of at least one team member? This newspaper construction exercise is an excellent cooperative learning activity.

For another problem-solving opportunity, pick a story from the news of the day that presents a problem to be solved. Ask the students, working in groups, to use the creative problem-solving model (see chapter *I*) to work through the problem found in the news. For example, the city of Denver, Colorado, is building a new international airport. The city recently sponsored a contest among students to find creative ideas to solve its problem of what to do with a soon-to-be-obsolete airport.

The creativity model that has been shared in this chapter allows and encourages TalentEd teachers and media specialists to more easily develop the creative attitudes and abilities of gifted, talented, and creative children and adolescents. It is not intended that all fifteen attitudes and abilities outlined in the model be addressed in every daily classroom lesson. Obviously, that would not be an achievable or even desirable goal. Rather, as educators plan instructional units, such as the creation of a unit based on the newspaper, this creativity model can serve as a reminder to consciously plan activities and experiences that recognize, attend to, and enhance the fifteen attitudes and abilities of creative people over time. When teachers do this, creative talent will flourish in TalentEd classrooms. Creative promise will be realized. Moreover, with the development and enhancement of creative talent, the net result will be the strengthening of the all-important self-concept.

Notes

[1] Arnold Toynbee, "Is America Neglecting Her Creative Minority?," in *Widening Horizons in Creativity: The Proceedings of the Fifth Utah Creativity Research Conference*, ed. Calvin W. Taylor (New York: John Wiley, 1964), 4.

[2] Anne B. Crabbe's model first appears in her book *Creating More Creative People* (Aberdeen, N.C.: Think, 1986). Information about the model and related products can be obtained by writing THINK, Inc., P.O. Box 85, Aberdeen, NC 28315.

[3] Gary A. Davis, *Creativity Is Forever*, 3d ed. (Dubuque, Iowa: Kendall/Hunt, 1992), 70-72.

[4] Part of the text in this chapter first appeared in a three-part series, "Creativity and Curriculum: A Partnership" by Anne B. Crabbe and Jerry D. Flack in *THINK* 3, no. 1 (October 1992): 17-22.

[5] Carl Rogers quoted in Don Fabun, *You and Creativity* (Beverly Hills, Calif.: Glencoe Press, 1971), 3.

[6] Emile Chartier quoted in Roger von Oech, *A Kick in the Seat of the Pants* (New York: Harper & Row, 1986), 30.

[7] Abraham Maslow, *Toward a Psychology of Being*, 2d ed. (Princeton, N.J.: D. Van Nostrand, 1962), 139-140.

[8] Von Oech, 14-15.

[9] Von Oech, 28.

[10] Ibid.

[11]Madeleine L'Engle, *A Circle of Quiet* (New York: Farrar, Straus & Giroux, 1972), 20-21, 66.

[12]Milton Larson, "Humbling Cases for Career Counselors," *Phi Delta Kappan* 54 (February 1973): 374.

[13]Rick Hansen and Jim Taylor, *Rick Hansen: Man in Motion* (New York: Viking Penguin, 1987); Patricia McKissack, *Mary McLeod Bethune: A Great American Educator* (Chicago: Childrens Press, 1985); Leslie Scrivener, *Terry Fox: His Story* (Toronto: McClelland and Stewart, 1982).

[14]E. Paul Torrance, *The Search for Satori and Creativity* (Buffalo, N.Y.: Creative Education Foundation, 1979), 74-83.

[15]Jon Scieszka, *The True Story of the 3 Little Pigs by A. Wolf*, illus. by Lane Smith (New York: Viking Kestrel, 1989).

[16]An account of Coleridge's dream and the creation of "Kubla Khan" may be found in D. N. Perkins, *The Mind's Best Work* (Cambridge, Mass.: Harvard University Press, 1981), 10-11.

[17]Donald MacKinnon, *In Search of Human Effectiveness: Identifying and Developing Creativity* (Buffalo, N.Y.: Creative Education Foundation, 1978), 172.

[18]Jacob Getzels and Philip W. Jackson, *Creativity and Intelligence: Explorations with Gifted Students* (New York: John Wiley, 1962), 75.

[19]Fabun, 5.

[20]Thomas Edison quoted in von Oech, 28.

[21]H. D. Lasswell quoted in Fabun, 3.

[22]MacKinnon, *In Search of Human Effectiveness*; Torrance, *The Search for Satori*; Davis, *Creativity Is Forever*.

[23]Graham Wallas, "The Art of Thought," in D. N. Perkins, *The Mind's Best Work* (Cambridge, Mass.: Harvard University Press, 1981), 183.

[24]Frank Williams, "The Cognitive-Affective Interaction Model for Enriching Gifted Programs," in *Systems and Models for Developing Programs for the Gifted and Talented*, ed. Joseph S. Renzulli (Mansfield Center, Conn.: Creative Learning Press, 1986), 461-484; Torrance, *The Search for Satori*, 65-72.

[25]Getzels and Jackson, 15-22.

[26]Howard Gardner, "An Interview with Howard Gardner," *Gifted Child Today* (*G/C/T*) 13, no. 6 (November/December 1990): 28.

[27]Von Oech, 82.

[28]Erich Fromm quoted in Fabun, 4.

# Is for Olympics

Citius, Altius, Fortius!

(Faster, Higher, Stronger!)

Motto of the Paris Olympics, 1924
Selected by Baron Pierre de Coubertin

Every four years, people all over the globe celebrate their humanity and the union of body, mind, and spirit by staging the Olympic Games. The Olympic Games trace their history back to Greek mythology and the battles waged by the god Zeus. Mortal Greeks began the Games and Rites at Olympia, Greece, in 776 B.C. The Roman emperor, Theodosius, banned the ancient games in A.D. 393. Through the indefatigable efforts of the baron Pierre de Coubertin of France, the modern Games began in Athens, Greece, in 1896. In 1924, the French hosted the first Winter Games. Beginning with the XVII Winter Games at Lillehammer, Norway, in 1994, the winter and summer Olympic Games occur in alternating even years. Additional Olympic facts are on pages 167-169.

The Olympic Games are wonderful spectacles full of suspense, excitement, and drama. Despite geographical barriers, varying stages of political, economic, and social development among nations, and the obstacle of different languages among participants, the modern Olympic Games have grown to include participation by virtually every country on Earth in less than a century. The principal reason for this astounding success may well be that the Olympics are a demonstration of idealism in action. In an age of materialism, there are, fortunately, many individuals who still believe there are things in life more important than monetary reward, and who see the Olympics as a hope for uniting the world.

The ideals and traditions of the Olympic movement provide a perfect framework for promoting self-esteem, encouraging positive attitudes toward life, and fostering goal setting in TalentEd students. Simultaneously, educators can create an awareness of the similarities in human experience as well and the wonderful cultural diversity that exists in humanity.

The frequency with which the colorful and exciting Olympic Games occur (every two years) is a cause for celebration for TalentEd teachers. These dramatic events offer rich opportunities that allow teachers to connect with a great many areas of concern in school reconstruction. Opportunities abound for the skillful employment of cooperative learning. The study of the Olympics is so rich and varied that every student's predominant learning style can be addressed. Moreover, any study of the Olympics is bound to be interdisciplinary. The integration of new knowledge and information can be woven into significant concept and knowledge base building.[1]

160 O Is for Olympics

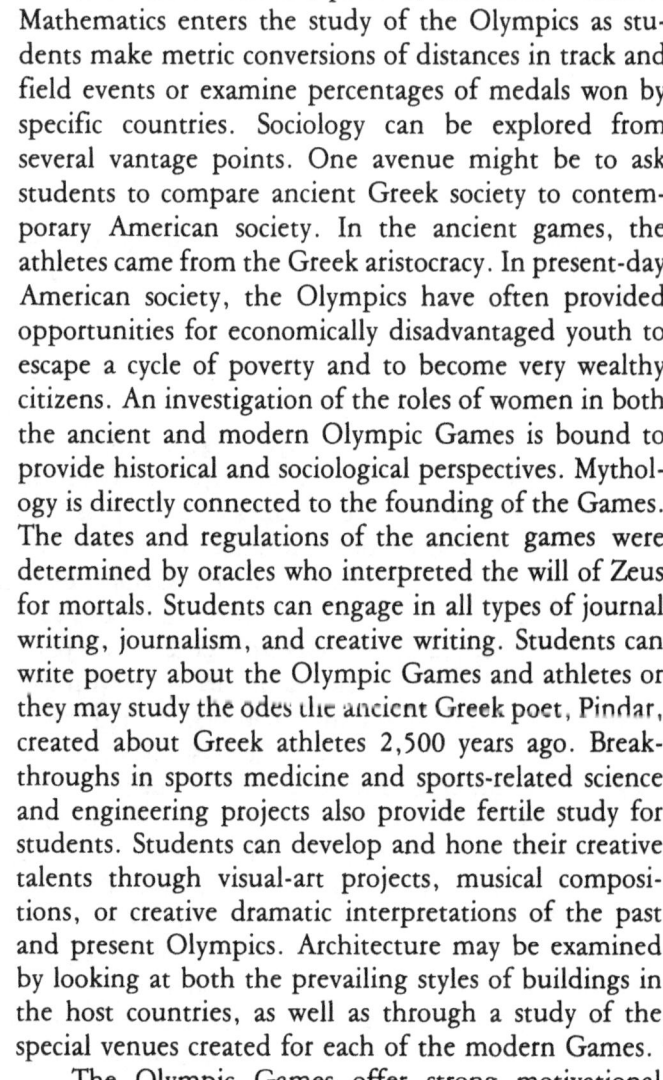

A study of the Olympics involves teaching history. The ancient games were of such magnitude in the lives of the Greeks that the founding date of the first Olympic Games in 776 B.C. was considered to be the beginning of historical time. The modern Games have often been cancelled or boycotted because of historical events such as World Wars I and II and the Soviet Union's invasion of Afghanistan. Economics can be examined in terms of the advertising associated with the upcoming Games. The currencies and their values of the participating nations may be studied and compared. Geography is accentuated when students examine maps and atlases to note the host sites of former, present, and future Games. Mathematics enters the study of the Olympics as students make metric conversions of distances in track and field events or examine percentages of medals won by specific countries. Sociology can be explored from several vantage points. One avenue might be to ask students to compare ancient Greek society to contemporary American society. In the ancient games, the athletes came from the Greek aristocracy. In present-day American society, the Olympics have often provided opportunities for economically disadvantaged youth to escape a cycle of poverty and to become very wealthy citizens. An investigation of the roles of women in both the ancient and modern Olympic Games is bound to provide historical and sociological perspectives. Mythology is directly connected to the founding of the Games. The dates and regulations of the ancient games were determined by oracles who interpreted the will of Zeus for mortals. Students can engage in all types of journal writing, journalism, and creative writing. Students can write poetry about the Olympic Games and athletes or they may study the odes the ancient Greek poet, Pindar, created about Greek athletes 2,500 years ago. Breakthroughs in sports medicine and sports-related science and engineering projects also provide fertile study for students. Students can develop and hone their creative talents through visual-art projects, musical compositions, or creative dramatic interpretations of the past and present Olympics. Architecture may be examined by looking at both the prevailing styles of buildings in the host countries, as well as through a study of the special venues created for each of the modern Games.

The Olympic Games offer strong motivational interest to students. TalentEd teachers and school library media specialists can help youth win lots of gold medals for creative thinking and production in the coming Olympic years. These glorious spectacles offer educators a special opportunity to help youth reflect and focus upon the enobling spirit of people trying to be at their very best.

Activities and Projects

An exciting place to begin a study of the Olympic Games is through study and possible dramatization of Greek myths depicting the origins of the ancient Olympics. In cooperative learning groups, students can research and then dramatize Greek myths such as the battle between Zeus and Cronos, Pelops and Oenomaus, and Heracles and King Augeas. Students should examine Greek mythology for clues to the development of the rites and games of the Olympics.

It's Greek to me. Language symbol development is enhanced if students investigate and work with the Greek alphabet. Students can create name tags using the Greek alphabet. They can also research the derivation and definitions of these words:

| *athlete* | *Olympiad* | *pentathlon* | *decathlon* | *hippodrome* |
| *spartan* | *marathon* | *stadium* | *promethean* | *gymnasium* |

Olympic sleuths can create codes or messages about the Olympics, past and present, utilizing the Greek alphabet. The Greek alphabet has twenty-four letters while the English alphabet has twenty-six letters. Because the Greek and English alphabets do not have direct equivalents, some creative coding may have to be done. Olympic sleuths can also search advertising, textbooks, and other sources for uses of Greek alphabet letters. The ancient Olympics were halted by the Romans. This fact may prompt other students to investigate Latin, the language of the Romans.

Give self-esteem a boost. Good sportsmanship is the central theme of the Olympics. Ask students to brainstorm all the words and phrases they can think of to tell someone they are great or that they have done a good job. Students should enter their lists in their journals and refer to them often.

A study of the Olympics is yet another opportunity for students to create alphabet books. Students can research the history of both the modern and ancient Games. Using the names of Olympic sites, customs, events, and personalities, they can create alphabet books that celebrate the Olympics, A to Z. The best Olympics ABC books should be laminated and cataloged in the school library media center for the enjoyment and education of other students. Imaginative students may also create catalogs (see chapter *C*) related to Olympic themes.

Creative writers can use personification to write about dramatic events in the history of the Olympics from the point of view of vital pieces of sports equipment. For example, Susan may pretend to be the blades on the skates of Kristi Yamaguchi in the 1992 Albertville Winter Olympics. She describes the thrill and excitement of the competition and the glory of winning the gold medal. David may write from the perspective of one of the track shoes worn by Carl Lewis in the 100 meters at the 1984 Los Angeles Summer Olympics.

O Is for Olympics

Creative youth can suggest whimsical and creative alternatives to equipment utilized in Olympic events. For example, what kitchen instruments might be substituted for track and field equipment? Could one substitute a paper plate for the discus, a broom for a javelin, or a scouring pad for the shot put? Brrrrr! Welcome to the Ice Cube Olympics. Before the invention of refrigerators, people thought of many ingenious ways to preserve winter's ice for use during the warmer months. Hold an Ice Cube Olympics. Who can construct a container that will keep ice solid the longest? Kitchen Olympics of various kinds can be fun.

More fun can abound when students consider what might happen if the animals had their own Olympic Games. What events might challenge animals and which animals would be heavy favorites to win these events? Who would win the gold medal in the diving competition, for example? Who would win the marathon? Share excerpts from Howard Smith, Jr.'s *The Animal Olympics*. Creative students may want to design school-year calendars that portray different animal Olympians for each of the school-year months.

What other kinds of unique Olympic Games might be held? Encourage students to speculate on the kinds of events that might occur in winter games using equipment from the school cafeteria. Perhaps the game of basketball could take on a new twist if students used paper wads as balls. Set up two baskets, one inside the other; an empty tin can placed inside a laundry basket, for example. Students receive two points for every paper wad that makes it into the smaller can and one point for each paper wad that scores in the laundry basket. These games may provide perfect opportunities to teach the metric system of measurement. If drinking straws are used for javelins, for example, how many meters did the farthest-placed straw travel?

Invite students to create a new honor or award that will be awarded in future Olympic Games. They should design a medal and tell why and how it will be awarded. Next, students can write a *Sports Illustrated* feature story about the first recipient of the honor. Perhaps an award should be given to the athlete who best promotes harmony among all the athletes from all the nations represented in the Games, or perhaps the honor might go to the woman or man who exhibits the greatest degree of courage or sacrifice.

Sadly, some of the recent summer Olympic Games have fallen victim to political boycotts and even terrorist activity. Such activities have kept young people from around the world from forging positive bonds and experiencing the brotherhood and sisterhood the modern Olympics were designed to foster. In one tragic incident at the 1972 Munich Olympics, terrorists killed young Israeli athletes. Ask students to examine this question: Have the Olympic Games lost their value for forging international cooperation and respect? Should they be changed in some way? Encourage students to practice creative problem solving (see chapter I) to explore this subject and to forge creative solutions to assure that future Games remain peaceful and nonpolitical. Students may want to send a statement of their final plan to the International Olympic Committee and United States Olympic Committee.

Invention can play a role in an Olympics unit. Ask students to imagine that stopwatches do not exist; no one ever invented one. How might Olympic officials clock contestants in events found in alpine skiing and track and field? Encourage students to invent new ways to time sporting events. They should be able to describe their inventions and explain how they work. They should also create drawings or diagrams of their inventions. Teachers may also want to challenge creativity with this prompt: You are an inventor. A sporting-goods corporation has commissioned you to develop a new shoe to be used by athletes to improve their performance in one of the Olympic track and field events. Design a superior sports shoe. What would it look like? What special features would it have? What name will you give this special shoe?

Take inventors into the future. Ask students to invent new sports for the 2096 winter or summer Olympic Games. Invite students to describe the events, the equipment and facilities needed, and the particular skills future athletes will need to succeed in the 2096 activities. They should write newspaper stories about the 2096 competitions and winners, complete with illustrations of gold medal winners. What symbols or logos can students create for the 2096 Olympic Games?

For another future twist, ask students to imagine that they are living in the year 2096. NASA scientists have made contact with life beyond Earth. Indeed, they have made contact with life forms on several planets. Have student groups create new formats for the Galaxy Olympics. Olympic planning groups should create games or events that allow the different planetary species to compete on common footing. Provide each group with these charges: Create a universal symbol for any new sport. Devise some events that might take place in a weightless environment. What devices might be used to time or measure such events? Draw a picture that captures the scene of the first gold medal winner participating in one of the new events. How would some of the current Olympic events be conducted on Mars? On Jupiter? Create an exciting and visually stimulating travel brochure that will make Earth citizens want to travel to the Jovian Olympics in 2292.

A study of the Olympics is a fine occasion for reading biographies. Ask each student to select a favorite athlete to study. Students should engage in sufficient research to be able to tell each Olympian's story. How did the subjects become great athletes? In which Olympic Games did the athletes excel? What other things happened to the subjects beyond their Olympic triumphs? Students should note the Olympic records or feats of their subjects. During forthcoming Olympic Games, they can then compare the records made by their subjects with new times, distances, and scores. A class historian might also want to investigate and determine what events have been dropped from the Olympics over time. Why were these events dropped? Should they be reinstated? For example, the founder of the modern Olympics, Baron Pierre de Coubertin, proposed that artistic events be included in the Olympics. They were added in 1912, but dropped in 1948. Imagine that artistic entries will be reinstated in future Games. Encourage students to create poetry, songs, and artwork to enter in these future art Olympic categories.

Art activities can also flourish when students examine the many Olympic mascots. "Misha" the Bear was the official mascot of the 1980 Moscow Olympics. "Sam" the Olympic Eagle was created for the 1984 Los Angeles Games. "Hodori" was the 1988 Seoul, Korea, tiger mascot, and Barcelona, Spain chose "Cobi" as their mascot. What animal is "Cobi"? Solicit designs from students for official mascots of future Olympic Games.

Artists all over the world create special items to help people enjoy and remember the Olympic Games. Invite students to create a series of postcards for future Olympic sites and events. Special postage stamps are created in many countries, including the United States, to honor the Olympics and Olympians. Students can also become stamp designers and create stamps to celebrate past and forthcoming Olympic sites, events, or athletes. Be sure to ask them to include the names of the origin countries of their stamps and their costs. This is an excellent springboard activity for discussing varying currencies used worldwide. Moreover, while students are still in the design mode, have them create T-shirts for any of the present and future Olympic Games, including the Galaxy Games in 2096!

Math story problems can be created utilizing the enormous amount of statistical data found in the Olympic Games. Comparisons of times and distances and weights can be made in the same events across several different years. The increased percentage of women participating in the Olympics in the 1990s can be compared to that of women competing in the 1950s. The possibilities for imaginative problem creation as well as problem solving are great in a classroom Olympics unit.

Use the backdrop of the Olympic Games to have students create a mystery story or play. On the opening day of the Atlanta Games, for example, all of the gold medals are found to be missing! There are no immediate suspects. Each story or play should include the standard mystery elements or questions to be answered: Who? What? When? Where? Why? and How?

Building on the ideas students create for the activities described in chapter *K* (pages 113-117), encourage students to create a brand new country or kingdom that wants to enter its first Olympic competition. Promoters for new countries or kingdoms should create maps of their countries, and establish governments, constitutions, and laws for their countries. They should create national flags. In which events will its citizens be most likely to compete? What souvenirs or native products will the athletes from this new country take to the Olympic Games to exchange with athletes from other nations? In the opening ceremonies of the Olympic Games, which citizen from their kingdom will carry the new flag? Why has this individual been so honored?

Direct students to examine color photographs of the Olympic flag that flies at Olympic sites. Explain the significance of the interlocking rings. The five interlocking rings represent the five continents and the colors black, blue, red, green, and yellow represent at least one color found in the flags of all the nations. In small groups, give students the task of designing other flags that could symbolize unity, friendship, and cooperation. Have older students create a Big Book telling the story about the existing Olympic flag or a new friendship flag that could then be utilized in a whole language lesson with younger readers. Similar Big Books can be created that will explain the history of the Olympics, recount the heroics of a particular Olympian like Jesse Owens, or explain some of the geography involved in the Olympic competitions.

A TalentEd teacher in Maine says that the five interlocking rings remind him of the famous magician's trick where separate rings are held up to magically form a chain. He says, "I love trying to figure out how tricks are done but this one keeps me humble. The rings look completely solid to me." Are there any TalentEd students who are willing and eager to become the classroom magic experts? Can they learn to perform this trick or figure out how it is accomplished? Yet another avenue for the creative classroom is a classroom magic Olympics.

Nutritional habits are critical in the overall training programs of most Olympians. Have students research and explore the nutritional habits of Olympic athletes and design a diet for a male or female athlete in a chosen sport. Next, they should go to a grocery store and engage in some price shopping. How economical is the recommended diet? What kind of a monthly budget is needed to sustain the diet?

The whole class can participate in making a classroom mural that shows scenes of everyday life or dramatic landmarks in many of the nations that participate in the Olympic Games. Each student chooses a country and is given a section of the mural to complete after engaging in plenty of research about the chosen nation and its citizens and attractions.

Students might also create a mural that functions as a timeline. At the beginning they can draw pictures of what an Olympic event might have looked like in 776 B.C. They continue the timeline on around the room right up to the present date. Indeed, they may even extrapolate from the present and move the timeline into the future. They may draw a scene representative of the 2096 Olympic Games.

Make geography an integral part of a study of the Olympics. Ask students to find Olympia in Greece. Next, have them locate on a map all the host countries of the Olympic Games since 1896. What are some of the travel routes the Olympic flame has taken in 100 years? Using a world map, students can connect all the countries to Olympia in Greece where the Olympic flame originates.

Clever TalentEd students can ply their humor in a study of the Olympics, and practice writing parody (see chapter *P*, pages 176-177). Classroom humorists can dream up whimsical sporting events. They can tell the history of their sport and where it originated. For example, historians of the Olympics may be surprised to know that the "spitball-blown-through-a-straw" sporting event was created in a middle school classroom in the United States. The launch in this event may take place only when teachers are writing on the chalkboard with their backs to the class. The purpose of the event is to annoy educators. Those who sit farther back in the classroom receive handicap points as they have to blow harder to have any chance of actually having their spit wad hit teachers dead on.

The popular and much-acclaimed British film *Chariots of Fire* was highly successful at movie box offices. Tell students that a movie producer wants to make another hit movie and thus seeks their advice. *Chariots of Fire* tells the Olympic saga of two of England's competitors in the 1924 Paris Olympics. Ask students to describe the plot, the major settings, the main characters or subjects, and to point out any special shots, effects, or images they desire to accentuate in the new film they are recommending to the producer. Will they tell the story of Wilma Rudolph, Greg Louganis, Mary Lou Retton, Jesse Owens, Florence Griffith Joyner, or the 1980 United States gold medal-winning hockey team? Perhaps they will choose yet another dramatic story to film.

O Is for Olympics

The culminating activity for an Olympics unit in a TalentEd classroom might well be goal sheets students create that symbolize their individual pathways to gold medal lives. The marathon event in the first modern Games in 1896 was run, in part, on ancient Greek cobblestone streets. Challenge students to think of each cobblestone that they may touch on their pathways to success. In other words, what price success? What does it take to be a champion, to be a victor not just in athletics but in academics, in making friends, and as a leader? In an Olympics unit, TalentEd students should be challenged to create their own symbolic cobblestone roads to becoming gold medal winners in life. A sample cobblestone road to success might include these milestones:

The Olympics present an occasion for encouraging youth to be their absolute best. A celebration of these Games represents a wonderful time to call for excellence from and for gifted, talented, and creative youth. A focus on the Olympics should cause educators to remind youth to always strive to be their best, and that there is nothing wrong with perfectionism so long as it embodies the drive for excellence and does not become paralyzing or crippling. Celebrating the Olympics also affords educators a splendid opportunity to share with youth the motto of the University of Pennsylvania, which was so important in the life of Olympian Eric Liddell whose story was told in *Chariots of Fire*:

> In the dust of defeat,
> as well as in the laurels of victory,
> there is a glory to be found
> if one has done his best.

The Olympics should remind both educators and students of how similar their goals are to those of Olympic coaches and athletes. The belief in developing creativity, the intellect, problem-solving skills, teamwork, and interdependence among people all over the globe regardless of race, creed, color, or nationality is a remarkably worthy and appropriate goal of education.

Olympic Facts

ANCIENT OLYMPICS

Women were not allowed to participate in the ancient games at Olympia. They were forbidden, on penalty of death, from even observing the events.

The notorious Roman emperor Nero participated in the ancient Olympics. When his chariot overturned during a race, the other contestants stopped and waited for him to begin again, fearful that they might otherwise win the race and incur his wrath.

SUMMER OLYMPICS

Although the concept of the modern Olympic Games belonged entirely to the French baron Pierre de Coubertin, politics prevented him from being recognized or accorded any place of honor at the first modern Games held in Athens, Greece, in 1896.

No women participated in the 1896 Athens Olympic Games, but women participated in a lawn tennis event in the 1900 London Games. In the 1988 Seoul Summer Games 2,438 women competed.

The first use of electronic timing devices and a public address system occurred in the 1912 Stockholm Games. Photo-finish camera equipment and automatic timing devices were first used in the 1932 Los Angeles Games. Television was first used in the 1936 Berlin Games.

During the time of the ancient Olympic games wars ceased so that the games could be held. In the modern era, the reverse has been true. The 1916 Games were cancelled due to World War I, and defeated nations in World War I, which included Germany, Austria, and Turkey, were not allowed to have representatives in the 1920 Antwerp, Belgium, Olympic Games. No Games were held in 1940 or 1944 because of World War II. The 1980 Moscow Games and the 1984 Los Angeles Games were disrupted by the respective political boycotts of the United States and the Soviet Union.

The creator of the modern Games, the baron Pierre de Coubertin, selected the motto for the Olympic Games. "Citius, Altius, Fortius!" (Faster, Higher, Stronger!) was first read at the 1924 Paris Games. The Olympic pledge was first read at the 1920 Antwerp, Belgium, Games. It reads:

> In the name of all competitors, I promise that we will take part in these Olympic
> Games, respecting and abiding by the rules which govern them, in the true spirit
> of sportsmanship, for the glory of sport and the honor of our teams.

Bob Mathias was the youngest person in history to win a gold medal in men's track and field events. Mathias won the prestigious decathlon (ten events) in the 1948 London Summer Games. Four years later he won a second gold medal in the decathlon at the 1952 Helsinki Games.

Australian swimmer Shane Gould won three gold medals in the 1972 Summer Games in Munich, Germany. She was just fifteen years old.

Nadia Comaneci won three gold medals in gymnastics at the 1976 Montreal Summer Games. In doing so she became the first person in the history of the sport to receive gymnastics' perfect score of 10.0 from the judges. She received a total of seven perfect scores of 10.0 in the 1976 Olympics.

WINTER OLYMPICS

In the 1924 Winter Games in Chamonix, France, eleven-year-old Sonja Henie competed in figure skating. She did not win a medal then (in fact, she placed dead last), but she won the gold medal in the next three Winter Olympic Games held, respectively, in St. Moritz, Switzerland (1928), Lake Placid, New York (1932), and Garmisch-Partenkirchen, Germany (1936). She then turned professional and became an American film star.

The International Olympic Committee (IOC) originally did not approve of the idea of winter games. However, France, the designated host for the 1924 Summer Olympics, ignored the IOC and invited athletes to participate in winter games at Chamonix in 1924. These games were so popular that the IOC decided in 1925 to sanction winter games. They retroactively declared the 1924 Chamonix Games as the first official Winter Games. In 1928, the II Winter Games were held at St. Moritz, Switzerland.

Billy Fiske was just fifteen years old when he became the youngest man ever to win a gold medal in the 1928 St. Moritz Winter Games. He captained the American four-man bobsled team. He won a second gold medal in the same event in the 1932 Lake Placid Winter Games. Tragically, he would later become the first American pilot to die in Europe during World War II.

Russian women's speed skater Lydia Skoblikova won four gold medals in the 1964 Innsbruck, Austria, Games.

Speed skater Eric Heiden became the first person to win five gold medals in a single Winter Olympics competition in the 1980 Lake Placid Games. Heiden won a gold medal in every men's speed skating distance event.

The 1980 Winter Games were also notable for what may have been the greatest upset in the history of the Winter Games, the United States hockey team's defeat of the powerful Soviet team. The young American team went on to win the gold medal.

British ice dancers Christopher Dean and Jayne Torvill became the first persons to receive figure skating's perfect score of 6.0 from all nine judges in Olympic competition following their famed dance to Ravel's "Bolero" at the 1984 Winter Olympic Games in Sarajevo, Yugoslavia.

Note

[1] Material that appears in this chapter first appeared in Jerry D. Flack, "In Search of Serendipity," *Understanding Our Gifted* 4, no. 2 (November/December 1991): 17-18; and Jerry D. Flack, "The Olympics," *THINK* 2, no. 4 (April 1992): 23-31.

Teacher Resources

Aaseng, Nathan. *Great Summer Olympic Moments*. Minneapolis, Minn.: Lerner Publications, 1990.

The heroics of Olympians such as Jesse Owens are shared with younger readers. See also the same author's *Great Winter Olympic Moments* (Minneapolis, Minn.: Lerner Publications, 1990).

Carlson, Lewis, and John Fogarty. *Tales of Gold: An Oral History of the Summer Olympic Games Told by American Gold Medal Winners*. Chicago: Contemporary Books, 1987.

One of the American Olympians interviewed in this splendid work is the famed pediatrician Benjamin Spock, who won a gold medal in the 1924 Paris Olympics.

Conway, Geoffrey S., trans. *The Odes of Pindar*. London: J. M. Dent & Sons, 1972.

The "Olympian Odes" of Pindar reveal much of the glory of ancient Greece and the original Olympics.

Finley, M. I., and H. W. Pleket. *The Olympic Games: The First Thousand Years*. New York: Viking, 1976.

Excellent graphics help tell the story of the art and history of the ancient games.

Glubok, Shirley, and Alfred Tamarin. *Olympic Games in Ancient Greece*. New York: Harper & Row, 1976.

A children's book about the history of the ancient games.

Grunfeld, Frederic V. *Games of the World*. Zurich: Swiss Committee for UNICEF, 1982.

This wonderful book is not about the Olympics per se, but it is about the everyday games children and adults play all over the world. It may be ordered from UNICEF, an agency of the United Nations, or from bookstores.

Johnson, William Oscar. *The Olympics: A History of the Games*. New York: Time, 1992.

Johnson has created a gorgeous picture book of the Olympic Games for *Sports Illustrated*.

MacAloon, John J. *This Great Symbol: Pierre de Coubertin and the Origins of the Modern Olympic Games*. Chicago: University of Chicago Press, 1981.

> A scholarly treatment of the founder and the founding of the modern Games.

Ramsey, Russell W. *God's Joyful Runner*. South Plainfield, N.J.: Bridge, 1987.

> There are many wonderful biographies of great Olympians. This excellent authorized biography tells the story of Eric Liddell, the Scottish hero of the movie *Chariots of Fire*. The story of Harold Abrahams, the other hero portrayed in *Chariots of Fire*, may be found in Robert Slater's *Great Jews in Sports* (Middle Village, N.Y.: Jonathan David, 1983).

Segrave, Jeffrey, and Donald Chu, eds. *The Olympic Games in Transition*. Champaign, Ill.: Human Kinetics Books, 1988.

> Gifted middle school and secondary school students can profit from the editors' examination of the history, growth, and controversy found in both the ancient and modern Olympic Games.

Smith, Howard, Jr. *The Animal Olympics*. Garden City, N.Y.: Doubleday, 1979.

> John Lane's illustrations help to make this book a delight. The question posed is: Which animals would be especially successful in all the human events found in the Olympic Games? A case in point: The broad jump would be won by the snow leopard, which can span a distance of 49 feet in a single leap.

Wallechinsky, David. *The Complete Book of the Olympics, 1992*. Boston: Little, Brown, 1991.

> A complete list of events, winners, and sites of the modern Olympics from 1896 to the present is included in this fine resource. The author updates this title every four years.

Most public libraries have a variety of resources related to the Olympics and biographies of many great Olympians, past and present. In addition to the many print resources, teachers and library media specialists may wish to consult video resources, such as the Academy Award-winning best picture *Chariots of Fire*, or documentary works that record highlights of past summer and winter games.

School libraries and individual teachers may wish to subscribe to *The Olympian*, the magazine of the U.S. Olympic Committee. Current subscription rates may be requested from the U.S. Olympic Committee, *The Olympian Magazine*, 1750 East Boulder Street, Colorado Springs, Colorado 80909-5760.

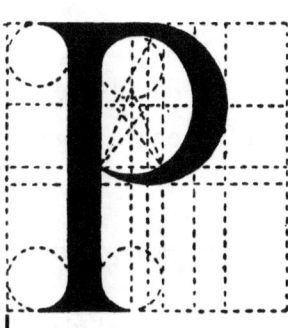Is for Pigs, Parody, and Puns

> Humor is emotional chaos remembered in tranquility.
> —James Thurber

> He deserves paradise who makes his companions laugh.
> —The Koran

> Laughter is the closest thing to the grace of God.
> —Karl Barth

A characteristic of TalentEd classrooms is the presence of frequent laughter. Humor is a vital ingredient in any life equation. In recent years, medical, educational, and creativity experts have come to appreciate the role humor plays in reducing stress and anxiety, in improving performance on tests and tasks, and even in aiding the healing process in people with illness. In a world often filled with stress, humor is a creative coping tool. As humor educator Joel Goodman says, "She who laughs, lasts."[1]

One of the most common traits identified with gifted, creative, and talented students is their unique sense of humor. In writing a profile of a gifted child in her classroom, a Colorado first-grade teacher writes that the most remarkable sign that a six-year-old in her classroom was distinctly different from his peers was the frequent evidence of his remarkably sophisticated sense of humor.[2] She is not alone. All over the country teachers recognize that an advanced sense of humor is a signal trait of many gifted, talented, and creative students. Due to their advanced, comprehensive, and sophisticated vocabularies, gifted students often understand and create puns and other forms of humor that escape the attention of other children their age. They also love parodies and enjoy creating them.

There are many ways TalentEd teachers can capitalize on the wit their creative students possess. They can share books and articles that involve humor and humor making. Joke and riddle books for all ages can easily be found in the school library media center and in the humor section of bookstores. Some classic examples of humor include:

P Is for Pigs, Parody, and Puns

Gordon, Harvey C. *PUNdemonium: Puns Are Everywhere!* Glenview, Ill.: Punster's Press, 1983.

> Just a few of the many, many places this punster finds puns is at the doctor's office, on the stage, in Americana, and at sporting events.

Larson, Gary. *The PreHistory of the Far Side: A 10th Anniversary Exhibit.* Kansas City, Mo.: Andrews and McMeel, 1989.

> A most talented cartoonist shares his best work and tells how he finds humor in unusual places.

McMillan, Bruce A. *Punography.* New York: Penguin Books, 1978.

> McMillan uses three or four photographs on each page to reveal a witty, visual pun. The simplicity of the photography suggests the possibility for students to imitate his clever work.

Thurber, James. *The Thurber Carnival.* New York: Dell, 1964.

> Happily, the work of the man who is easily one of the two or three best humorists America has produced stays in print. His work has special appeal to the sense of humor gifted junior and senior high school students adore.

Watterson, Bill. *The Essential Calvin and Hobbes: A Calvin and Hobbes Treasury.* Kansas City, Mo.: Andrews and McMeel, 1988.

> America's most precociously gifted child is the source of much humor in Watterson's work.

When Pigs Fly!

Students will enjoy humorous and creative encounters with pigs. Their first task is to redesign the pig to make it fly. The tool used is morphologically forced connections. Using this popular creativity tool, inventors, designers, or problem solvers take an object and analyze it according to its basic attributes or component parts. Next, problem solvers consider all possible values of each of the separate attributes. Once all the possible values of each attribute are listed, new product configurations are suggested by making random connections among them. Morphologically forced connections are most easily made when a grid is constructed and used. Across the horizontal axis, problem solvers list the various body parts of the pig: snout, ears, legs, tail, and so on (see fig. P.1). Next, they brainstorm all kinds of possible variations for each part and they place these responses in the vertical boxes. Finally, they select from among the many options the new configuration of parts needed to make the pig fly. An example is shown in figure P.2, page 174. The pig's tail functions as a rotary blade and lifts the pig helicopter-fashion.

Students should note that this process, used here in a humorous way, may be used in a more serious manner to redesign a school desk, a ballpoint pen, or any other object. For examples and additional explanations of morphologically forced connections, see *Conceptual Blockbusting* by James L. Adams, and *The All-New Universal Traveler* by Don Koberg and Jim Bagnall.

Once students have genetically engineered the pig to fly, they need to promote their newly invented product. Perhaps they can create an advertising campaign for Pigs Airlines modeled on the advertising ploys discussed in chapter E.

Fig. P.4. How to make pigs fly and other marvels of creativity.

Attribute	Snout	Ears	Legs	Tail	Body
Values	pointed, stiff	floppy	muscular	rotary	inflatable
		large, floppy		propeller	sleek
		drooping	winglike		

P Is for Pigs, Parody, and Puns

Fig. P.2. Pig lifted like a helicopter by way of his rotarylike tail.

As a result of the wealth gained from Pigs Airlines, the Pigs have become one of America's wealthiest families. However, they have been largely unsuccessful in their attempts to break into Newport society. How might the great psychologist Pigmund Freud help the Pigs overcome the stigma of their family name and history?

Challenge students to use their humor and creativity to imagine how the Pig family might take advantage of their wealth to employ some of the following experts.

How might society writer Porcina von Slop of the *Animal Farm Gazette* write an account of the wedding of Priscilla Pig to Porker "Razorback" Swiney?

What sort of grand mansion might the famous architect, Frankfurter Lloyd Wright, design for the Pigs?

The great artist, Pigcasso, is going to create a giant mural for the entryway to the new Pig Mansion featuring the Pig family crest. Help Pigcasso design the Pig family crest.

Pretend to be the famed poet, Swineburn. Create an ode to celebrate the Pigs' newfound fame and glory.

P Is for Pigs, Parody, and Puns

The Pigs are having a grand ball to honor notable swine. What notable names can students add to this preliminary list of honored guests in figure P.3?

Fig. P.3. The pig hall of fame.

Sir Francis Bacon	Albert Einswine
Pigmund Freud	George and Ira Gershwine
Hamlet, Prince of Danish Hams	Miss Piggy
Wilbur	John Philip Sowsa
Gertrude Swine	Frankfurter Lloyd Wright
Kevin Bacon	Frankenswine

■ ■ ■

As a conclusion to this tomfoolery with pigs, students may want to read from, as well as add to, the following list of pig tales, or classics of swine literature. Beware: Some of the following titles, cities, and publishers have been made up to suggest how students may create their own porcine bibliographies.

Anno, Mitsumasa. *Socrates and the Three Little Pigs*. New York: Philomel, 1986.
   The great Japanese illustrator introduces statistics and probability to young readers using the familiar tale.

Krensky, Stephen. *Perfect Pigs: Introduction to Manners*. Illus. by Marc Brown. Boston: Little, Brown, 1983.
   A clever cast of pigs demonstrate good manners for children.

Lobel, Arnold. *The Book of Pigericks*. New York: Harper & Row, 1983.
   Thirty-eight delightful rhymes of porcine dimensions.

McPhail, David. *Pig Pig Goes to Camp*. New York: Macmillan, 1983.
   Pig Pig gets lost in the woods, cooks over a campfire, and learns to love frogs.

Nissenson, Marilyn, and Susan Jonas. *The Ubiquitous Pig*. New York: Harry N. Abrams, 1992.
   A glorious celebration of the everpresent pig in photographs and art.

Scieszka, Jon. *The True Story of the 3 Little Pigs by A. Wolf*. Illus. by Lane Smith. New York: Viking, 1989.
   This scurrilous account by A. Wolf is not taken lightly by members of the Pig family. They would like to see it banned.

Shakespeare, William. *Hamlet*. England: Boarshead Folios, 1603.
   Source of the famed "To eat or not to eat" soliloquy.

Shaw, G. B. *Pigmalion*. Loindon: Loindon Books, 1918.
   See also *My Fair Lardy*.

Van Leeuwen, Jean. *Amanda Pig on Her Own*. Illus. by Ann Schweninger. New York: Dial Books for Young Readers, 1991.

Amanda learns to cope when brother Oliver goes off to school.

White, E. B. *Charlotte's Web*. New York: Dell, 1952.

Wilbur and company in a classic.

Wiesner, David. *Tuesday*. New York: Clarion Books, 1991.

Primarily, this 1992 Caldecott Medal book is about flying frogs, but readers should definitely not miss the final two pages of whimsy.

Yolen, Jane. *Picnic with Piggins*. Illus. by Jane Dyer. New York: Harcourt Brace Jovanovich, 1988.

The Sherlock Holmes of Swinedom solves another case.

Parody

Parody is a farcical imitation of a person, event, piece of literature, or cultural icon or artifact. TalentEd students with rich imaginations can create highly original and very funny parodies.

Newspaper tabloids, virtually parodies themselves, come in for some funny scrutinizing and imitation parody from creative students. Students enjoy poking fun at the kind of incredible stories that appear in sensation-based tabloids like the *National Enquirer*. They write unbelievable stories of UFO sightings and celebrity exploits.

Students love to write advice columns of the Dear Abby type found in daily newspapers. As demonstrated in the following example, they greatly exaggerate the personalities and problems that are the typical fare of such newspaper features.

Dear Abby,

The other day when I was cleaning out our cat's bedroom, I discovered her diary under her catnip pillow. From reading the diary, I could deduce that she is smoking a package of cigarettes daily behind our backs. What should I do?

Puzzled in Cleveland

Dear Cleveland,

Put the cat's diary back immediately before she discovers that you are a snoop.

Abby

The horoscope column also attracts good-natured lampooning. Here are two brief samples of the type of horoscope parody students may create:

Aries (March 21-April 20)
You will accomplish next to nothing today. You will also have the opportunity to greatly embarrass yourself in public. You deserve to feel depressed.

Capricorn (December 22-January 20)
This is your unlucky day. Your eccentricity will attract lots of attention. Beware of people in white coats.

Students also enjoy panning music and movie fan magazines for teenage audiences. One student invented a form letter that might appear in the classifieds of such magazines. The form letter purports to save busy teens the trouble of composing their own love letters. All teenagers have to do is circle or underline their choices.

Dearest darling _____ (fill in the name),

You are everything to me. I will never love anyone else. You light up my days with your smiling (blue / black / green / hazel / pink) eyes. I will live forever in the magic of your (money / presence / new car / motorcycle). It is surely fate that we have come together. As I write this note, I feel like I can reach out and touch your (long / greasy / wavy), (blonde / green / brown / red) hair. Our love will surely (endure through eternity / last until the end of the week / be around tomorrow through sixth period).[3]

The author's students have written parodies of famous poems, too. Henry Wadsworth Longfellow's "Paul Revere's Ride," Clement Clark Moore's "A Visit from St. Nicholas," and Robert Frost's "The Road Not Taken" are among the many classic poems students love to parody. One TalentEd student described a humorous scene in which Longfellow's teenage daughter helped her father immortalize Paul Revere's ride when the poet developed writer's block.

Self-help books and guides also become targets for student fun. Students enjoy creating guides such as "So You Want to Play Tennis," by U. Cheetum, and "Twenty Ways to Get Out of Doing Your Homework," by I. M. Cool. Mail-order catalogs, such as those mailed by L. L. Bean and Eddie Bauer, likewise receive good-natured ribbing. Students create wildly ridiculous camping gear and wilderness clothes for city dwellers who either want country chic or who fear the unknown outdoors.

Environmentally conscious students may move from parody to satire and make powerful social statements. One of the author's seventh-grade students created a notebook collage called "America the Beautiful." Each page featured a line from Katharine Lee Bates's patriotic verse. The illustrations portrayed just the opposite of the mental pictures the words suggest. Scenes of polluted rivers, smog-choked cities, traffic jams, and despoiled mountainsides accompanied Miss Bates's lines about spacious skies, purple mountain majesties, and fruited plains.

Puns

Students who love language are bound to enjoy and use puns. TalentEd students love to be inventive with homonyms and to joyfully play with language in other novel ways to create puns. Learning the geography of a state? Why not invite some creative students to create a list of the cities of a state? Here are some examples of Colorado towns and cities.

To cheat a few _____ (Gypsum)

Milder, humbler _____ (Meeker)

Route followed by Bambi _____ (Deer Trail)

Cupid's earth _____ (Loveland)

Baseball fans will love this punny game. The player has to determine the mascot of the professional baseball teams. The teacher will hear groans as well as chuckles when these examples are provided.[4]

Army insects _____ (San Francisco G. I. Ants)

Dead relatives of Edgar Allen _____ (Montreal Ex-Poes)

Past tense of meet _____ (New York Mets)

Charles and Lady Di _____ (Kansas City Royals)

Sad relatives of Is and Ks _____ (Toronto Blue Js)

Pastry costs _____ (Pittsburgh Pie Rates)

Want to know the names of the elements in the periodic table? Here are some puns for the science classroom.[5]

Name a famous masked man's horse. (Silver)

What do you call a funny prisoner? (Silicon)

What do you call a policeman? (Copper)

What do you call an automobile-shaped roll? (Carbon)

Pooling their ideas, student groups can write silly stories or letters using puns that are related to a particular subject or topic, such as the opening paragraph of this story based on food puns.

Today I asked my sister, Margarine, to caraway me in her bleu carp to my friend's house. The moment I stepped into her carp I knew that I smelt something egg salad like a dead sole. I turned to pear into the back seat to see what smelt so bad. The smelt was unbearable! I hated to beef but human beans can go bananas if lox in a carp with such a smelt! I began to veal sick. I was really in a pickle. Ice creamed, "Lettuce stop!"

The following story has been a favorite of the author for many years and has served as a catalyst for many of his students to create their own humor about everyday life annoyances, such as those awful white tags on pillows that advise against removal. It is reprinted here with the kind permission of its author, P. R. Tedesco (Phyllis Reynolds Naylor).[6]

Under Penalty of Law

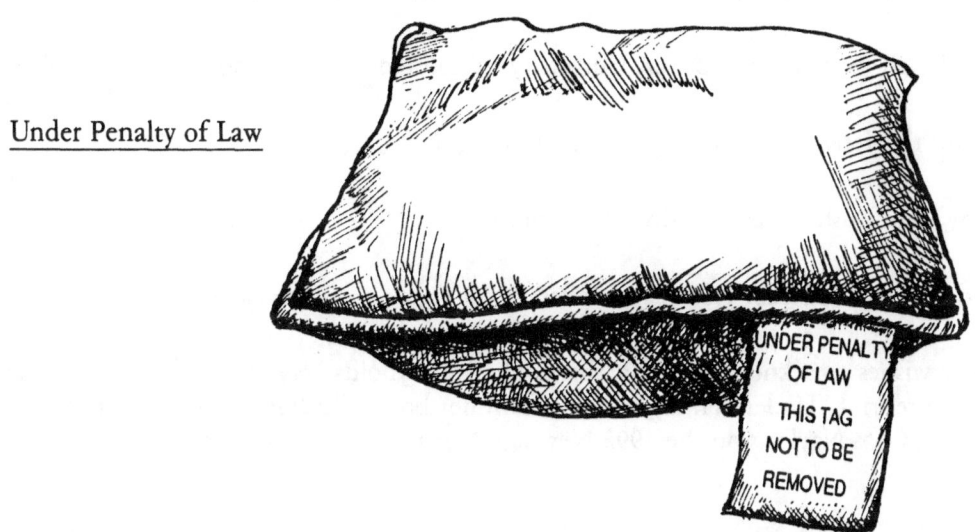

Every so often I rebel. Every so often I'm filled to the gills with "Don'ts" and "Do Nots" and am driven by a strange compulsion to go on a law-breaking spree. If a sign says, "Do not walk on the grass" I put my foot on it. If a sign says, "Employees only" I go in. If a sign says, "Do not fold" I fold. And if a sign says, "Use other door" I don't. I mean, the human spirit can only be fettered so long and then it must be allowed to romp or it'll go completely berserk.

So yesterday when I bought Mom a green satin pillow for her birthday, I didn't notice till I got home that a big white tag was sewed on one end with the words, "Do not remove under penalty of law."

Now this was perfectly ridiculous. How in the world was my mother going to put that green pillow on the coach with that hideous white tag sticking out like a kite? And suddenly my spirit began to rattle its chains and my lips began to smile, and slowly, carefully, in the privacy of my room, I cut off the tag. Then I lit a match, burned it in my wastebasket, and sat watching the dying embers with a great unfettered feeling of freedom.

This morning, after church, we all gave Mom her presents.

"I'll bet you spent a lot of time looking for this," Mother said, turning the pillow around in her hands.

"You bet I did," I smiled. "Tried every store in town."

"It's beautiful," said Mother, "but I am afraid it won't do—not in a turquoise living room. Could you take it back and exchange it for a white one?"

I stared at Mom. I stared at the green satin couch pillow. "I can't," I bleated, "I burned the tag."

"Not the 'do not remove' tag!" she gasped.

"Not the 'under penalty of law' tag!" screamed my sister Kate.

"The same," I moaned.

The upshot was that I had to use next week's allowance for another pillow for Mom, and the first green satin pillow with the tag removed resides on the top shelf of my closet. Every night when the moon is full, I take it down and stick it full of pins in some weird ritual that only an idiot like me can understand.

Notes

[1] Joel Goodman is president of the Humor Project, Inc., 110 Spring Street, Saratoga, NY 12866. This organization sponsors research related to humor, holds humor conferences, publishes a quarterly magazine, *Laughing Matters*, and produces a fine catalog of humor books and materials.

[2] Wendy S. Schall, unpublished paper, University of Colorado at Colorado Springs, October 23, 1991.

[3] The idea for this letter was first suggested by Judy Ripley.

[4] Created by Jeree Bushnell and used with permission.

[5] Suggested by Cynthia Miller-Horacek, *Science Scope* 15, no. 3 (January 1992): 43.

[6] The author wishes to acknowledge and thank Phyllis Reynolds Naylor, writing as P. R. Tedesco, for permission to reprint "Under Penalty of Law" from her book *The Private I* (Philadelphia, Pa.: Fortress Press, 1969), 64-65. Naylor won the 1992 Newbery Medal for her novel *Shiloh*.

Teacher Resources

Adams, James L. *Conceptual Blockbusting: A Guide to Better Ideas*. New York: W. W. Norton, 1979.
    A creative engineer describes means to limber up the mind.

Koberg, Don, and Jim Bagnall. *The All-New Universal Traveler*. Los Altos, Calif.: William Kaufmann, 1976.
    A book of self-help creativity tools.

Is for Questions

> Teaching the answers without first raising the questions takes most of the meaning out of learning.
>
> —Francis Slater, London School of Education

As teachers search for strategies to meet the cognitive needs of all students, let them learn from, be inspired by, and emulate great teachers. Let them be ever mindful that the greatest teachers ever known to the world—Jesus, Socrates, and Confucius—used simple but powerful teaching tools such as parables and questions, and simple but profound statements of ideals. Teachers do not necessarily need elaborate and expensive equipment or extensive classwork in instructional methodologies to be effective teachers.

Certainly one of the great teachers whom today's teachers might emulate is Socrates, who was skillful in the art of questioning. Questions can be the most powerful tool teachers of talented students have at their disposal. Through the power of her questions, a teacher can move students to continuously newer and higher levels of knowledge, discovery, and understanding. TalentEd teachers have at least three rules they like to follow when using questioning strategies with all students.

First, teachers should ask questions that require students to think. TalentEd teachers use Bloom's *Taxonomy of Educational Objectives. Handbook I: Cognitive Domain* in posing questions and planning curriculum experiences for students. They routinely move students from knowledge-based questions to thoughtful analysis, synthesis, and evaluation questions at the higher levels of this taxonomy of thinking skills.

The taxonomic hierarchy that has come to be known as Bloom's Taxonomy is the product result of a meeting of college examiners attending an American Psychological Association convention in Boston in 1948. These college examiners were concerned about developing a uniform set of standards and terminology that would allow for more effective communication of learning goals and objectives of professionals across virtually all academic fields. They sought a means of exchanging ideas and materials without succumbing to the use of nebulous terms that made clarity of meaning among professionals like themselves difficult to achieve. What, for example, did teachers and scholars mean when they said they wanted their students to "comprehend," to "really understand," or to "grasp the meaning of" core knowledge in their disciplines?

The college examiners, led by Benjamin Bloom of the University of Chicago as editor, elected to design a taxonomy that was in many ways analogous to the taxonomies of the biological world that allow biologists to classify all living matter into the categories of phyllum, class, order, family, genus, and species. It was determined that such taxonomies should be designed for the constructive use of helping educators build curricula with a variety of intended cognitive, affective, and psychomotor outcomes. *Cognitive* is understood to include mental activities such as remembering and recalling knowledge, thinking, problem solving, and creating. After many informal meetings, the hierarchical taxonomy of educational objectives for the cognitive domain was published as a handbook by Longman, Green in the early 1950s.[1] Subsequent handbooks for the affective domain and the psychomotor domain were also published.[2] Figure Q.1 lists the six hierarchical levels of Bloom's Taxonomy with representative action verbs.

Fig. Q.1. The six hierarchical levels of Bloom's Taxonomy.

Knowledge	**Comprehension**	**Application**
Define	Discuss	Illustrate
List	Explain	Demonstrate
Recall	Review	Translate
Name	Report	Sketch
Repeat	Locate	Dramatize
Memorize	Identify	Operate
Cite	Generalize	Complete
Recognize	Translate	Solve
Report	Summarize	Show
Label	Illustrate	Practice

Analysis	**Synthesis**	**Evaluation**
Analyze	Create	Judge
Experiment	Design	Compare
Contrast	Construct	Evaluate
Diagram	Compose	Rate
Inspect	Propose	Select
Solve	Plan	Assess
Differentiate	Redesign	Decide
Interpret	Hypothesize	Verify
Classify	Translate	Rate
Categorize	Imagine	Determine
Dissect	Fashion	Appraise

■ ■ ■

These action verbs prove extremely handy and useful to teachers who want to stretch and develop the thinking skills and behaviors of their students. The action verbs may be used in the stems of questions teachers ask as well as in the prompts teachers give to students to provoke higher levels of thinking in the products and projects they create. Good teachers skillfully utilize questions the answers to which will require ever more powerful levels of cognition. Wise teachers realize they save time when they use questions from across the spectrum of Bloom's Taxonomy. Analytical, synthetic, and evaluative questions require more answering time and provoke more discussions; thus, teachers can reduce the number of questions they need to create for any given lesson or unit.

Rather than asking a question such as "Where did the story take place?" a skilled TalentEd teacher redirects the question to read, "How did you know where the story took place?" or "Why do you think the author chose to set her story in the woods, or on a cloudy day?" An intellectually gifted student can often answer the first question correctly merely by studying the book illustrations, rather than actually reading the text! The second question requires not only a reading of the story, but comprehension and analysis as well.

Rather than asking social studies students to date when Lincoln gave the Gettysburg Address, the wise teacher may ask students to discuss the significance of Lincoln's address to the history of democracy in the United States. In other subject areas, teachers might ask students questions like these: "What new things did you learn from reading the chapter that you did not know before?" "What questions do you have now that you did not have before?" "How does the new information you have learned fit with the knowledge, information, and values you already have?"

While on the subject of thinking and Bloom's Taxonomy, teachers should also take pains to avoid the trap of confusing teaching students about thinking with teaching students to think. When the author was writing his dissertation in Indiana, he met a highly gifted junior high school student who was embarrassed by the activities he and the other students in his so-called gifted program were forced to do. He cited as one example the fact that he and the other students were made to memorize and sing a jingle that had the purported effect of helping them memorize the six levels of Bloom's Taxonomy. Hoping for some ray of sunshine in this dreadful account, the investigator continued, "Well, what did you do with Bloom's Taxonomy once you had it memorized?" "Nothing, absolutely nothing," was his response.

An extreme example, one hopes. But it should serve as a reminder to teachers not to become so caught up in teaching Bloom's Taxonomy, creative problem-solving models, critical-thinking paradigms, futures wheels, and the like that they forget that such pedagogical tools are means to ends and desired outcomes and not ends in themselves. Good teachers are ever mindful that their goal is to develop thinking students.

The second rule TalentEd teachers follow when questioning their students is to allow students adequate **time** to respond to all good questions they ask. Mary Budd Rowe's research relative to this point should be familiar to every educator. She found that the average wait time that guides teacher behavior is one second or less. That is, teachers allow one second or less to pass after they have posed a question before they rephrase the question, provide an answer, go to another student for a response, or take some other similar action. When teachers increase the average length of wait time to as few as three seconds, dramatic shifts in student behavior and achievement occur, including

- The length of student responses improves between 300 and 700 percent.
- The incidence of speculative reasoning increases.
- Students' responses reflect more inferential thinking, and more inferences are supported by evidence.

- The number of student questions and student-proposed experiments increases.
- Students' failure to respond decreases.
- Disciplinary moves decrease.
- Student self-confidence improves.
- Student-to-student exchanges increase.[3]

In some American classrooms teachers appear to abhor silence. Perhaps they fear that those fiendish-minded bright children are plotting a takeover of the class! Yet all good teachers know from experience that silence is critical to reflective thinking.

The third questioning rule good teachers observe is to invite and encourage bright and inquisitive students to **ask questions often**. Moreover, they do not feel intimidated if they do not have a ready answer for every question that is brought into the classroom. Perhaps the best thing teachers can do when they encounter a question for which they do not have an immediate answer is to say to students "I do not know, but that's a good question. Let's find an answer."

Encourage all students to ask questions.

Teach children how to ask questions that help them focus on what they want to learn, what they need to know, and how they can access information. One fine TalentEd teacher challenges her students to develop an effective question-asking attitude by telling them at the beginning of each school year, "I will always answer your questions truthfully, but I will not tell you what you do not ask." Once students realize the import of her statement they quickly learn to hone and sharpen their own questioning strategies.

Some other good classroom management tools when using questions include the following. To prevent highly verbal and competitive students from dominating class discussions and question-and-answer sessions, direct questions to specific students. Instruct the named students to quietly think about the response they want to give for a minute or two. Direct all the other students to write down on paper their response to the same question. This procedure results in at least three separate and positive consequences: it encourages greater reflection and yields more thoughtful responses, it discourages domination of class discussions by one or two students, and it prevents one student's response from contaminating the thinking of all the other students.

Teacher who want to develop the creativity of their students also infuse some creative questioning strategies into their teaching practices. Creative questions include what if? questions such as these:

- What if all roads were underground?
- What if the weather never changed?
- What if once a light bulb were turned on it never would burn out?
- What would happen if there were no trees in the world?
- What would happen if spiders were the strongest creatures in the world?
- What would happen if grass were available in decorator colors?
- What would happen if birds could talk to humans?
- Suppose you could spend $10 million to help save an endangered species. What would you do?

Creative questions can be used for roll taking, too. A creative teacher may take roll by asking students questions like these:

Would you rather be

- a school bus or a bright, red sports car?
- the Pacific Ocean or the Mississippi River?
- a bird or a flower?
- an eagle or a diamond?

With whom would you rather dine,

- Albert Einstein or Emily Dickinson?
- Abraham Lincoln or Leonardo da Vinci?

- How is a leaf like a song?
- Which is deeper, a tree's roots or loneliness?
- Which is faster, gossip or a bird?

Teachers do not always have to be the sole questioners in TalentEd classrooms, either. Once teachers have used several creative questions with their students, the students will soon know how to make up their own creative questions to ask their peers. Assign different students the task of being, for a week, the Provocative Question Procurement Officer. This student is responsible for creating provocative what if? questions for the week. The Provocative Question Procurement Officer may even ask some "Reversiquestions." Reversiquestions are simple answers or statements that may be acceptable replies to many different questions. For example, if the Reversiquestion answer is "In the middle," a variety of questions may be imagined, including "Where is the filling in a sandwich?" "Where is the white in an Oreo cookie?" "Where is your belly button?" and "Where is the hole in a donut?"

Questions that are effectively phrased and used can stimulate the imaginations of students and fuel their curiosity. Questions cost nothing but yield wonderful and powerful returns in the development of talent and creative and critical-thinking skills. A popular bumper sticker reads "Minds are like parachutes. They only function when open." A TalentEd teacher opens minds with the skillful and frequent use of good questioning strategies.

Notes

[1] Benjamin S. Bloom, ed., *Taxonomy of Educational Objectives. Handbook I: Cognitive Domain* (New York: Longman, 1977). Throughout this book, Bloom's Taxonomy is the label used to describe the hierarchy of ways of knowing that is outlined here.

[2] David R. Krathwohl, ed., *Taxonomy for Educational Objectives: The Classification of Educational Goals: Handbook 2: Affective Domain* (New York: Longman, 1964). Anita J. Harrow, ed., *A Taxonomy for the Psychomotor Domain: A Guide for Developing Behavioral Objectives* (New York: Longman, 1972).

[3] Mary Budd Rowe, "Wait Time—Slowing Down May Be a Way of Speeding Up," *The Journal of Teacher Education* 37, no. 1 (January-February 1986): 43-44.

# Is for Recipe

Talented young writers should have the opportunity to experiment with many types of writing formats such as essays, short stories, newspaper stories, and verse. When students write often and experiment with many formats from among a wide array of possibilities, they find both their own writing voices and build competence in their writing skills. One of the writing formats that the author has used successfully with his students is the recipe. Using the recipe format, students can produce creative and powerful writing.

A great beginning resource to use with students of all ages is *Smashed Potatoes: A Kid's-Eye View of the Kitchen*, edited by Jane Martel. Martel shares the words and pictures of small children as they tell how to make their favorite foods like skabbetti, black steak, chops, banilla cake, and basketti with macaronis. TalentEd writers will find the recipes of small children funny and refreshing and they will quickly join in the creative mood of wanting to invent their own imaginative recipes. Teachers will find that it is an easy and smooth transition to move from talking about literal recipes for popular foods to experimenting with the recipe format to create inventive recipes for nonfood items such as world peace, happy homes, perfect parents, blind dates, best friends, and hundreds of other things.

Encourage TalentEd students to experiment with writing original recipes. Suggested topics include unbeatable football teams, grade-A teachers, democracy, popularity, love, school spirit, friendship, courage, great coaches, and summer vacations.

Recipes that extol the virtues of loving parents, grandparents, and good friends make especially touching and warmly received gifts. Students may create recipes for perfect mothers to give on Mother's Day. Tributes in the form of recipes can be shared with grandparents on Christmas or Hanukkah. Recipes for best friends make perfect birthday gifts.

TalentEd teachers who are searching for tasty new fare to spice up the creative writing their students do should definitely add recipe writing to the menu of composition options they offer students.

Bon appétit!

R Is for Recipe

Half-Baked School Lunch

25 teachers	400 report cards	25 chalk erasers
25 red pencils	400 achievement tests	10 tardy bells
400 cartons sour milk	5 clocks (not working)	150 wads dried bubble gum

Bring sour milk to a boil. Add chalk erasers and broken clocks and let mixture stand until cool. Grate teachers slowly and cautiously and let simmer in their own juices. In a separate bowl, shred achievement tests and report cards and fold shredded mixture into stewing teachers. Combine all of these ingredients into one large baking dish and place in hot oven for 180 days. Set tardy bells to ring after 90 days. Meanwhile, collect bubble gum wads and shave red pencils. When the tardy bells ring, remove half-baked stew and garnish with spit wads, dried bubble gum, and red pencil shavings. Serve to tired, hungry principal.

Teacher Resource

Martel, Jane, ed. *Smashed Potatoes: A Kid's-Eye View of the Kitchen*. Boston: Houghton Mifflin, 1974.

# Is for Service

>Service is the rent you pay back to God for the time and space you spend on Earth.
>
>—Betty Siegel

True success is not measured by how much money people accumulate, the monetary value of their homes and automobiles, nor the status of the jobs they hold. Real success if determined by the way people use their talent, time, and treasures in service and stewardship to humanity, nature, and the very planet Earth itself.

>There is no higher religion than human service. To work for the common good is the greatest creed.
>
>—Albert Schweitzer

Service and stewardship offer youth pathways to more meaningful lives. Moreover, according to school researchers Dan Conrad and Diane Hedin, students who engage in service develop "a heightened sense of personal and social responsibility, more positive attitudes toward adults and others, more active exploration of careers, enhanced self-esteem, growth in moral and ego developments, more complex patterns of thought, and greater mastery of skills and content."[1] Service and stewardship empower both the giver and the receiver. The server often helps the recipients to be better able to solve their problems. In doing service, servers also develop a greater appreciation for their own gifts and the good that they can do.

The gift is meant to be shared.

Awareness

> One goal of education should be the process of helping everyone to discover his uniqueness, to teach him how to develop that uniqueness, and then to show him how to give it away, because that's the only reason for having anything.
>
> —Leo Buscaglia

One of the first ways TalentEd teachers can develop good attitudes toward service and stewardship in gifted, talented, and creative students is to build student awareness of the value of stewardship and the many ways that one may engage in service. Teachers can build awareness by taking classroom time to share stories of service with young people. The library media specialist can be of great assistance to teachers in locating print biographies as well as films of people who are models of lives lived in service to others, such as Clara Barton, Albert Schweitzer, Tom Dooley, Mother Theresa, Dag Hammarskjöld, Jane Addams, and Coretta Scott King. Just as many fine TalentEd teachers use oral reading and creative and critical-thinking activities during the first and last five minutes of class, they may also use similar time periods to share brief stories of people who have used their lives for the greater good of humanity and the planet.

Some awareness activities take no class time. Teachers can write quotations about service and stewardship, such as those that appear in this chapter, on the chalkboard or in the margins of activity and assignment sheets they prepare for student distribution. Similarly, bulletin boards that display newspaper and magazine articles about people cleaning up the environment, helping the homeless, or coaching Special Olympics athletes can be powerful yet silent reminders of the value of using one's time and talent for the good of others.

When teachers and library media specialists recommend good books to students, they can make conscious attempts to include titles of biographies and other works about service and stewardship. *Kid Heroes: True Stories of Rescuers, Survivors, and Achievers* by Neal Shusterman is one recent book filled with stories about young people who have selflessly used their gifts to aid others. Books such as John Javna's *50 Simple Things Kids Can Do to Save the Earth*, Billy Goodman's *A Kid's Guide to How to Save the Planet*, and Barbara A. Lewis's *The Kid's Guide to Social Action* provide students with ideas for service projects as well as models of people fruitfully engaged in stewardship.

Young people may erroneously believe that they are not able to make significant contributions until they are older. Nothing could be further from the truth. TalentEd teachers and library media specialists can share many stories of youthful service with younger students.

A Swedish youth, Roland Tiensuu, age twelve, is one of seven inhabitants of our Earth who received the Goldman Prize, the ecological equivalent of the Nobel Prize, on Earth Day 1991. Roland's accomplishment was a creative service project in which Swedish children purchased more than 17,000 acres of Costa Rica's rainforests. Roland's action has served to inspire youths in Japan, Germany, and the United States to take similar action. A part of the rainforest, now known as Children's Eternal Forest, has been saved.[2]

More than a decade ago, a young Canadian, Terry Fox, galvanized an entire nation into action with his Marathon of Hope. Having lost his right leg to cancer at the age of eighteen, Terry Fox began running across the more than 5,000-mile expanse of Canada on his left leg and an artificial limb. While Terry Fox tragically never lived to complete the cross-continental journey himself, he did live to see his service project earn more than $20 million in contributions. In the past ten years, well over $50 million for cancer research has been raised in Terry Fox's memory in Canada alone. Terry Fox marathons are run annually around the world and continue to raise millions annually for cancer research.[3] Moreover, Terry Fox inspired another young man, Rick Hansen, a paraplegic, to begin his personal service project, the Man in Motion Tour, in 1985. His goal *and* accomplishment was to hand roll his wheelchair 25,000 miles around the globe in order to earn millions of dollars for spinal cord research and rehabilitation.[4]

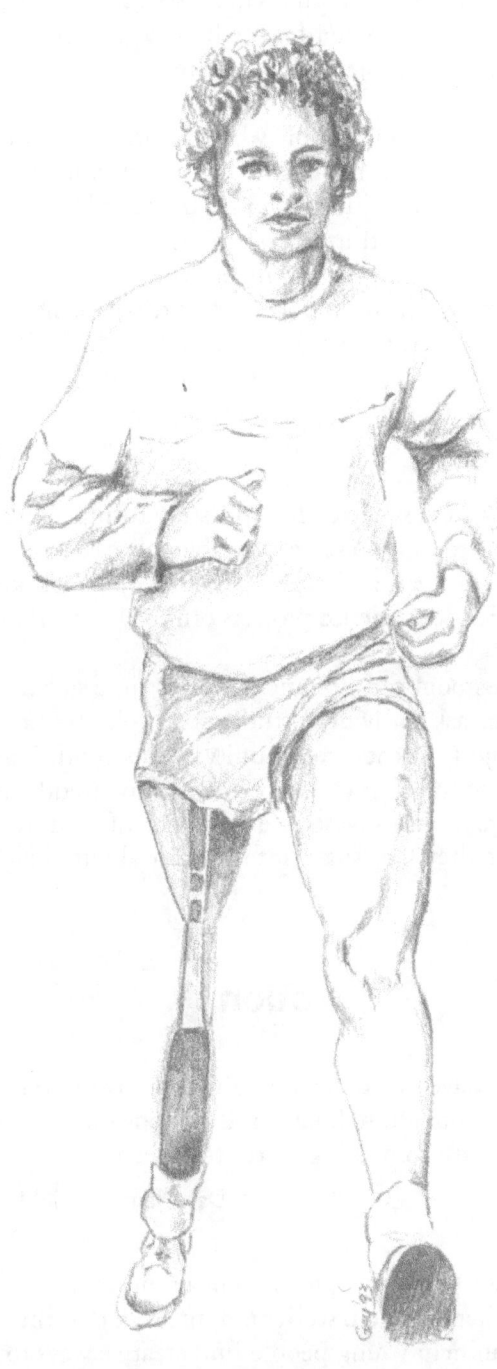

Terry Fox

Michelle Alexander was only nine years old when she invented the "Give Peace a Chance" board game that furthers her dream of growing up in a peaceful world. She has played her game with world leaders, and her game has been translated into several foreign languages, including Russian.[5]

A few years ago, Trevor Ferrell, then a sixth-grade youth in Philadelphia, saw a local early evening news program about the homeless in his city. He was so disturbed by the plight of people much less fortunate than he that he took the pillow and blanket from his own bed that same night and gave it to a homeless person in inner-city Philadelphia. The next night he gathered more blankets and pillows in his neighborhood and distributed them to Philadelphia's homeless. Before the school year was over, an army of volunteers joined his efforts and a new shelter for the homeless, appropriately called "Trevor's Place," was opened. Replications of Trevor's project were created by both children and adults in other communities.

History is filled with examples of young people who have made significant difference through their service. Louis Braille was only fifteen when he invented a system to help the blind read. Sacajawea was only sixteen when she served as a guide and interpreter for Lewis and Clark's exploration of the Louisiana Purchase. John Quincy Adams was only thirteen when he served as secretary to the United States' ambassador to Russia, and Joan of Arc was just seventeen when she commanded the armies of France.[6]

These examples of service accentuate an important point. One is never too young to serve. Youths need not wait until they reach adulthood to begin making a difference. One of the author's best friends grew up in a home in which the family creed was "Only you can make the difference that only you can make."[7] Age was never considered a condition for conscious service or caring or positive action. Each person's stewardship was valued, no matter how great or small. It is a creed most worthy of sharing with young people.

Teachers can also increase awareness of service and stewardship by encouraging their students to research service organizations and people who serve, as viable means of earning class and extra credit. For current events projects, students can read and report about people who are helping the homeless and senior citizens have better lives. Student science projects can focus upon individuals who are helping to save the planet.

Just as each student in a classroom can become an expert in a given area or skilled as outlined in chapter X, TalentEd teachers can ask individual students to volunteer to research and report on the specific volunteer and service projects in their community and beyond. Perhaps David can become the classroom expert on the activities of the Sierra Club, or Anne can attend a meeting of the local Kiwanis or Lions club. Still another classmate may investigate the kinds of volunteer services available to senior citizens in the community. Later they can share information about their service activities with their classmates.

Action

> You have not done enough, you have never
> done enough, so long as it is still possible that
> you have something to contribute.
>
> —Dag Hammarskjöld

There are many creative ways young people can engage in meaningful service and stewardship. Through awareness activities, teachers can help students appreciate that their gifts are best realized when they are shared. Next, teachers can help young people find creative ways to use their God-given talents in helping others.

Students can brainstorm ways that they can serve. The following are but a few beginning prompts.

Create learning games, puzzles, and problems that will help make learning more enjoyable and profitable for younger or less able learners.

Use free time in class to help other students come to better understand difficult materials, skills, and processes.

Older students can adopt younger students for unique projects. Sixth-grade students, for example, may adopt first-grade students. The older students interview the younger students to determine their likes, interests, and personal backgrounds. Then each sixth-grade biographer writes a short biography of a first-grader that is illustrated, laminated and bound, and given to the younger child as a gift to be treasured.

During lunchtime, recess, and on other special occasions, older students can also play educational games with younger students, using games found in books such as *Helping Kids Care* by Camy Condon and James McGinnis. The games in this book teach young people how to resolve conflicts peacefully and respect diversity.

Brainstorm twenty-six things that students can do to help others. Use this information to make an ABC poster for the classroom bulletin board that may serve as a daily reminder of ways people can serve each other.

An important caution. It should be noted that examples such as these should encourage the generous sharing of talent, rather than exploitation. Unfortunately, one of the results of the sometimes hasty implementation of cooperative-learning strategies in middle schools across the nation is that gifted students have often been exploited. Gifted and talented students are placed in small groupings with students of average and below-average scholastic abilities and are subsequently made to be responsible for both the grade the group receives and the lion's share of the work. These outcomes were never the intention of the proponents of cooperative learning and typically result through the lack of careful monitoring by classroom teachers. The sad result of such misuses of cooperative learning is that the brighter students feel abused and exploited. Rather than seeing the value of service, which is one of the values of well-orchestrated cooperative learning, these students are turned off to service, wanting nothing more to do with it.

While students are naturally interested in such global service projects as saving the Earth, they also need to recognize that often the most effective and important service begins at home and in the classroom. Students can brainstorm twenty or more ways that they can serve to help their mothers and fathers, siblings, grandparents, neighbors, teachers, principals, library media specialists, and classmates. For example, what are five things youths can do to help their parents with lawn care this summer? What are ten things they can do in the classroom to help each other and the teacher?

Help students recognize that often simple and unheralded actions can do at least as much good as public demonstrations and campaigns. What simple activities and steps can they take to improve the environment and the lives of others? Can they eliminate the use of at least one aerosol product from their lives? Can they adopt a block and routinely pick up trash on that block on their way to and from school every day? Can they spend time on a weekend cleaning their closets and donating clothes they have outgrown to an agency that will distribute them to more needy persons? How about toys? Do they have clean and well-cared-for stuffed animals they can give up so that children less fortunate than they may have nice toys? Can they take the simple daily step of closing window blinds in their classrooms and homes in the summer to keep out the sun's heat and opening the same in the winter to let in the sun's warmth? Such a simple act helps preserve the Earth's resources. What other simple steps to service can students take? Wise teachers can devote a classroom bulletin board to such suggestions and encourage students to continuously add new ideas to the list.

Additional skills are enhanced when students research local, state, national, and international service groups. Letter-writing skills, for example, are utilized when students write to service organizations to learn more about their activities and ways that they can serve the named agency or group. Communication skills are addressed when students organize the information they receive from these agencies into lucid and interesting reports to their classmates. Organizations of interest to students include the following:

194 S *Is for Service*

The Nature Conservancy
1815 North Lynn Street
Arlington, VA 22209

Greenpeace, USA
1436 U Street NW
Washington, DC 20009

National Wildlife Federation
1400 16th Street
Washington, DC 20036

Sierra Club
730 Polk Street
San Francisco, CA 94109

National Audubon Society
950 Third Avenue
New York, NY 10022

Save the Whales
P.O. Box 3650
Washington, DC 20007

World Wildlife Fund
1250 24th Street, NW
Washington, DC 20037

Wildlife Preservation Trust
34th Street and Girard Avenue
Philadelphia, PA 19104

Kids for Saving Earth
P.O. Box 47247
Plymouth, MN 55447-0247

Students Against Driving Drunk
P.O. Box 800
Marlboro, MA 01752

Habitat for Humanity
121 Habitat Street
Americus, GA 31709

CARE (Relief)
660 First Avenue
New York, NY 10016

School and public library media specialists can be especially helpful in assisting students in finding addresses and phone numbers for service agencies in their communities and across the nation.

Service enhances life and makes living more enjoyable and fruitful. TalentEd teachers find countless opportunities to increase student awareness of stewardship and to help their students find means of service action. They help young people find creative ways to serve and truly make a difference.

> Man at his best, like water,
> serves as he goes along.
> —Lao Tzu, *The Way of Life*

Notes

[1] Dan Conrad and Diane Hedin, "School-Based Community Service: What We Know from Research and Theory," *Phi Delta Kappan* 17, no. 10 (June 1991): 749.

[2] "Saviors of the Planet," *Time*, 29 April 1991, 66.

[3] For more information on Terry Fox's service, see Leslie Scrivener, *Terry Fox: His Own Story* (Toronto: McClelland and Stewart, 1981), and the video *The Terry Fox Story* (HBO Premier Films, 1983).

[4] For a personal account of Rick Hansen's around-the-world trek, see Rick Hansen and Jim Taylor, *Rick Hansen: Man in Motion* (New York: Puffin Books, 1987).

⁵The story of Michelle Alexander and other youthful heroes such as Ryan White are told in Neal Shusterman, *Kid Heroes: True Stories of Rescuers, Survivors, and Achievers* (New York: Tom Doherty Books, 1991).

⁶The stories of youthful achievers such as Sacajawea and Louis Braille may be found in Dennis B. Fradin, *Remarkable Children: Twenty Who Made History* (Boston: Little, Brown, 1987).

⁷The Rev. Herbert Swaby, father of Dr. Barbara Swaby, personal communication.

Teacher Resources

Condon, Camy, and James McGinnis. *Helping Kids Care: Harmony Building Activities for Home, Church, and School*. Bloomington, Ind.: Meyer-Stone Books, 1988.

Dozens of ideas, many incorporating the use of puppets, that help children learn about people who are different, whether by age, disability, race, or nationality.

Goodman, Billy. *A Kid's Guide to How to Save the Planet*. New York: Avon Books, 1990.

The author provides concrete tips on how students can take personal action to improve the environment and protect endangered species.

Javna, John. *50 Simple Things Kids Can Do to Save the Earth*. New York: Andrews and McMeel, 1990.

Strategies all people can employ in their daily lives.

Lewis, Barbara A. *The Kid's Guide to Social Action: How to Solve the Social Problems You Choose and Turn Creative Thinking into Positive Action*. Minneapolis, Minn.: Free Spirit, 1991.

This fine resource provides teachers and their students with strategies and tools for problem solving and a wealth of addresses for networking with individuals and groups that care about making today's world a safe and better place.

Shusterman, Neal. *Kid Heroes: True Stories of Rescuers, Survivors, and Achievers*. New York: Tom Doherty Books, 1991.

Stories of youth such as AIDS victim Ryan White, and Michelle Alexander, who invented the game "Give Peace a Chance."

# T Is for (No) Television

Radio comedian Fred Allen said, "Television is a device that permits people who haven't anything to do to watch people who can't do anything."[1] And architect Frank Lloyd Wright called television "Chewing gum for the eyes."[2] However it is defined or described, there is strong evidence that television plays something less than a beneficial role in the development of creativity and talent in today's youth. As such, it is a subject of serious concern for parents and educators who wish to foster the development of the gifts, talents, and creativity the nation's youth possess.

Big World, Small Screen: The Role of Television in American Society, edited by Aletha C. Huston and others, reports the findings of a recent American Psychological Association study that confirms decades of earlier research findings in terms of the vast amounts of time students expend watching television, the effect of television advertising on children, and the types and degrees of violence and stereotyping they witness. For example:

- American children spend more time watching television than they do in school.[3]

- The most conservative estimate is that the average U.S. child watches about three hours of television every day.[4]

- In the typical American household, the television set is on seven hours a day.[5]

- Children are exposed to at least an hour of television commercials for every five hours of commercial programming they view.[6]

- Children who are heavy viewers of television show high concern about getting sick and have heightened perceptions of the relief they can get from medicines.[7]

- Both experimental and longitudinal studies support the hypothesis that viewing violence is causally associated with aggression.[8]

- By the time the average child graduates from elementary school, she or he will have witnessed 8,000 murders and more than 100,000 other associated acts of violence. Depending on the amount of television viewed, youngsters could see more than 200,000 violent acts before they hit the schools and streets of the nation as teenagers.[9]

- Children, elderly people, minorities, women, and gays and lesbians are often underrepresented or portrayed in narrow, stereotyped roles on television. Underrepresentation and negative portrayals may influence the self-concepts and images of their own group for members of affected categories, and may also generate attitudes and beliefs about such groups among members of the general public.[10]

It is not just the amount of television viewing or the viewing fare that should be of concern to educators. Most television programming by its very nature is antithetical to the educational aims of TalentEd teachers.

Television viewing is the opposite of reading. It requires a passive rather than active response. Television provides action rather than character development. Television does not encourage young viewers to use their imaginations. The screen provides all the images. In a book, the author's words invite young readers to imagine what characters and settings look like. With television, all viewers see are the sets and actors chosen by one producer.[11]

Television too frequently promotes stereotypes, often the very stereotypes educators are trying to counteract in the classroom. Moreover, popular role models of youth portrayed in television comedies and dramas frequently disparage academic excellence and intellectual pursuits. The student who takes education seriously is often portrayed as being a "nerd" or, at the very least, as lacking in popularity.

Television does not engage children. They can neither ask questions nor participate in conversation with the television medium. Language development is hardly fostered in such a climate. Conversation, games, and books invite children to ponder ideas, strategies, situations, and consider alternatives. Television does not require such active thinking. Television tosses images and messages at children rapidly, and allows no time or opportunity for questions or feedback.

Television tends to promote deceptive and simplistic thinking. Have a headache? No problem. Simply go to the medicine chest, take a couple of tablets, and presto, the headache is gone. Or more perniciously, adults are shown to consume several alcoholic beverages within a thirty- or sixty-minute drama with little or no impairment to their speech, mobility, or behavior toward others.

Taming the Beast

How can parents and teachers work together to counter the intrusive and pervasive medium of television? First, encourage students to determine their personal level of television viewing. Ask students to keep a viewing log for a minimum of one week. At the end of the week, students should be able to assess the amount and kinds of television viewing in which they engage. Challenge young people to personally beat the national average for youth: 22.4 hours a week of television viewing compared with 5.1 hours of reading outside school.[12] Can they reverse this appalling statistic and read 22.4 hours a week and watch 5.1 or fewer hours of television weekly?

As a second step, help students consider alternatives to television viewing. Ask students to brainstorm all the things they can do when not watching television. The lists students generate may include these possibilities: building models, creating scrapbooks, writing letters, taking walks, visiting museums and libraries, playing games, putting puzzles together, visiting neighbors, planning family vacations, and, of course, reading.

Help young people see the opportunities that are missed when they spend vast amounts of time, zombielike, in front of a television set. Hispanic author Abelardo Delgado attributes his career as an author to not having a television set as a child. "I owe my having become a writer to having grown up without a television set. The biggest factor was my great-grandmother Andrea. She was near a hundred years old and was bedridden. She was blind but she could spin a yarn, or *cuento* as we call them in Spanish. Her stories kept me close to her bed. I got to the point where she would start a *cuento* and my imagination would take off and finish it."[13]

T Is for (No) Television

Many TalentEd schools and teachers across the nation have had success with television black-out weeks or similar designs to stave off the pervasive influence of television. One elementary school in Colorado sponsors family campouts in the school on given Friday evenings. Parents and their children bring games and good books, as well as their sleeping bags, to school on Friday evenings. A giant read-in is staged. Classrooms are set aside for playing board games, storytelling, group reading, and parent-child reading activities. The main goal is to move students away from perceiving television as the main means of entertaining oneself.

Of course, not all television viewing is bad. Selective television viewing can be highly entertaining as well as educational. Public television specials bring the natural world into America's living room, allowing students to enter worlds and see places they could never visit otherwise. The coverage of special events such as the Olympics and dramatic political happenings such as the fall of the former Soviet Union allow students to be eyewitnesses to history.

The following activities involve limited television viewing, but change the viewer's perspective. Active involvement and the use of the imagination are necessary and prized.

 Ask students to defend their favorite television program. Suggest the notion that a new law severely restricts the amount of television people may watch. Each person is only allowed sixty minutes of viewing per week. What program(s) will they choose to watch? Why do they want to watch this particular program? What benefits may be accrued from watching the named program(s)? This activity is good for teaching students to marshall critical thinking to justify their choices.

TalentEd Examine the image current television programming presents of the United States of America and its citizens to the rest of the world. Look carefully at a single evening of television programming. What shows are broadcast during prime time? Do most American families truly resemble the ones portrayed in the programs seen during this time period? How are American families, churches, schools, teenagers, parents, workers, police officers, physicians, and teachers portrayed on American television? Are lawyers and physicians overrepresented among the careers portrayed? Do the teachers and parents found in television prime-time programming resemble the real parents and teachers students know? How many minority groups are portrayed in prime-time programming? Are people in wheelchairs featured in major television programs? How many blind and hearing-impaired persons are represented? How many individuals over the age of sixty-five are shown to be living happy and productive lives? Once again, the critical thinking students need to employ to complete this activity represents a fair exchange for the amount of viewing time required.

TalentEd Television is said to promote negative stereotypes of women, minorities, and the elderly. At the same time, critics of television programming argue that these same groups are underrepresented. Ask students to critically evaluate these charges. Ask students to become television watchdogs for a selected population group such as women, the elderly, the physically impaired, or a racial or ethnic group. Over a one- or two-week period, students should pay special attention to the manner and frequency with which the selected group is portrayed on television. How much and in what ways is the group the focus of news, sports coverage, advertising, and entertainment programming? From their focused viewing of television, students should be able to build a profile of how a selected group of citizens are portrayed in the television medium.

TalentEd Following up on their critical evaluations of television programming, encourage students to write letters of concern or support to commercial television networks, public television stations, and even advertisers. The addresses of television agencies can be found in weekly television guides or can be supplied by the school library media specialist.

TalentEd Ask students to model the creative advertising techniques they see in television advertising to create a one-minute razzle-dazzle commercial to extol the virtues of their favorite school subject or book. The same techniques may be employed to create a highly imaginative "commercial" to celebrate the birthdays of parents, grandparents, and siblings, or other family events.

TalentEd Encourage students, individually or collectively, to write a script or scenario for a special episode of their favorite television entertainment program. Many years ago a junior high school English class in California wrote a Christmas story episode for the television comedy "Room 222," a situation comedy about a high school teacher and her students. The producers of the series used the student-created episode. Another creative response to viewing favorite television programs might be the creation of board games based on popular situation comedies. Students can design playing boards, create game rules, maneuvers, and payoffs for playing their games. What kind of board game, for example, might students create to complement "The Wonder Years"?

TalentEd Highly imaginative youth can create parodies and satirical treatments of television viewing and television fare. The movies *Splash* and *Being There* both lampooned television's impact on society. Ask a creative student to create a television "everyperson" who is a compilation of all the clichés found in television programming. Send this "everyperson" character out into the real world. How does he or she fare? What happens to the character? Can he or she find a solution to every problem in a thirty-minute time frame? Can every physical ill be cured with a quick trip to the bathroom medicine cabinet? What other kinds of satire or parody might be created?

TalentEd Encourage students to utilize a television comedy or drama as an occasion for engaging their families in some creative problem solving. The family should choose one program to watch together on a given evening. The family watches the program halfway through to its conclusion. They tape the remainder of the program for later viewing. In the meantime, they turn the sound off or move to another room in the house and engage in a family creative problem-solving session. First, each family member predicts how the program's characters will solve their problems or dilemmas. Then, the family pretends to be advisers. How could the characters best solve the problems they face? The family concludes the activity by watching the last half of the taped program to determine the similarities and differences in problem-solving skills of the program's characters and their family.

TalentEd Ask students to take a radio break from television. Most public libraries have fairly extensive audiotape collections that often contain classic examples of old-time radio broadcasts such as "The New Adventures of Sherlock Holmes," "Burns and Allen," and the "Jack Benny Show." Alternatively, teachers can tape and replay contemporary National Public Radio programs. Instead of watching entertainment, ask students to *listen* to entertainment. Today's students are so visually oriented that they may have trouble concentrating on the single auditory stimulus. It may be useful to provide each student with drawing paper and request that they draw pictures of what they hear as they are listening.

TalentEd Engage students in news analysis. Assign students to evaluate the coverage of a single news event as covered by cable networks, commercial networks, public television, and in non-television media such as radio and newspapers. How does television coverage of news events vary from coverage of similar stories in other media? How do public television, cable television channels, and the major commercial network news programs and formats differ?

Parents and educators who desire even more information and ideas about the effect of television on young people and how to turn the medium into a powerful teaching tool will want to consult *Visual Messages: Integrating Imagery into Instruction* by David M. Considine and Gail E. Haley. In this outstanding book, authors Considine and Haley provide a finely detailed and well-researched chapter on using television effectively.

Time is a precious commodity. It should not be squandered. In every TalentEd classroom in America, students should be challenged to make the most of every moment of their lives. TalentEd teachers show young people ways to develop and use their special gifts, creativity, and talent for the good of themselves and others. Exciting, challenging, fun, and self-enhancing activities and pursuits are encouraged, and impediments to the realization of such talent—such as excessive television viewing—are discouraged.

Notes

[1] Fred Allen quoted in Jon Winokur, *The Portable Curmudgeon* (New York: New American Library, 1987), 269.

[2] Frank Lloyd Wright quoted in Winokur, 267.

[3] Aletha C. Huston et al., eds., *Big World, Small Screen: The Role of Television in American Society* (Lincoln, Nebr.: University of Nebraska Press, 1992), 1.

[4] Ibid., 11.

[5] Ibid., 52.

[6] Ibid., 80.

[7] Ibid., 67.

[8] Ibid., 55.

[9] Ibid., 53-54.

[10] Ibid., 22, 33.

[11] James Trelease, *The New Read-Aloud Handbook* (New York: Penguin Books, 1989), 121-128. Trelease outlines and persuasively discusses many of the serious problems television creates for children who view it excessively.

[12] Richard Louv, "TV Generation Sapped of Creativity," *Rocky Mountain News*, 30 December 1991, 4.

[13] Abelardo Delgado quoted in Linda Padilla, "Hispanic Writer Reveals Many Sides in Autobiography," *La Voz Hispana De Colorado* 18, no. 20 (May 13, 1992), 12.

Teacher Resources

Considine, David M., and Gail E. Haley. *Visual Messages: Integrating Imagery into Instruction*. Englewood, Colo.: Teacher Ideas Press, 1992.

> The authors provide an outstanding overview of media images and how media shapes contemporary lives. The authors examine the topics of media and visual literacy and focus on such vital subject areas as television, advertising, the news media, and movies.

Huston, Aletha C., et al. *Big World, Small Screen: The Role of Television in American Society*. Lincoln, Nebr.: University of Nebraska Press, 1992.

> A collection of eminent scholars examine the positive and negative influences of television in contemporary society.

T Is for (No) Television

Television viewing can become a springboard for reading and further inquiries. Many of the fine public television programs appear in book form. Examples include Geoffrey C. Ward's *The Civil War: An Illustrated History* (New York: Alfred A. Knopf, 1990) and Daniel Goleman, Paul Kaufman, and Michael Ray's *The Creative Spirit* (New York: E. P. Dutton, 1992). School library media specialists and local reference librarians can help students, teachers, and parents find such fine resources.

Is for Understanding a Word

> The investigation of the meaning of words is the beginning of education.
>
> —Antisthenes

> Words are, of course, the most powerful drug used by mankind.
>
> —Rudyard Kipling

Just as students in a TalentEd classroom should be continually expanding their vocabularies through work with ABC books and other vocabulary-building exercises, they should also pause long enough in their acquisition of words to be able to appreciate the richness and beauty of language. They should learn to experience and savor language in the same way that an art student might contemplate a painting by Renoir, or a music student might listen intently to a Bach fugue. An excellent word assignment that invites students to do just that is the Understanding a Word Project. By coming to know one word intimately and understanding its multiple levels of meaning, students will be able to gain a greater appreciation and understanding for the way all words are utilized. Their explorations become lessons in both the denotative and connotative meanings of words.

First, students choose one word, typically an abstract noun, that they would like to know better. Sample words include *loneliness*, *beauty*, *femininity*, *patriotism*, *genius*, *masculinity*, *power*, *ignorance*, *love*, *talent*, *youth*, *faith*, *hope*, *perfection*, *nature*, *brotherhood*, *warmth*, *failure*, *justice*, *equality*, *honor*, *wisdom*, *creativity*, *enthusiasm*, *pride*, *simplicity*, *death*, and *freedom*.

> **Man does not live by words alone, despite the fact that he sometimes has to eat them.**
>
> —Adlai Stevenson

U Is for Understanding a Word

Words WORDS WORDS WORDS WORDS WORDS
WORDS WORDS WORDS WORDS WORDS
WORDS WORDS WORDS
WORDS WORDS
WORDS **WORDS** WORDS
WORDS
WORDS WORDS WORDS WORDS WORDS WORDS WORDS
WORDS WORDS WORDS
WORDS WORDS WORDS WORDS **WORDS**
WORDS WORDS WORDS WORDS WORDS WORDS WORDS WORDS WORDS
WORDS WORDS WORDS WORDS WORDS
WORDS WORDS WORDS WORDS WORDS
WORDS WORDS WORDS WORDS WORDS WORDS

Once students choose a word, they should then find out everything they can about their word by following the steps outlined in figure U.1. The instructions are written directly for students for ease of use by teachers.

An older student might compose a poem similar to "Meditation on the Meaning of Spring" (see page 206) if the word she chose was *memory*, *nature*, or *spring*. She might create a collage of pictures of nature or spring, or better still, create her own drawings of the pine boughs and spring trees bursting with buds. Many other figural and verbal components would make up her word book.

Still another student might prefer to take a more humorous approach to defining words or exploring their meanings using a format like that found in *The Weighty Word Book* by Paul M. Levitt, Douglas A. Burger, and Elissa S. Guralnick (Longmont, Colo.: Bookmakers Guild, 1985), a sophisticated and very creative ABC book referenced in chapter A (see page 13). Words such as *felicity*, *coruscate*, and *juxtapose* are defined by way of imaginative and funny stories.

These assignments are popular with students. It is not uncommon for middle school students to create word notebooks that are twenty, thirty, or even forty pages in length. Students often pour their hearts out in the pages of their notebooks. There is a significant affective component in this project and teachers should be forewarned to "grade" this project with considerable circumspection. In coming to know one word, it seems that students often come to know themselves better, too.

Fig. U.1. Steps toward understanding a word.

1. Write your own definition of the word. What do you think the word means?

2. Find pictures, news articles, and other materials and create a collage that suggests or represents your feelings about the meaning of the word.

3. Write about a personal experience in which the word or its meaning played a large part.

4. Either write or find a story, poem, or song that illustrates the meaning of your word.

5. Ask at least five other people what they think your word means. Record their answers on paper or on tape. Attempt to interview people representative of different age groups.

6. Make up an entirely new word that you would like to include in the dictionary as a synonym for your word. For example, a new word for "old age" might be "goladdy" from "Go gently into the sunset of your years old man and take with you the warmth of your days as a lad."

7. When you have completed all of the above tasks, look in a dictionary for the denotative meaning of your word. Also attempt to find its derivation. Include this information in your word notebook.

8. Compile all your writings into a book with an appropriate cover design. You will have your own complete history and meaning of a word.

Meditation on the Meaning of Spring

I went out walking tonight
To celebrate winter's death.
The air felt good in my lungs
And I felt giddy.
Silliness and gaiety were mine.
They must have been sleeping
In me all winter long
(like dreams I lose track of).

I felt kin to the buds
Spring brought forth
On the branches of the
Trees in our woods.

I walked in the woods and the
Lyrics of song I had almost
Forgotten came back to me.

The loneliness of winter's doubts
Left me, and dreams I had
Misplaced came back.

The faces of friends and the
Laughter we had shared
Came rushing before me in
Remembrance.

Moods within me changed.
I was like the pine boughs trying to
Adjust to the newness of the
Spring breezes.

There was sadness, too.
Remorse for a friend no longer here.
She will never walk these woods again.

A patch of snow appeared before me
Not yet touched by spring's warm days
(sheltered by overhanging pines).

I leaped onto it and kicked it free of
Its winter bondage.

I laughed even though
There was no one to
Hear me.

I thought how lonely winter is
And how glad I am
To be in love with spring.

Is for Verse

> Poetry is the achievement of the synthesis of hyacinths and biscuits.
>
> —Carl Sandburg

People live today in an age that is concerned with the search for truth, yet, sadly, people turn less and less to poets and to poetry for help in finding their way. Poetry, or verse, instructs. It entertains. It enlightens. In an increasingly complex and busy world, poets startle the reader with their remarkable capacity to distill all that is around them into simple, powerful statements of truth. In their magic of language, poets also offer words of comfort when solace is needed, and expressions of joy when it is fitting to celebrate life's fine deeds and good moments.

Verse is a most appropriate area of study for talented, creative youth who so often seem to have come into the world madly in love with words. Poetry should be an integral part of the education of youth; it should not be something "extra" tacked on to the curriculum for one week each school year. Moreover, verse should not just be encountered in language arts lessons. Poets have written mightily of science, historical events and figures, and, yes, even mathematics. One exceptional TalentEd teacher uses poetry on a near-daily basis in her seventh-grade science classroom. Her students encounter their science lessons not only through the biology text but through the verse of Robert Frost, Carl Sandburg, Shakespeare, and Emily Dickinson. At the end of a period she may have her students summarize the new information they have learned during the hour by writing their own haiku or cinquain poems. The experiences with verse of this teacher's students increase their creative observation skills as students of science. By consciously using all of their senses to mine expressive words and phrases about the weather, the seasons, and other natural phenomena for haiku, for example, her students are sharpening observations skills they can apply on another day to further scientific inquiry.

The vast majority of students will not necessarily choose to read or create their own verse without teacher direction. Just as students need a guided and structured introduction to fine fiction and nonfiction, so too they need to be introduced to great verse and fine poets. In accepting the opportunities suggested in chapters *A* and *U*, TalentEd students are moving toward the creation of verse through their active acquisition of new words as well as their developing understanding of the denotation and connotation of words. Similarly, students who actively keep journals, as recommended in chapter J, have already begun the work of poets by recording their favorite images, colorful phrases, and ideas for poems.

One fine method or strategy for introducing students to creating their own verse is the use of model poems. Beginning poets benefit from both structure and example. Structure is provided through shared models of verse such as haiku and cinquain. Students are given boundaries and structures within which to ply their creativity through word and image choices. Examples of such forms and structures provide students with acceptable models on which to pattern their own verse. The author finds it especially useful to have the class as a whole create an example of the model. Collectively, for example, the students create a class haiku that the teacher writes on the chalkboard or an overhead transparency.

Many poets will confirm that their own writing is often sparked by reading the models and examples other poets provided through published verse. The act of publishing student verse is worth further comment. Student poetry should be published. The author has always collected and published the verse of his students in annual class or school anthologies. These teaching anthologies celebrate the talent of the current students. Moreover, a classroom set of the anthologies can become the text models for the forthcoming school year. That is, the haiku, cinquain, and "Imagine Me" verse of one group of students can serve as the guide models for the following year's pupils.

The verse forms and models shared here are not exhaustive, but do represent some of the fine beginning points for moving students to the creation of their own verse. An annotated list of outstanding poetry anthologies and texts is also shared at the end of the chapter. Teachers will find many outstanding models as well as composing techniques in these fine resources.

Haiku

The haiku is a three-line verse form that originated in Japan centuries ago. The complete poem is written in three lines that total seventeen syllables. There are five syllables in the first line, seven in the second line, and five again in the final line. Typically, haiku is written about nature, as in poems about the seasons of the year. Because the format is easy for students to comprehend and utilize, it is a good beginning point for using the model poem approach. The following are examples of haiku.

> The wind blows fiercely.
> It screams and bangs the windows
> Like a fearful man.

> Spring
>
> Budding leaves on trees,
> Birds singing, flowers blooming,
> A new year begins.

> Autumn
>
> Red-gold reminders
> Upon the vast mountainsides—
> Leaves fall near Aspen.

> Great, mysterious
> Shadows danced at midnight; tree
> Limbs silent at dawn.

Classical haiku finds its topics in nature, but students who like to experiment with this form occasionally enjoy using the format to write about things close to them personally as in these examples.

Father

Always loving me.
Always there when I need him.
He can fix all things.

Life is beautiful.
Life is sweet, and sometimes life
Is too good to keep.

Cinquain

Early in the twentieth century, Adelaide Crapsey learned that she was suffering from a terminal illness. In the final year of her life, she walked the woods and hills of northern New York State. As she walked, she composed five line poems about life, death, and nature. She invented the cinquain. Cinquains are poems of five lines that follow this pattern:

Line 1: One word for the title.

Line 2: Two words that describe the title.

Line 3: Three words that express an action.

Line 4: Four words that express feelings.

Line 5: One word that repeats the title or a synonym.

These models of the cinquain form address topics as diverse as nature, patriotism, sports, and the human face.

Rainbows
Prism colors
Stretching in the sky
Remembered loveliness and beauty
Rainbows

America
Our nation
People living free
Wonderful and beautiful land
America

Flag
Stars, stripes
Furling, flying proudly
One nation under God
Glory

Football
Autumn sport
Kicking, passing, tackling
The team's passionate quest
Victory!

Faces
Beautiful, handsome
Smiling, frowning, crying
Expressing joy and sorrow
Masks

Eagle
Proud symbol
Gliding, flying, soaring
Representing freedom throughout America
Eagle

Newspaper Verse

Another five-line verse form is a newspaper poem which answers the newspaper reporter's five Ws. Each line answers one of the five Ws: Who, What, When, Where, and Why. Here are some stark examples:

A desperate man
Holding up a 7-11
On a muggy summer night
Food for his hungry children
Stocking over his head; cold metal in his hand

Baseball player
Hitting the ball
In the 9th inning
Over the left-field wall
To win the big game

Diamanté

A diamanté poem is created with seven lines that visually form a diamond. Change is often indicated midway through the verse. The pattern is as follows.

Line 1: One word (subject noun)

Line 2: Two words (adjectives)

Line 3: Three words (participles)

Line 4: Four words (nouns related to the subject)

Line 5: Three words (participles)

Line 6: Two words (adjectives)

Line 7: One word (often opposite of title word)

```
               Leaves
            Green, Shiny
        Growing, thriving, living
   Sun,    Water,    Wind,    Air
        Changing, dying, falling
            Amber, brittle
               Leaves


               Kitten
           Fluffy, playful
       Pouncing, rolling, jumping
   Whiskers,    fur,    eyes,    claws
        Growing, stretching, stalking
             Bold, hungry
                Cat
```

Cafeteria Verse

Cafeteria verse is fun to create in cooperative-learning groups or as a whole class activity. It is perhaps best written in collaboration. Students imagine colorful and unusual things that may be going on in the cafeteria food line as students and teachers choose their school lunches.

Teachers are odd at my school:

> The math teacher estimates the number of calories in her carrot sticks.
>
> The science teachers try to tell students they're eating atoms instead of hamburgers.
>
> Mrs. Miller, my social studies teacher, folds Kraft cheese slices into little boats and pretends to sail them like Christopher Columbus.
>
> Mrs. Lopez, the geometry teacher, tries to carve a hexagonal pizza from a circular one.
>
> Mr. Chung tries to teach his french fries Latin.
>
> The music teacher foolishly tries to sing with peanut butter in her mouth.
>
> And, our anthropology teacher demonstrates the baboon's mating call to a fish stick.

I play it safe.

I bring my lunch from home and avoid the cafeteria line!

Young poets can easily use their friends' names in place of their teachers' names in cafeteria verse, too.

Imagine Me Verse

Imagine Me verse has no hard and fast rules save that the first line always begins with the words "Imagine Me" plus the poet's name. The remainder of the verse explores an imagined adventure or event in the life of the poet. Imagine Me poems are especially fine follow-up responses to the daydream project fully described in chapter D. Here are two examples of Imagine Me poems.

>Imagine Me, Michelle
>Playing the piano at Carnegie Hall.
>Hours of practice!
>Imagine me, soaring through a
>Beethoven composition,
>Just breezing along,
>Making no mistakes,
>Giving a flawless interpretation.
>Just perfect!   Ah........

>Imagine Me, John
>Winning the Nobel Prize.
>Imagine me standing on the stage,
>Receiving the prize.
>Thousands watch.
>Do they see how nervous I am?
>The tears of joy and happiness
>Well up in my eyes.
>Years of hard work rewarded.
>I have done it!

Limericks

Limericks are popular with wordsmiths of all ages. A limerick is created with five lines and often is nonsensical. Lines one, two, and five rhyme and contain more words or syllables than do lines three and four, which also rhyme. Limericks frequently begin with the words, "There once was a..."

The following limericks were written by the author and a seventh-grade poet.

>There once was a Dame name of Christie
>Penning mystr'y on mystr'y on mystr'y
>As her sleuths dug for clues
>And unraveled each ruse,
>The villains were vanquished to histr'y.[1]

>There was a poor train from Kazoo
>Who just couldn't say his choo-choo.
>The reason was this:
>The poor thing had a lisp
>And the choo-choo came out as thyoo-thyoo.[2]

Impression Poems

Impression poems are fun to write, and provide a good outlet for student creativity. There is no set form. Students choose a subject, and first brainstorm all the impressions — sights, sounds, smells, tastes, feelings — they have about the chosen topic. Then, they order their impressions in an eye-pleasing arrangement. The following impression poem was created by the author for his book *Mystery and Detection* to honor great detectives. Students might create impression poems about such diverse topics as basketball, school, dating, summer, the ocean, nature, birthdays, jobs, boyfriends (or girlfriends), sports cars, music stars, or their families.

Detectives

Bloodhounds, shadows
Private eyes,
Mousers,
Dicks, Gumshoes,
Snoops

Corpulent East Side tender of orchids
Inspector Queen's scion,
Parisian pipe-smoking Maigret,
Father Brown,
White-haired spinster snoop

Knitted tea cosies,
Prized mustaches and spats,
Inverness cape and deerstalker cap,
Trench coats and trenchant speech,

It's Elementary!

They are our latter day knights
Righting wrongs
O, what skullduggery they unearth,
What vile plots and
Fiendish rogues
They unmask

They are our heroes
The great detectives![3]

Personalized Verse

Personalized poems, also called acrostics, use names of people or things important to poets. The name or word is written on the page, vertically, one letter per line. Next, descriptions of the subject, words beginning with each corresponding letter of the subject, can be written on each line, horizontally, to complete the poem.

214 *V Is for Verse*

For his book *Lives of Promise*, the author created the following personalized poem about himself.

        Joyous

        Electric and enthusiastic

        Rare

        Resourceful

        Youthful outlook

        Full of energy

        Lively!

        Activity-oriented

        Curious

        Kinetic![4]

For his book *Mystery and Detection*, the author created this personalized poem honoring Agatha Christie's heroine Miss Marple.

        Mild mannered

        Inquisitive and

        Snooping spinster of

        Saint

        Mary Mead

        Artful

        Resourceful

        Prober of mysteries—

        Legendary

        Englishwoman[5]

Found Verse

Many students enjoy searching for poems or verse that are already written. Found poems are poems created from words found in prose on labels, in advertisements, on billboards, and elsewhere in the environment. The poet rearranges the found words to create verse. All of the words in the following poem were found on the front page of a newspaper.

The SUNDAY Denver Post
Voice of the Rocky Mountain Empire
April 5, 1992
1892 — Centennial Year — 1992
75 cents
Sunny and warm
Complete weather: 8C
Gangs: Grim Life
Gang Members Gunned Down
Eulogized As Heroes
Sports: It's Duke v. Michigan
for NCAA Title
<u>Inside the Post:</u>
Business 1-12H
Movies 1-8D
Crossword 7E
Denver & West 1B

Home Delivery ...
832-0900

Concrete Poetry

Eugen Gominger, a Swiss poet, is considered to be the father of the verse form known as concrete poetry. A concrete poem is intensely visual. The poem becomes a picture of the thing it describes. A concrete poem about a tree is written in the shape of a tree. Poems about kites drift across the poet's page, and verse about waterfalls visually trickles. The shape of the verse allows the poet to use word placement as well as words themselves to express an idea. Variations of concrete poems include verse written in crossword puzzle format and rebus word constructions. Here is a concrete poem about the sun, found on page 216.

(Notes follow on page 217.)

216 *V Is for Verse*

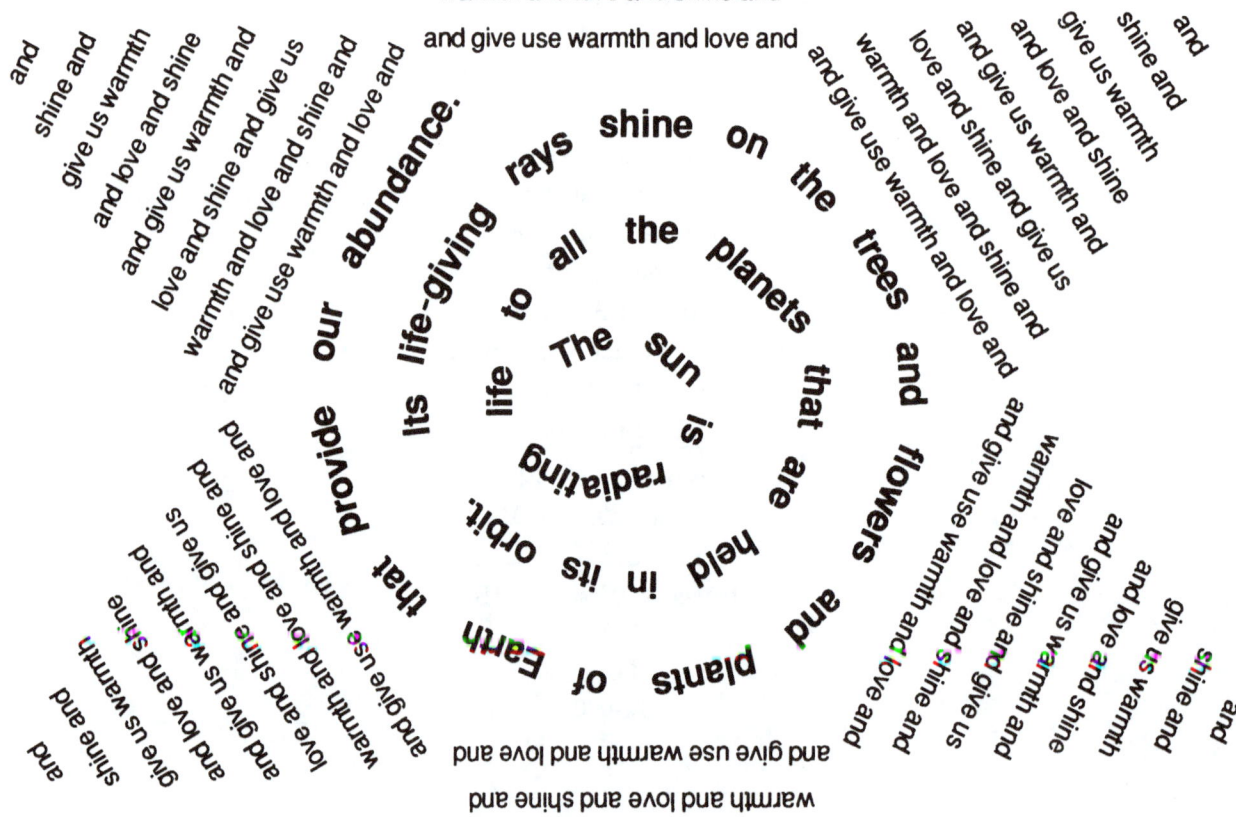

Notes

[1] Jerry D. Flack, *Mystery and Detection: Thinking and Problem Solving with the Sleuths* (Englewood, Colo.: Teacher Ideas Press, 1990), 51.

[2] Martha Dewey. Used with permission.

[3] Flack, *Mystery*, 52.

[4] Flack, *Lives of Promise: Studies in Biography and Family History* (Englewood, Colo.: Teacher Ideas Press, 1992), 30.

[5] Flack, *Mystery*, 50.

Teacher Resources

Calkins, Lucy. *The Art of Teaching Writing*. Portsmouth, N.H.: Heinemann Educational Books, 1986.
  Calkins's excellent writing strategies include a chapter on the writing of verse.

Denman, Gregory. *When You've Made It Your Own: Teaching Poetry to Young People*. Portsmouth, N.H.: Heinemann Educational Books, 1988.
  A celebration of the art of embracing, loving, caring for, and teaching children about the magic of verse.

Dickinson, Emily. *I'm Nobody! Who Are You? Poems of Emily Dickinson for Young People*. Illus. by Rex Schneider. Owings Mills, Md.: Stemmer House, 1978.
  Beautiful illustrations invite readers to share in Dickinson's time and place and to share her love of language.

Heard, Georgia. *For the Good of the Earth and the Sun: Teaching Poetry*. Portsmouth, N.H.: Heinemann Educational Books, 1989.
  A fine book about teaching poetry at all levels, primary to adult.

Koch, Kenneth. *Rose Where Did You Get That Red? Teaching Great Poetry to Children*. New York: Random House, 1973.
  Koch provides classic selections of verse and the formulas for sharing them with children.

―――, *Wishes, Lies, and Dreams: Teaching Children to Write Poetry*. New York: Random House, 1970.
  Fine, easy-to-use ideas to stimulate students to think about words, sights, sounds, and writing their own verse.

Koch, Kenneth, and Kate Farrell. *Sleeping on the Wing: An Anthology of Modern Poetry*. New York: Random House, 1982.
  An extension of the first author's works *Wishes, Lies, and Dreams* and *Rose Where Did You Get That Red?* this time for high school students. Emily Dickinson, Walt Whitman, T. S. Eliot, and Leroi Jones are among the twenty-three poets featured.

———. *Talking to the Sun: An Illustrated Anthology of Poems for Young People*. New York: Henry Holt, 1985.

Koch and Farrell use art treasures of the Metropolitan Museum of Art to illustrate verse by Shakespeare, Dickinson, Basho, John Keats, e. e. cummings, and other poets.

Merriam, Eve. *A Sky Full of Poems*. New York: Dell, 1986.

A terrific modern poet begins this anthology with her delicious verse selection, "How to Eat a Poem," and ends by telling young people how to write poetry. In between, she shares her wonderful verse.

O'Neill, Mary. *Hailstones and Halibut Bones*. Illus. by John Wallner. New York: Doubleday, 1989.

Wallner's terrific illustrations complement the wonderful poems about colors. Students can successfully model O'Neill's color poems.

Pilon, Barbara. *Concrete Is Not Always Hard*. Middletown, Conn.: Xerox Educational, 1972.

Wonderful examples of concrete poetry by modern poets.

Prelutsky, Jack. *The Random House Book of Poetry for Children*. New York: Random House, 1983.

William Blake, Christina Rossetti, A. A. Milne, Robert Frost, and Lewis Carroll are among the many poets represented in 572 selections about nature, children, the four seasons, and dogs, cats, and bears.

———. *Something Big Has Been Here*. Illus. by James Stevenson. New York: Greenwillow Books, 1990.

Humorous illustrations and funny poems that can serve as models, as students reflect on their own everyday experiences, including mother's meatloaf, brother's appetite, and being sorry for squashing a banana in bed!

Vender, Helen, ed. *The Harvard Book of Contemporary Poetry*. Cambridge, Mass.: Harvard University Press, 1985.

Thirty-five present-day poets are represented by works in this fine collection of verse for older students. Poets represented include Theodore Roethke, Anne Sexton, Sylvia Plath, and James Dickey.

Volavkova, Hana. *I Never Saw Another Butterfly*. New York: Schocken Books, 1978.

An extraordinary collection of children's poetry and drawings from the Terezin concentration camp, 1942-1944. It is impossible to read this work and not be deeply moved.

Willard, Nancy. *A Visit to William Blake's Inn: Poems for Innocent and Experienced Travelers*. Illus. by Alice Provensen and Martin Provensen. New York: Harcourt Brace Jovanovich, 1981.

This book had the rare distinction of winning the Newbery Medal and also being named as a Caldecott Honor Book. The poems are about exciting happenings at an imaginary inn run by William Blake.

 # Is for Writing

Writing should be the keystone of the curriculum structure that educators build for the talent development process. Students who cannot communicate their ideas with both skill and ease are greatly handicapped. Not long ago, the author spoke with the head of the chemistry division of an international pharmaceutical company who said he had reached a point in his hiring practice where, faced with choices among equally qualified young chemists (all with Ph.Ds from the nation's finest schools) for job openings with his company, he increasingly looked for candidates with good writing skills. "I do not have time to edit and rewrite my employees' reports," he said. The point is that no matter how gifted, talented, and creative students are in art, mathematics, chemistry, or any other field, they must still be able to articulate ideas, and the primary medium used for communication is written composition.

In research interviews with highly gifted students in Michigan and Indiana, the author had the occasion to talk to young people about their school experiences. One of the most appalling things he learned was the infrequency with which these gifted students were given writing practice and composition assignments. Incredibly, one extremely gifted young man's total output in two years of junior high school had been one book report. Anyone who has ever been a writer knows that there is a strong correlation between the frequency with which one writes, the ease with which one writes, and the resulting quality of composition. That is, the more people write, the more easily and more competently they write. If written composition is an integral part of all aspects of a TalentEd program, it is only reasonable to expect that these students will become better writers.

When teachers talk of talented writers, they need to consider more than just one kind of writing talent. For most educators, the first student that comes to mind as a talented writer is the student who is an exceptional creative writer. This is the student whose writing is rich in imagery and metaphor. This is the student who can, as by magic, create a wonderful story out of the mere building blocks of random words. This also may be the student who composes startling images with his or her poetry. Teachers, however, should also be on the lookout for students gifted in writing nonfiction prose. Which student can pen a description of an ant hill that is sublime? Which young writer describes processes with unusual clarity and precision? In the TalentEd classroom, teachers should seek evidence of advanced vocabularies well used. They should look for students who use language expressively, too. They should look for students who are not stingy with words. Which students provide good detail and elaboration in their writing?

How do teachers teach composition to students? First, there is simply no substitute for continuous writing practice. One cannot become an accomplished swimmer if one never gets into the pool. Similarly, the way to develop and enhance writing talent is to have lots and lots of practice. Teachers should find any and every opportunity to get students to write. The only way students will find their own writing voices is through frequent writing practice and opportunity. Students should write in their journals on a daily basis. Writing in class should be an everyday expectation. More polished writings should go into class anthologies and school newspapers and literary magazines. Encourage students to write in a variety of formats. A TalentEd language arts teacher in Colorado Springs encourages her students to express their views on social and political issues through letters to the editor of the city's major newspaper on a regular basis. There are legions of writing contests for students. Encourage students to enter as many of these competitions as possible. Winning is not overly important. The experience of writing often and for a variety of audiences is the important factor. Encourage students to keep portfolios of all their writings. Most of the finer colleges and universities in the nation require at least one writing sample as part of the application process. Prize-winning writing samples can be most impressive. TalentEd teachers create a climate where writing is natural and where students love to share their writing with each other and even wider audiences.

Of course, final products are not all that matter in a good writing program. Far from it. Process is at least as important as product in the development of writing talent in youth. Writing processes that include prewriting exercises, discussions, warm-ups, long periods of writing, and critical editing and revision phases should be taught to students and constantly utilized. Happily, in the last two decades education for writing has gained momentum in schools thanks to the work of talented people such as Nancy Atwell, Donald Graves, and Donald Murray, all of whom emphasize the process of writing.

Some students are more at ease with the writing process than others. Many talented students write with ease and need little encouragement or motivation to write. But what are teachers to do with reluctant writers? Two approaches may be considered. The first is not to allow noncomposition options or excuses from reluctant writers. Frequent writing practice and assignments should be a natural part of the classroom routine. More than a few former students have ultimately thanked teachers who did not allow them to dodge composition requirements. Some of life's sweetest victories come from learning to become competent in skills for which people initially believe they have little talent.

Second, TalentEd teachers should provide assignments for students that are exciting, challenging, thought-provoking, and fun. When teachers give dull assignments (e.g., What did you do over summer vacation?), they should not be very surprised if their students are reluctant to respond. TalentEd teachers are always on the hunt for new, exciting, and creative prompts to extend to young writers that will engage and ignite their imaginations. Students need never be bored if they learn to use their writing talents wisely.

Wise teachers also realize that no two students are alike. The continual practice of writing should be individually guided and based upon a diagnosis of each student's strengths and weaknesses in composition. TalentEd teachers build upon strengths and help students remedy weaknesses. Ultimately, teachers need also to communicate to students the joy of writing. Creating something new and unique is one of the supreme pleasures anyone can derive from living. Students who come to love writing understand this and give writing the daily practice it deserves.

The writing ideas in figure W.1, pages 222-226, should aid TalentEd teachers in providing students with creative and challenging writing ideas. The directions are written directly for students for ease of use by teachers.

W *Is for Writing* 221

(Teacher Resources follow on page 226.)

Fig. W.1. Writing ideas for young writers.

 Recall a childhood prank, accident, adventure, or incident that seemed terrifying or devastating at the time, but can now be looked upon with a sense of humor. One beginning to a written piece might be, "I felt terrible the day I ..."

 Celebrate the months of the school year with your pen and your imagination. From September's Labor Day festivities to May's more reflective and somber Memorial Day, the calendar's holidays offer many opportunities for creative writing.

- September: Imagine what might happen if all the inanimate objects in school were to come to life and form a labor organization, The United Mind Workers. Who might their spokesperson be? Write a Labor Day oration that the classroom computer, pencil sharpener, or wastepaper basket might deliver on Labor Day.

- October is a frightful season for pumpkins. First, people come along and carve them up, and then Halloween ruffians steal them off people's porches and smash them in the streets. Write an obituary for a prominent pumpkin who has been vilely treated.

- November is the month turkeys hate, and with good reason! But now there is Super Turkey! Create a cartoon strip or a funny story about the exploits and adventures of Super Turkey as she comes to the rescue of distressed turkeys everywhere.

- December is the occasion for singing the beloved Christmas song, "The Twelve Days of Christmas." Write a new version of the song for the year 2095. What gifts might a suitor present for the twelve days of Christmas or the eight days of Hanukkah a century hence?

- January is the time for writing New Year's resolutions. Take a fresh look at the world. Write a list of things to do in the new year that will require real creativity and ingenuity on your part.

- February is the time for Valentines. Engage in a little research about some of the famous duos down through history: Romeo and Juliet, Antony and Cleopatra, Abbott and Costello, and the Wright brothers. Write two letters that the chosen twosome might have penned to one another.

- "Beware the Ides of March!" Plan and write an original murder mystery story in which the soothsayer's admonition should have been heeded. (For background information on the origin of the saying "Beware the Ides of March," read William Shakespeare's play *Julius Caesar*.)

From *TalentEd: Strategies for Developing the Talent in Every Learner*, © 1993 Teacher Ideas Press, P.O. Box 6633, Englewood, CO 80155-6633

- April affords an opportunity to describe your work as a genetic engineer. Redesign the Easter Bunny. Think of the attributes or parts of a rabbit: nose, whiskers, ears, body, and tail. Now create a new kind of bunny by changing all these parts. Maybe the Easter Bunny should have a wagging tail rather than a powder puff. Once the new bunny is created, write a quasi-scientific paper describing the merits of the new animal, or describe your advertising campaign to introduce the new bunny to the world.

- To complete the school year in May, write a thoughtful poem or an essay that is a memorial tribute. Memorials do not just have to be about people. Recall a special pet that you loved very much. Or, perhaps write a sad farewell to a lost ideal or a broken friendship.

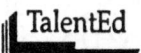 You are applying for a dream job for which you must submit a resumé. The prospective employer is a very particular and very busy executive. This executive insists that your resumé be brief and absolutely to the point. It must be *exactly* sixty-four words in length. Be concise! Proofread and edit carefully. Write a sixty-four-word personal resumé.

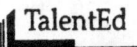 Read a story and then react to the story in one of the following ways:

Rewrite the story as a press release.

Create a poem one of the characters might have penned.

Assume the role of one of the characters and write a letter seeking help from an advice columnist such as Ann Landers.

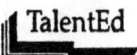 Locate and peruse a book about American art. Carefully examine a painting that appeals to you. Study the detail. Once you have established a "feeling" for the painting, write a story, play scene, essay, or poem about the people, animals, objects, or events portrayed in the painting. Imagine, for example, the lives of the people in Grant Wood's *American Gothic* before and after the moment caught in time by the painter.

TalentEd Rosy Hue was an extraordinary artist of great talent, but she was also very eccentric. After her death and subsequent funeral, her friends went to Rosy's artist's studio to sort through her personal possessions. It turned out to be a real problem-solving task. You see, Rosy not only had a cluttered apartment—she never threw anything away—she also used things in unique ways never envisioned by their creators. Thus, all the items listed below and found by the late artist's friends were used in unusual but creative ways. For example, Rosy would fill an empty milk bottle with sand (colored, of course) and use it as a doorstop. Can you determine what use these items had in

(Fig. W.1 continues on page 224.)

Fig. W.1 – *Continued*

Rosy's scheme of things? Imagine how each item was used and write a short article for either an art magazine or a home decorator's journal describing such uses. The items Rosy Hue's friends found included

- twelve rocks
- fake fur coat
- garden hose, 25 feet
- thirty postcards from the Grand Canyon
- ten turkey tail feathers
- two strings of Christmas tree lights
- a coffee table minus one leg
- clay statue of a St. Bernard dog
- six decorated tin canisters
- basketball-size ball of twine
- plastic dish drainer

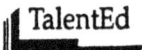 What would happen if people didn't have watches or clocks? Write an essay, story, or poem about the perceived or real importance of time-keeping devices. Or, write an article for a newspaper or magazine explaining what time is. Is time, for example, perceived the same way by all people? Do you procrastinate and have trouble managing time? Write a funny story about a student who faces one calamity after another because he or she lacks good time management skills.

 Read the Bill of Rights in the Constitution of the United States of America. Now, think of a population that needs similar kinds of protection of their rights. What rights do they have? What responsibilities? What protection do they need? Compose a bill of rights for children, endangered species, Olympic athletes, or dyslexic students.

 Rewrite history. Write a story that explains why the capital city of the United States should be your hometown, or why the blue jay should be the national bird.

 Create an autobiography for a famous invention. Imagine that you are the first television, automobile, running shoe, microwave oven, or fast-food burger. Tell your life story. Use the first-person voice to describe how you came to be and the impact you have had on the world, for better or worse.

TalentEd Consider your hometown or city. Choose one of the following writing activities as a means of celebrating your hometown:

- Write a poem celebrating the beauty of your city.

- Research the life of one of your hometown's most famous citizens. Compose a diary or journal entry he or she might have made.

From *TalentEd: Strategies for Developing the Talent in Every Learner*, © 1993 Teacher Ideas Press, P.O. Box 6633, Englewood, CO 80155-6633

- Which season is your favorite time to be in your city? Write an ode or a haiku poem celebrating the city and the season.

- Fine restaurants hire writers to describe menu items in appealing and tantalizing ways. Choose five attractions or sites in your city and describe each as appealingly and colorfully as you can.

- What might happen in your city if Superman or Batman resided there? Write a newspaper account of how one of these comic book heroes solves a community problem.

- Write a script for a television commercial that promotes your city as a tourist attraction or convention site.

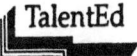 Examine several contemporary magazines that address a variety of audiences (e.g., working women, hunters, teens, tennis players, cat lovers). Note the kinds of articles and features and advertising found in the periodicals. Once you have a grasp of the idea of creating a magazine for a special audience, create a brand new magazine for your family, your school, or your community. Create a sample table of contents with the names of at least five to ten articles or features. Design a cover for your magazine. Make up a list of possible advertisers. Finally, write one of the articles listed in your imagined table of contents.

 Pretend that you have been shipwrecked and marooned on a Pacific island. Ten items have survived the shipwreck and are at your disposal. What ten items would you most want to save? Provide at least one reason for wanting each item. Write a creative story using all ten items in the narrative. Don't forget to recall the harrowing experience of the shipwreck.

 Choose an athlete whom you admire and follow his or her career over a period of at least two months. Imagine yourself to be a reporter working on a book or a serial feature article about the athlete. Structure a series of interviews with the subject. Each entry or passage should reflect events really occurring in the athlete's life. How does each victory or defeat affect the subject? What reasons are given for particular victories or defeats? Add creative illustrations to the overall profile. At the end of the two months, when the profile is complete, send a copy of it to the subject.

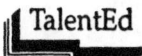 Summer camp escapades. Create a character who is unique. Perhaps this character might be an unusually precocious child or a very inquisitive person. Imagine yourself as the camp counselor primarily responsible for the care of this camper. Write a story collage about your experiences with the camper. A story collage might be composed of camp memos, letters home to friends and family, conversations with the camper, and imagined personal journal entries. All of the pieces of the story collage fit together to reveal a portrait of the unusual camper and his or her experiences.

(Figure W.1 continues on page 226.)

Fig. W.1—*Continued*

 Choose three people whom you trust and whose opinions you value. Make up a list of five to ten questions about yourself (e.g., what is my best personality trait? what three words best describe me?). Ask your three friends to complete the questionnaire about you. Also answer the questions yourself. Use the four separate responses to write a self-portrait.

 Work with your classmates to author a classroom "Who's Who." Interview one of your classmates about his or her life, likes, attitudes, dreams, and aspirations. Write a capsule biography of your classmate. Brevity is needed, so be sure to be especially concise in your writing and utilize your critical-thinking skills to determine the most vital pieces of information to include. Work with other students in your classroom to compile all the profiles into one classroom collection that features all your classmates, highlighting each person's uniqueness.

■ ■ ■

Teacher Resources

Atwell, Nancy. *In the Middle: Writing, Reading, and Learning with Adolescents*. Portsmouth, N.H.: Boynton/Cook, 1987.

  An eminently readable account of one teacher's literacy journey with eighth-grade students.

Fulwiler, Toby. *Teaching with Writing*. Portsmouth, N.H.: Boynton/Cook, 1987.

  Fulwiler provides outstanding teaching tips and advice on student journals, writing and learning connections, composing, revising, editing, and writing workshops.

Graves, Donald. *Writing: Teachers and Children at Work*. Portsmouth, N.H.: Heinemann Educational Books, 1983.

  Graves is one of the great advocates of starting children to write at an early age. This book tells teachers how to do it.

Murray, Donald M. *A Writer Teaches Writing*. Boston: Houghton Mifflin, 1985.

  A great writing teacher shares the methods of helping people learn to write well.

———. *Expecting the Unexpected: Teaching Myself and Others to Read and Write*. Portsmouth, N.H.: Heinemann Educational Books, 1989.

  A lifetime of writing and teaching writing is revealed in this highly readable work.

# X Is for Classroom eXperts

One of the critical strategies of TalentEd is the use of classroom experts. Being classroom experts provides students with opportunities as well as the challenge to be the best that they can be in at least one content area or skill. Consider a few examples.

Luis is a seven-year-old boy with a fascination for dinosaurs. He becomes the classroom expert on paleontology. All questions that come up in class about dinosaurs are referred to Luis. He supplies ready answers or engages in further research to find and provide answers. He coordinates the construction and arrangement of a classroom learning center about dinosaurs. He works with the school library media specialist to find an especially good film about dinosaurs that the entire class will enjoy and profit from viewing. He may start a dinosaur club that meets in the lunchroom once a week to share newly acquired dinosaur models and facts.

Studying language? Five-year-old kindergartners recently left the University of Colorado Super Saturday Program for gifted students, able to spell and recognize examples of *onomatopoeia*. Why not put a verbally gifted child in charge of finding and sharing with the class examples of onomatopoeia? Nations and states have poet laureates. So, too, can TalentEd classrooms have poets who commemorate birthdays, create get-well greetings, and honor special occasions with their verse.

When a class is studying invention, teachers may assign specific inventions or inventors to each student. It may be Josh's task to become the classroom expert on famous women inventors, and Mary's to develop expertise on the evolution of aerospace inventions. When biography is the topic focus, each student can become the classroom resident expert on the lives and times of different biographical subjects.

When Shakespeare is read in his classes, one TalentEd junior high English teacher requires that his students become experts on one of the many topics he shares with them. The topics include the geography found in *Hamlet*, everyday life in Elizabethan England, the Globe Theatre, Elizabethan witchcraft and magic, Renaissance philosophies, and Elizabethan views on the world.

There can be classroom experts at every grade level and in every subject and topical area of the curriculum. Expertise does not have to stop with content knowledge bases and interest areas. Skills and particular talents can also be celebrated and recognized. A Denver TalentEd teacher has resident artists in her classroom. These experts help other children develop their own drawings and lettering skills that they employ for posters in science fair projects and independent study reports. One young man, initially shy, blossomed under her guidance and in his new found classroom responsibility with its attendant respect from his peers. Sadly, he was not as fortunate the following year. His new teacher insisted that all students do their own work exclusively, without any assistance or help from others. His initial teacher said the young artist spoke not a word of protest, but artistically created a little sign for his desk that read: "Artist: Gone Out of Business."

There is no end to the topic and skill areas that can be addressed by classroom experts. Every classroom could profit from having classroom experts such as these:

Legal Rights Expert	Poet Laureate
State Historian	Space Scientist
Resident Artist	Shakespeare Scholar
Movie Critic	Football Pundit
Spelling Wizard	Grammar Guide
Computer Master	Music Virtuoso
Geography Guru	Olympics Authority
Math Mentor	Soccer Sleuth
First Amendment Attorney	Weather Forecaster

Many benefits accrue in classrooms where classroom experts are valued. First, the practice of honoring classroom experts allows all students the opportunity and the challenge to be continuously learning new information about a topic or skill that is a personal interest or passion. Moreover, it gives each child in a classroom both the responsibility and the pleasure of being the classroom best in something. This is no small matter where self-esteem is concerned. Every student comes to know that he or she is a vital and critically important member of the classroom community. Others depend upon their contributions to the whole.

The use of classroom experts is especially beneficial to gifted students. Having an area of expertise gives these students a purposeful avenue of inquiry to pursue when they have spare time in class. Students do not need to mark time waiting for others to finish class assignments. When they finish assigned work, they can move directly into reading, research, and creative works related to their chosen area of expertise. Acquiring this behavior promotes a belief in and practice of lifelong learning.

One junior high science student noted that his classmates were having trouble remembering the various muscles of the body. When he finished early with the class assignment, he created a song that would serve as a mnemonic tool to help his classmates. "Our Muscles" is sung to the tune of "My Bonnie Lies Over the Ocean."

Our Muscles

My bicep lies over my triceps
My deltoid is next to those two
Trapezius lines up behind them
To hold up my arm right to you.

Pectoralis, Pectoralis
This is a muscle on you-ou-ou
Pectoralis, Pectoralis
This is a muscle on you-ou-ou

Behind all those ribs is this muscle
We need it for everyday use;
But with this great muscle to help you
Your "bod" stays as loose as a goose.

Latissimus, Latissimus
Latissimus Dorsi behind you
Latissimus, Latissimus
Latissimus Dorsi behind you

The rectus femoris you run with
It gives you that smoothness and grace
But without this great muscle behind you
You never would place in a race.

The left leg, the right leg, they give
you the pride to stride ahead.
The left leg, the right leg, they give
you the pride to stride ahead.

The gluteus muscles you sit on
Shall finish this poor little song
Perhaps you do not like these muscles
Perhaps this poor song was too long.

Anatomy, anatomy
It is a science we all must learn
Anatomy, anatomy
It's the secret that makes the world turn.[1]

The young man's science teacher found the song to be so helpful to other students that he has given copies to students every year since it was composed. What a fine way for a gifted student to use class time. Is it not better for gifted students to use time developing their talents and sharing their gifts with others than it is for them to be assigned yet one more busywork ditto?

Another benefit of the practice of having classroom experts is that it helps to dispel the notion students may have that the teacher is always the repository of all knowledge and wisdom. One of the heroes of the author's youth was President John F. Kennedy. J.F.K. brought a certain grace and style to the White House. In the spring of 1962, President Kennedy invited all the living Nobel Prize-winners from the United States to a special White House dinner. He began his remarks to the august body of talent by saying, "I think that this is the most extraordinary collection of talent, of human knowledge, that has ever been gathered together at the White House with the possible exception of when Thomas Jefferson dined alone."[2]

In his time, Jefferson surely was a Renaissance man. He exhibited expertise in fields as diverse as agriculture, political science, history, and architecture. He was an inventor, an author, and a statesman. But, Jefferson lived in very different times. Today's youth are growing up in the Information Age. It is a time of knowledge explosions. What was fact or rule this morning may be inconsequential, or worse, invalid information by this afternoon. It is simply not possible for teachers or others to be experts in all fields today. Creating classroom experts gives children and adolescents a sense of the kinds of specializations they will be more and more likely to encounter in their adult lives. The practice of having classroom experts also helps students learn to "share the wealth," so to speak. Students learn from each other as well as from the teacher. No one classroom genius dominates the group, either. Every student has the opportunity to be "the best" or the expert on some topic or in some skill. Further, since the classroom experts will not always be able to provide immediate answers to all questions, students will quickly see the need to learn how to find out the answers to questions they raise. Students come to appreciate the role of the teacher as the facilitator rather than the dispenser of learning in the classroom.

The following represents just a few of the creative ways TalentEd teachers and school library media specialists can use the talents of student experts. TalentEd students may:

- conduct library searches and prepare bibliographies for their classmates for forthcoming units of study;

- set up and guide laboratory experiences;

- create and construct classroom learning centers;

- teach mini-lessons in areas of personal expertise;

- prepare fact sheets and other educational material about their areas of expertise;

- write computer simulations in areas of interest and expertise; create record-keeping programs for classroom and library media center use;

- serve as mentors to classmates or younger students in areas of expertise;

- edit and publish class anthologies that may include science fair journals, newsletters, and literary magazines;

- create audiovisual materials such as synchronized slide-tape presentations about course content or special interest subjects; and

- keep track of all dates of importance to the classroom, including the birthdays of all the students, school holidays, and important historical events.

Teachers and parents frequently voice concern about the phenomenon of "summer lag." Students seem to forget over the summer the basic skills taught in school the previous year. Two of the author's gifted seventh-grade students created a summer activities book for all their peers in their middle school. The boy and girl team of classroom experts designed and authored activities to help develop and reinforce basic skills in math, reading and language arts, social studies, and science that students might forget over the summer. They created math games, science experiments that could be performed at home, directed reading assignments about history and current events found in daily newspapers, poetry writing exercises, and the like. Max and Heather created a separate activity for each day of the summer. All 250 students in the school received a free copy of the book the final day of school. They were encouraged to complete the fun-oriented activities over the summer.

Summer activity books created by TalentEd students may be tied to themes the school wishes to emphasize. Suppose that the school theme is a focus on the future. TalentEd students can create math problems based on computing distances between planets, or population growth trends. Directed reading assignments might stem from futures scenarios (see chapter *H*) students write. The student authors can relate basic science principles to environmental concerns or describe future inventions space colonists will need. They may create haiku or cinquain poetry based on future images they project for civilization. TalentEd students can plan, create, publish, and distribute these summer activity books for their fellow students with only modest adult supervision.[3]

The ideas suggested in this chapter just begin to scratch the surface in terms of the myriad ways TalentEd students can be on both the giving and receiving ends of education in the classroom. One does not have to be an adult, hold teacher certification credentials, or possess a Ph.D. to have something worthwhile to contribute. TalentEd teachers and library media specialists embrace this notion and put the expert talents of their students to work daily. The learning that occurs in a TalentEd classroom is a joyous, shared experience.

Notes

[1]The author wishes to thank Bruce Rolfe, M.D., for permission to use his song lyrics. Readers may be interested to know that the young student who penned the lyrics about muscles is now an orthopedic surgeon in Seattle, Washington.

[2]John F. Kennedy, "Address to White House Dinner Honoring Nobel Prize Winners, April 1962," in *Bartlett's Familiar Quotations*, 15th ed. (Boston: Little, Brown, 1980), 891.

[3]For a more thorough discussion of the summer activity book see Jerry D. Flack, "With Summer in Mind..." *Gifted Child Today* (*GCT*) 40 (September/October 1985): 24-25.

Y Is for DictionarY and EncYclopedia Stories

A favorite writing task of students is the creation of encyclopedia or dictionary stories. Assign each student a letter of the alphabet. Next, provide each student with the corresponding letter volume from an encyclopedia set and a dictionary. The student's task is then to write a story chiefly made up of words, events, people, and places that begin with the assigned alphabet letter. With few exceptions, notably pronouns and prepositions, the key words and elements in the stories students create should be found in the volume of the encyclopedia each possesses.

Preparatory to writing, teachers should review the standard story elements: plot, character, setting, and theme. Either before or after the writing and sharing of stories, teachers can use this activity as a springboard for teaching students about the poetic device of alliteration. TalentEd teachers may want to share several entries found in Graeme Base's wonderful book *Animalia*. For example, Base's text for the letter *Y* reads, "Youthful Yaks Yodeling in Yellow Yachts."[1]

Before students begin to structure their stories, a good first step is to create columns for people, places, and things beginning with their given letters. If *Y* is Yolanda's chosen or given letter, her first steps may lead to a guide that looks like figure Y.1.

Fig. Y.1. A guide to people, places, and things that begin with the letter *Y*.

People	Places	Things
Yankee Doodle	Yakima	yacht
W. L. Yancy	Yalta	yak
Yaqui Indians	Yalu River	yawl
Chuck Yeager	Yemen	yeoman
Brigham Young	Yonkers	yoga
W. B. Yeats	Yosemite Falls	year
Yeti	Ypres	youth
Chen Ning Yang	Yukon	yeast
Elihu Yale	Yokohama	yogurt
Hideki Yukawa	Yuma	yttrium

Y Is for DictionaryY and EncYclopedia Stories

Yolanda may next turn from the encyclopedia volume to a dictionary and make a list of *Y* verbs for possible use in her story. Her verb list may include the words *yap*, *yank*, *yaw*, *yearn*, *yell*, *yield*, *yodel*, *yammer*, and *yawn*. She may even search for some adverbs like *yep*, *yes*, and *yet*.

The following *Y* story may be shared with students as one example of an encyclopedia or dictionary story.

Yolanda Young's Youth

Yolanda Young was a youth who yearned to yearly move around the world. She yammered about taking a yacht or a yawl to Yakima, Yalta, Yokohama, Yugoslavia, the Yalu River, and Yoruba. Yolanda yowled and yelled when she learned from her yoga teacher that youth could not go to Yemen or up the Yenisey River—not to mention Yellowstone Park—to look for Yeti. "Yipes!" Yolanda yowled in Yiddish, "If Yeats from Yonkers, Young from Yuma, and Yeager from Ypres can yell in Yemen, why can't I?" Yolanda's pet Yugoslavian yearling yak (born in the Yablonovyy Mountains) first yawned and then yowled in sympathy with her. Hideki Yukawa, a Yaqui Indian, and Yvonne Yalow came to Yolanda's rescue. They were heading up a joint YMCA-YWCA year-long study at Yale University of the element yttrium and its effects upon yellow-bellied sap suckers, yew, and yucca in the Yap Islands and in the Yucatan. Happily, Yolanda joined them and forgot all about Yemen, the Yenisey, and Yeti.

The End

From *TalentEd: Strategies for Developing the Talent in Every Learner*, © 1993 Teacher Ideas Press, P.O. Box 6633, Englewood, CO 80155-6633

Students love to share their stories with each other. Once students have had ample time to share their story drafts, and engage in editing, conferencing, and rewriting, a class anthology of stories, *A to Z*, can be compiled and published.

A note of caution. Assign especially difficult letters such as *Q* to creative and highly motivated TalentEd students. There are many alternatives or variations of this writing task. Teachers who want to introduce cooperative learning strategies may assign alphabet letters to pairs or groups of three or four students. Using dictionaries and encyclopedias, the pairs or groups collaborate to compose a story based on a given letter shared by all. The students work cooperatively in their research and writing. Obviously, when pairs or groups are used, it will take more time to achieve stories for each of the alphabet's twenty-six letters. In this case, perhaps several classes could work together to create a school anthology of encyclopedia stories.

A most creative resource TalentEd teachers may wish to consult is Jody Limscott's *Once Upon A to Z*, highlighted in recommended alphabet books featured in chapter *A*. In *Once Upon A to Z*, "Andy always ate an astounding amount." Moreover, he ate "artichokes, apples, avocados and apricots."[2] Where the letter *A* leaves off, the letter *B* takes over the story, telling its part of the tale with all words that begin with *B*. The story continues to unfold in this manner until the letter *Z* completes the saga.

Encyclopedia stories are fun to write and positively challenge the creative energies of TalentEd youth.

Notes

[1]Graeme Base, *Animalia* (New York: Harry N. Abrams, 1986), p. *Y*.

[2]Jody Limscott, *Once Upon A to Z*, illus. by Claudia Porges Holland (New York: Doubleday, 1991), 1.

Z Is for Zebras and Zoo Stories

Zipes! The alphabet is almost exhausted! Time for one more fun, creative, and productive activity. Zoo stories are student-made books that feature zoo animals. Each student in the class chooses a zoo animal about which to research, learn, and write. Each child spends several days utilizing science books, encyclopedias, and other resources to learn about a special animal he or she has selected for study. Habitat, history, and habits are pieces of vital information each student will want to find about his or her zoo animal. Once each student has considerable data about his or her animal, introduce students to the writing technique of personification. Using personification, each student writes a first-person or autobiographical account of his or her life as a zebra, gorilla, polar bear, kangaroo, or camel. Figure Z.1, page 236, is a sample of what might be the zebra's story. It is a model that may be shared with students. Once all the students have created their zoo animal accounts, place them all together in a zoo story anthology. Presto! The class has a creative and fact-filled zoo book for everyone to enjoy. If there are twenty-five students in the classroom, then the zoo book has twenty-five separate, creative, fact-filled stories that will enrich the learning of all.

TalentEd teachers need not stop with zoo stories. Once students are familiar with this form of individual research, creative writing, and collaborative sharing, the same plan can be used with almost any topic. Studying minerals in science class? Create a mineral storybook in which each student researches a mineral and tells its particular story. States, cities, nations, landmarks, flowers, insects, fish, birds, trees, endangered species, and many, many more broad topics can be the focus of this collaborative writing pattern.

Fig. Z.1. First-person account of life as an animal.

A Zebra Story

Hi! I am Zaragosa the Zebra. I am a member of the horse family Equidae, and the genus *Equus*. I live in the grassy areas of Africa, south of the Sahara desert. I am found in three families: Grevy's zebra, Burchell's zebra, and the mountain zebra. I stand proudly with a shoulder height of 4 to 5 feet, and have an average weight of 770 pounds. My most striking feature is my pattern of alternating black (or dark brown) and white stripes. I am striped from head to tail. Believe it or not, my stripes help me to hide from my chief four-legged enemy, lions. But, lions are not my worst enemy. Sadly, humans like my colorful hide, and my brothers and sisters and I have been hunted to near extinction in many parts of Africa.

I am herbivorous, preferring grasses and shrubs for my dinner. I like to live with a small group of my family members. I mingle with other peaceful grazing animals like wildebeests, antelopes, and even ostriches. When under attack, I am known to be both fast and dangerous. I can achieve a running speed of 40 miles per hour. When cornered, I can be a savage fighter. Despite the dangers, I like living in the wild. Attempts by humans to domesticate me for work, like my cousin the horse, have been unsuccessful.

From *TalentEd: Strategies for Developing the Talent in Every Learner*, © 1993 Teacher Ideas Press, P.O. Box 6633, Englewood, CO 80155-6633

Afterword

TalentEd: Strategies for Developing the Talent in Every Learner is the fourth book I have written for the Gifted Treasury series. In many ways, it is my personal favorite writing effort. Every page of the book was a joy to write because it represented an opportunity for me to put into one volume the ideas and strategies that I have used with students of many ages for more than twenty-five years as a teacher. Each idea or activity suggested by a letter of the alphabet was an occasion for sifting through papers and files of student work created over a period of more than two decades of teaching. Each moment was an opportunity to recall young people having fun while they were learning how to develop, sometimes awkwardly, sometimes reluctantly, yet often brilliantly, their God-given talents. What a wonder teaching is! What other career gives any person the opportunity to do work that is simultaneously so vital, so rewarding, and so much fun.

In creating this book, I had the opportunity to renew friendships with students I taught in junior high school settings across many years. I communicated with a young prosecuting attorney in New Jersey, a physician in Minnesota, a foreign policy graduate student at George Washington University, and a stage director in New York who uses drama to help officers of major corporations better appreciate and deal with issues of diversity in the workplace.

On the same day that I finished the last chapter of this book, I had the pleasure of having lunch with an extraordinarily talented former student I had taught in Kalamazoo, Michigan, in the 1970s. The young man, now a highly successful and dedicated attorney in Phoenix, Arizona, shared stories of legal cases he has taken on in recent years. In one case, he gave freely of his talent to help an impoverished elderly woman save her home. At the time of this writing, he is defending a seventeen-year-old youth who he believes has been wrongly accused of a gang-related murder. Listening to this attorney talk about his commitment to his work and to the principles of justice was both inspiring and revealing. His passion for justice and his personal pursuit of excellence were evident when he was twelve years old. It is a great pleasure to see how he has realized his great promise.

Of course, not every student I have taught has been so fortunate. A quiet, beautiful girl who wrote sensitive and mature poetry in my ninth-grade English class was brutally murdered this past year. A brilliant young man was unjustly imprisoned for more than a year. Another youth gave his life on a battlefield. None of them will ever realize the enormous potential their talents promised, and I am left asking the eternal question: Why?

Afterword

Not long ago I sat in a classroom where the teacher asked each student to imagine, and then share, his or her most ambitious dream. The students responded to the teacher's prompt with descriptions of idyllic visits to tropical isles, and heroic feats like flying jets at yet unconquered speeds. Although I was not called upon to share a response, I was glad for the opportunity to pause in an otherwise hectic week and give a bit of thought to the question. I don't often have the chance to stop and question the meaning of my life. My private response was simple, one so often given that it has sadly come to be thought of as a cliché. It is this: My dream is to use my life to make some contribution to the world, no matter how small, so that it may be a better place for my having been here.

That philosophy gives meaning to my life and to my teaching. I believe teaching is a trust. Education, religion, and the family are the primary means by which civilization is passed from one generation to the next. To fulfill the trust I must be many things. I need to be knowledgeable. The information I impart to students must be accurate and current, yet I cannot just dispense facts. I must model behavior that encourages not only the acquisition of information, but a love of learning. I need to be a scholar and contribute to the knowledge base that I teach. I need to be caring and perceptive. I love the smiles of recognition when a difficult concept has been grasped by my students. But, I also know the desolate feeling students experience when they do not understand that which seems so easily comprehended by others, and I know I need to help these students even more. I love smiling faces and eager students, as every teacher does. But, I have also had students who have suffered great losses, or who have felt pain so intense that suicide, for a time, seemed the only answer open to them; and I have put away the textbook and helped them as best I could. Learning the content is not all that should happen in a classroom. I teach problem solving, thinking skills, *and* people, as well as a discipline. If I model excellence, tolerance, patience, enthusiasm, kindness and respect, cooperation, and other attributes that are the hallmarks of what it is all about to be human, then I will have taught well and will have honored the trust undertaken.

I like to think of teaching as the immortal profession. Other workers more easily witness the fruits of their labors. A composer hears the music, a bricklayer sees the finished home, a physician heals a patient. Teachers rarely know the full measure or value of their work. The understanding I help a student achieve, the excitement for learning I impart to another human being, the encouragement as well as criticism I gently offer, will be circulating among my students and their students and beyond. This is an awesome responsibility that I do not take lightly. I am proud to be a teacher. Through my work and my belief in the importance of that work, I am building tomorrows I will never see, through the lives of those I teach and touch today.

JERRY D. FLACK

Index

Aaseng, Nathan, 41
A B C books, 8, 11-15, 33, 48, 147, 161, 204
ABC Exhibit, 13
Abecedarian Book, 12
Abercrombie & Fitch, 33
Ability grouping, 3, 8
A, B, See!, 13
Academic talent, 69-73, 75-76
Acceptance finding stage of creative problem
    solving, 101-2
Adams, James L., 99, 172
Adams, John Quincy, 105, 192
Addams, Jane, 190
Adler, David, 130
Advertising activities, 52-55
Advertising contract, 53 (fig.)
Advertising techniques, 52
Afghanistan, 160
Ahlberg, Allan, 61-62
Ahlberg, Janet, 61-62
Albertville, France, 161
Alexander, Michelle, 192
Alison's Zinnia, 14
All Creatures Great and Small, 34
All-New Universal Traveler, 172
Allard, Harry, 130
Allen, Fred, 196
Alphabet grids, 16
Alphabet Puzzle, 13
Alphabetics, 14
Amanda Pig on Her Own, 176
"America the Beautiful" (song), 177
American folklore, 113
"American Gothic" (painting), 223
American Library Association, 100, 119, 122
American Psychological Association, 181, 196
Americans, 160
Amway products, 41
Amy, Ben, and Catalpa the Cat, 12
Anderson, Sherwood, 113
Angria, 113
Ann Landers (newspaper column), 12, 154, 156, 223

Animal Olympics, 162
Animalia, 12, 232
Anne Frank: The Diary of a Young Girl, 123
Annemarie Johansen (fiction character, *Number
    the Stars*), 123
Anniversaries and Holidays, 24
Anno, Mitsumasa, 12
Anno's Alphabet, 12
Antics! An Alphabetical Anthology, 13
Antisthenes, 203
Antler, Bear, Canoe, 12
Apple Computers, 42
Arabs, 153
Arbor Day, 78
Archambault, John, 14, 15
Arilla Adams (fictional character, *Arilla
    Sundown*), 121
Arilla Sundown, 121
Armstrong, Neil, 110
Arthur, Malcolm, 61
Ashanti to Zulu: African Traditions, 14
Aster Aardvark's Alphabet Adventures, 15
Asteroid B-612, 113
Athena, 114
Athens Games, 167
Atlanta Games, 164
"Atlantic Bermuda," 114
Atlantic Ocean, 114
"Atlantis," 114
Atwell, Nancy, 220
Austria, 167
Aylesworth, Jim, 12

Babe Ruth. (*See* Ruth, George Herman)
Baghdad, 153
Bagnall, James, 172
Baker, Russell, 123
Barcelona Games, 163
Barchers, Suzanne, 60
Barth, Karl, 171
Barton, Clara, 190

Base, Graeme, 12, 232
Bates, Katherine Lee, 177
"Batman" (cartoon character), 225
Beagle (ship), 105
Being There (movie), 200
Bently, Edmund C., 19
Bertholdi, A., 98
Bethune, Mary McLeod, 151
Bible (Old Testament), 89
Big World, Small Screen, 196
Bill of Rights, 224
Biography, 19-31
Biography activities, 20
Black Enterprise, 55
Bloom, Benjamin, 5, 72, 182
Bloom's Taxonomy, 5, 72, 119, 181-83. See also *Taxonomy of Educational Objectives: Handbook I: Cognitive Domain*
Bloom's Taxonomy, 73 (fig.), 182 (fig.)
Blos, Joan W., 20
Book of Days, 24
Book of Pigericks, 175
Book sharing ideas, 125-26 (fig.)
Boulder, Colorado, 109
Bowen, Betty, 12
Boxen, 113
Boys Town (movie), 26
Bradford, Richard, 123
Braille, Louis, 192
Braque, Georges, 150
Breakthroughs, 102
Brennan, Justice William, 75
Brian Robeson (fiction character, *Hatchet*), 110, 124
Bridge to Terabithia, 120
Brigham Young University, 36
Brontë, Anne, 113
Brontë, Branwell, 113
Brontë, Charlotte, 113
Brontë, Emily, 113
Brooks, Bruce, 121
Brown, Kenneth A., 99
Brown, Molly, 20
Buck, Pearl, 129
Bunting, Eve, 130
Burger, Douglas A., 13, 204
Burr, Aaron, 137
Buscaglia, Leo, 190
Business Week, 55

C Is for Colorado, 14
Cabot Spooner (fictional character, *Midnight Hour Encores*), 121
Cafeteria verse, 211
Caldecott medal, 14, 60
Calvin O'Keef (fictional character, *A Wrinkle in Time*), 122
Camazotz, 113
Canada, 16, 17 (fig.), 190-91

Caney, Steven, 41
Cantillon, R., 41
CARE (Relief), 194
Care and Feeding of Ideas, 99
Caribou Alphabet, 14
Carlyle, Thomas, 27
Carrie Stokes (fictional character, *The Language of Goldfish*), 122
Carruth, Gorton, 23
Carter, Jimmy, 119
Castle Rock, Colorado, 107
CAT-scan, 97, 99
Catalogue activities, 33-35
Celebrity trash drive activity, 77
Celery Stalks at Midnight, 133
Chamonix Games, 168
Chariots of Fire (movie), 165-66
Charles Wallace Murry (fictional character, *A Wrinkle in Time*), 122
Charlotte's Web, 140, 176
Chartier, Emile, 148
Chase's Annual Events, 23, 24
Cherry, Lynne, 76, 123
Chicka, Chicka, Boom, Boom, 14-15
Children's Eternal Forest, 190
China, 150, 153
Chris Theodoraskis (fictional character, *The Westing Game*), 122
Christie, Agatha, 130, 137, 212, 214
Christmas, 187, 199, 222
Chronicles of Narnia, 113
Cinderella City Mall activity, 58-60
Cinquain verse, 208-10, 231
Circle of Quiet, 11, 150
Civil War, 21
Classroom experts, 3, 227-31
"Cobi" (mascot), 163
Coleridge, Samuel Taylor, 152
Collins, Marva, 3
Colorado, 21, 157, 171
Colorado Springs, Colorado, 106, 220
Colt, Samuel, 48
Columbus, Christopher, 21
Comaneci, Nadia, 168
Communicating talent, 69-70, 72-73, 76-77
Concept map. See Curriculum web
Conceptual Blockbusting, 172
Concrete verse, 215
Condon, Amy, 193
Confucius, 181
Congressional Record, 78
Conrad, Dan, 189
Considine, David M., 200
Constitution of the United States, 224
Coolidge, Calvin, 150
Coon, Alma S., 12
Cooperative learning, 11, 193, 234
Cooperative learning groups, 11, 98, 161
Costa Rica, 190
Cotton gin, 98

Coubertin, Pierre de (Baron), 159, 163, 167
Cousins, Norman, 93
Cox, Lynn, 12
Crabbe, Anne, 5, 146-47
Crapsey, Adelaide, 209
Crazy Alphabet, 12
Creative problem solving (CPS) model, 58, 99-102
   acceptance finding, 101-2
   data finding, 100
   idea finding, 101
   mess finding, 99-100
   problem finding, 100-101
   solution finding, 101
Creative questioning strategies, 184-85
Creativity catalogues, 33-35
Creativity model, 146, 147 (fig.)
   elaboration, 154-55
   expressiveness, 153-54
   flexibility, 149-50
   fluency, 148-49
   independence, 152
   intelligence, 155
   intuition, 152
   openness to ideas, 151-52
   originality, 153
   perceptiveness, 156
   persistence, 150
   positive self-concept, 148
   problem solving, 156-57
   sense of humor, 155-56
   tolerance for ambiguity, 149
Critical thinking, 129-30, 131 (fig.)
Cronos, 161
cummings, e. e., 119
Curie, Marie, 19, 97, 105, 155
Curriculum web, 5, 7-8 (fig.), 132 (fig.)
Curtis, Charles P., 118

da Vinci, Leonardo, 105, 134, 153, 185
Danish Resistance, 123
Darwin, Charles, 105
Data finding stage of creative problem solving, 100
Davis, Gary, 146, 153
Davis, Jim, 156
Day, Clarence, 127
Day in the life activity, 22-31
Daydreams, 8, 15, 36-40, 107, 109
dePaola, Tomie, 123
de Trevino, Elizabeth Borton, 121
Dean, Christopher, 169
Dear Abby (newspaper column), 22, 154, 156, 176
"Death and Life" (poem), 26
Decision-making talent, 69, 72, 83-84
Delgado, Abelardo, 197
DeMille, Agnes, 150
Denver, Colorado, 20, 157, 215, 227
Denver Post, 150, 215
Detective Pin (fictional character), 134
"Detectives" (poem), 213

Diamanté verse, 210-11
Dickinson, Emily, 123, 185, 207
Dictionary stories, 232-33
Dillon, Diane, 123
Dillon, Leo, 123
Disney, Walt, 102, 151
Don't Cross Your Bridges Before You Pay the Toll, 16
Dooley, Tom, 190
Doug Hoo (fictional character, *The Westing Game*), 122
Dow, Marilyn Schoeman, 44, 47
Downie, Jill, 13
Doyle, Arthur Conan, 130, 133-34, 137
Dr. Watson (fictional character), 129-31, 137
"The Dream" (story), 39
Duncan, Isadora, 153

E: Environmental Journal, 75
Earhart, Amelia, 71
Earth Day, 190
Earthsea, 113
Easter Bunny, 223
Eberle, Robert, 101
Ebony, 23
Eddie Bauer catalogue, 33, 177
Edison Thomas, 48, 90, 97-98, 105, 110, 153, 155
Eight Hands Round, 14
Einstein, Albert, 58, 90, 98, 105, 153, 185
Elaboration component of creativity model, 154-55
Eliot, T. S., 129, 133
Elizabethan England, 227
Ellen Rosen (fictional character, *Number the Stars*), 123
Elting, Mary, 13
Encyclopaedia Britannica, 36
Encyclopedia Brown (fictional character), 130, 134
Encyclopedia stories, 232-33
Entreprendre, 41
Entrepreneur, 41
Entrepreneurial Woman, 55
Entrepreneurs, famous, 42 (fig.)
Entrepreneurship, 41-57
   activities, 48
   fact finding form, 43 (fig.)
   self-study, 44, 45-46 (fig.)
Environmental Protection Agency (EPA), 106
Escalante, Jaime, 70
Essential Calvin and Hobbes, 172
Expressiveness component of creativity model, 153-54

Fabun, Don, 153
Fairy tale reading activity, 63-66 (fig.)
Fairy tales, 58-68
Farrell, Kate, 123
Father's Day, 27
Faulkner, William, 129
Ferguson, Charles W., 12

Ferrell, Trevor, 192
Ferris, Jeri, 20
Fifty Things Kids Can Do to Save the Earth, 76, 190
Fisher, Leonard, 13
Fiske, Billy, 168
Flack, Jerry, 214
Flexibility component of creativity model, 149-50
Fluency component of creativity model, 148-49
Folks in the Valley, 12
Folsom, Michael, 12
Forbes, 55
Ford, Henry, 21
Forecasting talent, 69, 72-73, 85-87
Fortune, 48, 55
Found verse, 215
Fox, Terry, 151, 190-91
France, 159, 168
Franklin, Benjamin, 105
Freedman, Russell, 20
French, Fiona, 61
Freud, Sigmund, 129
Frewin, Anthony, 24
Frog Prince Continued, 61
Fromm, Erich, 156
Frost, Robert, 118-19, 207
Fulwiler, Toby, 105
Future Problem Solving Program, 83
Futurist, 95

Galileo (Galileo Galilei), 153
Garbage, 69-88
Garbage activities, 69-88
Garbage: The Practical Journal for the Environment, 75
Gardner, Howard, 5, 69, 155
Garfield (cartoon character), 155
Garmisch-Partenkirchen Games, 168
Garrett, Sheriff Pat, 137
George, Jean Craighead, 124
Germany, 167, 190
Getty, Jean Paul, 48
"Gettysburg Address," 183
Getzels, Jacob, 152, 155
Gifted children and youth, 2, 4, 33, 44, 75, 113, 118, 166, 171, 190, 193, 207, 219, 227, 230
  as fictional characters, 120-22
Give Peace a Chance (game), 192
Glaciens, 114
Glasstown Confederacy, 113
Globe Theatre, 227
Goddard, John, 36, 37-38 (fig.)
Goldberg, Rube, 99
Goldilocks and the three bears, 58
Goldman Prize, 190
Gominger, Eugene, 215
Gondal, 113
Goodall, Jane, 21
Goodman, Billy, 190

Goodman, Joel, 171
Gordon, Harvey C., 172
Gould, Shane, 168
Graves, Donald, 220
Great Depression, 123
Greece, 159, 166
Greek alphabet, 161
Greek myths, 161
Greeks (ancient), 159-61
Greenpeace, USA, 194
Gregory, Ruth W., 24
Grimm Brothers (Jacob and Wilhelm), 59
Growing Up, 123
Grun, Bernard, 24
Guided Design, 100
Guralnick, Elissa S., 13, 204
Gutenberg, Johannes, 153

Habitat for Humanity, 194
Haiku, 208-9, 231
"Half-Baked School Lunch" (recipe), 188
Halloween, 222
Hamilton, Virginia, 120-21
Hamlet, 106-7, 119-20, 124, 175, 227
Hammarskjöld, Dag, 190, 192
Hansen, Rick, 151, 191
Hanukkah, 187, 222
Hardy Boys (fictional characters), 133
Hart, Michael, 123
Harvard University, 98
Hatchet, 110
Hausman, Gerald, 13
Hawthorne, Nathaniel, 105
Hedin, Diane, 189
Heiden, Eric, 168
"Helen Trent" (radio program), 25-26
Helping Kids Care, 193
Helsinki Games, 168
Hemingway, Ernest, 124
Henderson, Morgan, 95
Henie, Sonja, 168
Hepworth, Cathi, 13
Hera, 114
Heracles, 161
Hercule Poirot (fictional character), 129
Heroine of the Titanic, 20
Herriot, James, 34
His & Hers: The Fantasy World of the Neiman-Marcus Catalogue, 33
Historical Statistics of the United States, 137
Hoban, Tana, 13
The Hobbit, 115
"Hodori" (mascot), 163
Hope, 3, 89-95
Hopi (Native Americans), 123
How Things Work, 99
"How to Make Pigs Fly," 173 (fig.)
Howe, James, 133

Hughes, Langston, 123
Humor, 155-56, 171
Huston, Aleta C., 196
Hyman, Trina Schart, 60-61

I, Juan de Pareja, 121
Idea finding stage of creative problem solving, 101
Ides of March, 222
"Imagine Me" verse, 208, 212
Impression verse, 213
Inc., 55
Independence component of creativity model, 152
Indiana, 219
Innsbruck Games, 168
Intelligence component of creativity model, 155
International Olympic Committee, 162, 168
Intuition component of creativity model, 152
Invention, 97-102
Invention and innovation, 97-102
Invention journal, 107
Inventors at Work, 99
Isaksen, Scott G., 83, 99
Israeli athletes, 162

"Jack Benny Show" (radio program), 200
Jack Sun Run (fictional character, *Arilla Sundown*), 121
Jackson, Philip W., 152, 155
Jacob Have I Loved, 120
James, Jesse, 137
Jane Marple (fictional character), 129-30
Japan (Japanese), 119, 188, 190
Jarvik, Robert, 97
Javna, John, 76, 190
Jefferson, Thomas, 40, 95, 153, 230
Jesse Oliver Aarons, Jr. (fictional character, *Bridge to Terabithia*), 120
Jessica Fletcher (fictional character), 130
Jesus Christ, 123, 181
Jews, 123
Joan of Arc, 192
Jobs, Steve, 48
John Henry (folklore hero), 113
Johnson, Jeremy, 85, 86-86 (fig.)
Jolly Postman, 61-62
Jonas, Susan, 175
Journal of Academic T-Shirts, 33
Journal topics, 109-10 (fig.)
Journal writing, 105-9
Journals, 105-11
Journey, 124
Joyner, Florence Griffith, 165
Juan de Pareja (fictional character, *I, Juan de Pareja*), 121
Judy Blume Catalogue, 34
Julius Caesar, 222
Jung, Carl, 129
Junior Brown (fictional character, *The Planet of Junior Brown*), 121

Kalamazoo, Michigan, 212
Kayaks Down the Nile, 36
Keating, Jim, 106-7
Keillor, Garrison, 113
Keller, Helen, 120, 134
Kellogg, Steven, 13
Kennedy, John F., 230
Kenya, 124
Ketteringham, John M., 102
Kick in the Seat of the Pants, 150
Kid Heroes, 190
Kids for Saving Earth, 194
Kid's Guide to How to Save the Planet, 190
Kid's Guide to Social Action, 190
King Arthur, 1
King Augeas, 161
King, Coretta Scott, 190
King, Martin Luther, Jr., 19
King Philip IV (Spain), 121
King Solomon, 89
Kingdoms activity, 113-16
Kipling, Rudyard, 16, 129, 203
Koberg, Don, 172
Koch, Kenneth, 123
Koran, 171
Korea, 163
Korn, Jerry, 24
Krensky, Stephen, 175
"Kubla Khan" (poem), 152

Labor Day, 222
Ladies Home Journal, 23
Lake Placid Games, 168
Lake Wobegon, 113
Language of Goldfish, 122
Lao Tzu, 194
Larson, Gary, 155, 172
Lasswell, H. D., 153
LeGuin, Ursula K., 121
L'Engle, Madeleine, 11, 122, 150
Leslie Burke (fictional character, *Bridge to Terabithia*), 120
Letter writing, 193
Letter writing skills, 77-78
Levitt, Paul M., 13
Lewis and Clark expedition, 192
Lewis, Barbara A., 190
Lewis, C. S., 113
Lewis, Carl, 161
Lewis, Meriwether, 137
Library media center, 4, 19, 27, 171. See also Public libraries
Library media specialists, 4-5, 12, 23, 33, 78, 95, 102, 118, 160, 190, 193-94, 227, 231
Liddell, Eric, 166
Lillehammer, Norway, 159
Limericks, 212
Limscott, Jody, 13, 234

Lincoln, Abraham, 20, 129, 151, 183, 185
Lincoln: A Photobiography, 20
Literature, 118-24
Little Red Riding Hood (fairy tale character), 58-59
Little Red Riding Hood (Hyman), 60 (fig.), 61
Little Red Riding Hood (Marshall), 60
Lives of Promise, 21, 214
L. L. Bean (catalogue), 33, 177
Lobel, Anita, 14
Lobel, Arnold, 175
Locker, Thomas, 123
Lon Po Po, 60 (fig.), 61
London Games, 167-68
Longfellow, Henry Wadsworth, 177
Longmans, Green, 182
Los Angeles Games, 161, 163, 167
Louganis, Greg, 165
Louisiana Purchase, 192
Lowry, Lois, 123
Lucas, George, 113
Lyndon B. Johnson Space Center, 95

Macaulay, David, 99, 123-24
"Macavity: The Mystery Cat" (poem), 133
MacDonald, Sue, 14
MacKinnon, Donald, 152-53
MacLachlan, Patricia, 124
Making of a Scientist, 5
"Man with the Twisted Lip" (story), 130
Mann, Thomas, 16
Marathon of Hope, 190-91
Marcellino, Fred, 61
Mardi Gras, 23
Marin, Natasha, 39
Markham, Beryl, 124
Marshall, James, 60, 130
Marshall, Judge Thurgood, 75
Martell, Jane, 187
Martin, Jr., Bill, 14-15, 35
Mary Kay cosmetics, 41
Maslow, Abraham, 149
Massachusetts, 123
Mathias, Bob, 168
McCloskey, Dennis, 107
McGinnis, James, 193
McMillan, Bruce A., 172
McPhail, David, 175
McPherson, Stephanie Sammartino, 20
Mead, Margaret, 95
"Meditation on the Meaning of Spring" (poem), 204
Meg Murry (fictional character in *A Wrinkle in Time*), 122
Melville, Herman, 105
Memorial Day, 223
Merlyn, 1-2
Mesa Verde, 137
Mess finding stage of creative problem solving, 99-100
Metropolitan Museum of Art, 123

Michigan, 148, 219
Mickey Mouse (cartoon character), 151
Middle Earth, 113
Midnight Hour Encores, 121
Miller, Glenn, 25-26, 150
"Misha" (mascot), 163
Miss Marple (fictional character/poem), 214
Mitchell, Maria, 20
Moby Dick, 120
Mohammed, 123
Mona Lisa (painting), 134
Montagu, Ashley, 2
Montreal Games, 168
Moore, Clement Clark, 177
Morphological forced connections, 172, 173 (fig.)
Moscow Games, 163, 167
Mother Theresa, 190
Mother's Day, 27, 187
Mozart, Wolfgang Amadeus, 113
Mrs. Hudson (fictional character), 129
Multiple intelligences, 69
Multiple talents, 69-88
   academic talent, 75-76
   communicating talent, 76-77
   decision-making talent, 83-84
   forecasting talent, 85-88
   planning talent, 77-79
   productive-thinking talent, 79
Multiple talents action verbs, 72 (fig.)
Munich Games, 162, 168
Murray, Donald, 220
Musgrove, Margaret, 14
"My Bonnie Lies Over the Ocean" (song), 228
My Side of the Mountain, 124
Myers, Bernice, 61
Mystery, 129-40
Mystery and Detection, 131-32 (figs.), 213
Mystery desks, 135-36 (figs.)
Mystery literature, 129-30, 133-34, 137, 141-43, 212-13
Mystery race, 137 (fig.)
Mystery story starters, 138 (fig.)
Mystery web, 5, 132 (fig.)

Nancy Drew (fictional character), 130, 133-34
NASA. *See* National Aeronautics and Space Administration (NASA)
NASA CORE, 95
Nashua River, 123
Natalie Field (fictional character, *Very Far Away from Anywhere Else*), 121
Natalis Press, 25
Nation at Risk, 97
National Aeronautics and Space Administration (NASA), 95, 100, 114, 163
National Audubon Society, 194
National Council of Teachers of English, 105, 108
National Geographic Society, 99
National Inquirer (newspaper tabloid), 176

National Wildlife Federation, 194
Native American Doctor, 20
Nature Conservancy, 194
Nautilus equipment, 102
Navajo (Native Americans), 123
Nayak, P. Ranganath, 102
Naylor, Phyllis Reynolds (P. R. Tedesco), 179
Negotiating, 49
Negotiations simulation, 49-51 (fig.)
Neiman-Marcus catalogue, 33
Nero (Roman emperor), 167
Ness, Eliot, 137
Netsilik Eskimos, 114
"New Adventures of Sherlock Holmes"
New Business Opportunities, 55
New Dictionary of American Family Names, 24
New Mexico, 133, 148
New Year's resolutions, 222
New York State, 209
New York Stock Exchange, 151
New York Times, 23
Newbery Medal, 120-23, 150
Newspaper, 146-57
Newspaper activities. *See* Creativity model
Newspaper verse, 210
"Newsroom" (computer software), 25
Newsweek, 23, 40
Nile River, 36
Nissenson, Marilyn, 175
Nobel Prize, 129, 190, 230
Norway, 159
Number the Stars, 123

Oakley, Annie, 19
Oenomaus, 161
O'Keeffe, Georgia, 19, 21, 155
Old Possum's Book of Practical Cats, 133
Olympia, Greece, 159, 165, 167
Olympics, 8, 159-69
  activities, 161-66
  facts, 167-68
  Games, 4-5, 8, 159-69, 198
  motto, 159
  pledge, 167
Omaha, 20
Omni, 95
Once and Future King, 1
Once Upon A to Z, 13, 234
100: A Ranking of the Most Influential Persons in History, 123
Oneal, Zibby, 122
O'Neill, Gerard K., 95
Openness to ideas component of creativity model, 151-52
Oraker, Jason, 90, 91-92 (fig.)
Originality component of creativity model, 153
"Our Muscles" (song lyrics), 228-29
Outstanding books for college-bound students, 122

Owen Thomas Griffith (fictional character in *Very Far Away from Anywhere Else*), 121
Owens, Jesse, 164-65
Owens, Mary Beth, 14
Oxford Concise Dictionary, 122
Oxford Dictionary of English Christian Names, 25

Paget, Sidney, 134
Paris Games, 165
Parody, 176-77
Paterson, Katherine, 118, 120-21
Paul, Ann Whitford, 14
Paul Bunyan (folklore character), 113
"Paul Revere's Ride" (poem), 177
Paulsen, Gary, 110, 118, 124
Pelops, 161
Perceptiveness component of creativity model, 156
Perfect Pigs, 175
Perrault, Charles, 59, 61
Persistence component of creativity model, 150
Personalized verse, 213-14
Philadelphia, Pennsylvania, 192
Picasso, Pablo, 150, 152-53, 155
Picnic with Piggins, 176
Pig Pig Goes to Camp, 175
Pigs, 172-76
Pigs from A to Z, 13
Pindar, 160
Pinkerton, Allan, 137
Planet of Junior Brown, 121
Planning talent, 69-73, 77-79
"Playground of the Future" (scenario), 90, 91-92 (fig.)
Pliny the Elder, 89
Poe, Edgar Allan, 130
Poinsettia, 98
Pope Innocent X, 121
Pork Avenue Collection, 33
Positive self-concept component of creativity model, 148
PreHistory of the Far Side, 172
Presbury, Jack, 95
Problem finding stage of creative problem solving, 100-101
Problem solving, 129-30, 131 (fig.). *See also* Creative problem solving (CPS) model
Problem solving component of creativity model, 156-57
Problem solving model, 131 (fig.)
Prodigious proverbs, 15-16
Productive-thinking talent, 69-70, 72-73, 79-82
Public libraries, 23, 26
"Publish It" (computer software), 25
Pulitzer Prize, 123
PUNdemonium, 172
Punography, 172
Puns, 171-72, 178
Puss in Boots, 61

Q Is for Duck, 13
Queen Elizabeth I, 123
Question rules, 181-85
Questioning strategies, 5, 181-85
Questions, 181-85
Quotations, 190

Rain forests, 190
Raskin, Ellen, 48
Recipes, 187-88
Red Sky at Morning, 123
Retton, Mary Lou, 165
Revere, Paul, 177
Ride, Sally, 19
River Ran Wild, 76, 123
"The Road Not Taken" (poem), 177
Rockne, Knute, 150
Rodin, Auguste, 98
Roe, Ann, 5
Rogers, Carl, 148
Romeo and Juliet, 35, 107
Rooftop Astronomer, 20
"Room 222" (television program), 189
Roosevelt, Eleanor, 19, 36, 105
Roosevelt, Franklin D., 129
Rossetti, Christina, 123
Rowe, Mary Budd, 183
Rudolph, Wilma, 165
Russia, 192
Ruth, George Herman "Babe," 109

Sacajawea, 192
"Sam, the Olympic Eagle" (mascot), 163
Samuel W. Westing (fictional character, *The Westing Game*), 122
Sandburg, Carl, 36, 207
Sara Louise Bradshaw (fictional character, *Jacob Have I Loved*), 120
Saturday Evening Post, 23
Save the Whales, 194
Save Tomorrow for the Children, 95
SCAMPER, 101
Scarlet Letter, 105
Scarlet O'Hara (fictional character, *Gone With the Wind*), 152
Scenario writing, 85, 89-95
Scenario writing tips, 94-95
Schweitzer, Albert, 189-90
Scieszka, Jon, 60-61, 152, 175
Sears, Roebuck & Co. 1908 Catalogue No. 17, 33
Seattle Times, 44
Sendak, Maurice, 123
Sense of humor component of creativity model, 155-56
Seoul Games, 163, 167
Service, 189-94
Seventeen, 23

Shakespeare, William, 35, 106, 119, 123, 175, 222, 227-28
Shaw, George B., 129, 175
Sherlock Holmes (fictional character), 27, 129-31, 133-34
Shirley, Gayle C., 14
Shusterman, Neal, 190
Sibilance T. "Taxi" Spooner (fictional character, *Midnight Hour Encores*), 121-22
Sidney Rella and the Glass Sneaker, 61
Siegel, Betty, 189
Sierra Club, 75, 194
"Sitter with the Art Bag," 47 (fig.)
Skoblikova, Lydia, 168
Slater, Francis, 181
Sleuthing model, 131 (fig.)
Smallenberg, Carol, 40
Smashed Potatoes, 187
Smith, Elsdon C., 24
Smith, Howard, Jr., 162
Snodgrass, Mary Ellen, 41
Snow White and the Seven Dwarfs (movie), 26
Snow White in New York, 61
So, Hong J., 26
Socrates, 181
Socrates and the Three Little Pigs, 175
Solution finding stage of creative problem solving, 101
Soviet Union, 160
Spain, 121, 163
Special Olympics, 190
Splash! (movie), 200
Sports Illustrated, 40, 162
St. Moritz Games, 168
Stager, Robert, 100
Stand and Deliver (movie), 70
Star Wars (movie), 115
Starr, Belle, 137
Statistical Abstracts of the United States, 134
Statue of Liberty, 98
Steinbeck, John, 105, 129
Stevenson, Adlai, 203
Stinky Cheese Man and Other Fairly Stupid Tales, 61
Stockholm Games, 167
Students Against Drunk Driving, 194
Success, 55
"Sun" (concrete verse), 216
Super Saturday classes, 4, 227
Super Sensational Toy, 50 (fig.)
Super Turkey, 222
Superman (cartoon character), 225
Swiftly Tilting Planet, 122

Tabitha "Turtle" Wexler (fictional character, *The Westing Game*), 48, 122
TalentEd (philosophy), 1-5
TalentEd classrooms, 2-5, 8, 19, 36, 98, 102, 105, 109, 116, 118, 146, 171, 200-203, 219, 227

TalentEd teachers, 1-5, 8, 15-16, 21-23, 26-27, 33, 35, 40-41, 67, 70, 79, 92, 94-95, 102, 107, 109, 118, 129-30, 134, 148, 157, 159-60, 164, 171, 181, 183-85, 187, 190, 192, 194, 198, 207, 220, 227, 230-32, 234-35
Talents Unlimited, 69
Talking to the Sun: An Anthology of Poems for Young People, 123
Taming of the Shrew, 119
Taylor, Calvin, 5, 69-74, 88
Taxonomy of Educational Objectives: Handbook I: Cognitive Domain, 72, 181
Tedesco, P. R. *See* Naylor, Phyllis Reynolds (P. R. Tedesco)
Television viewing, 196-200
Television activities, 198-200
Terabithia, 120
Tesla, Nikola, 90
Theodosius (Roman emperor), 159
This Fabulous Century, 24
Three Little Pigs, 60
Thurber Carnival, 172
Thurber, James, 59, 171
Thurstone, L. L., 69
Tiensuu, Roland, 190
Time (magazine), 22
Timetables of History, 24
Tolerance for ambiguity component of creativity model, 149
Torrance, E. Paul, 95, 151, 153-54
Torvill, Jane, 169
Toynbee, Arnold, 146
Tracy, Spencer, 26
"Trash Collector" (scenario), 85, 86-87 (fig.), 90
Treffinger, Donald J., 83, 99
Trials and Tribulations of Little Red Riding Hood, 59
True Story of the 3 Little Pigs by A. Wolf, 60, 61, 152, 175
Truman, Harry S., 188
Ts'ai Lun, 153
Tuesday, 176
Turkey, 167
Turtle Island Alphabet, 13
TV Guide, 78
2081: A Hopeful View of the Future, 95
221 B Baker Street, 129-30

Ubiquitous Pig, 175
"Under Penalty of Law" (story), 179
Understanding a word activity, 203-4, 205 (fig.)
United States of America, 76, 183, 190, 199
United States Capitol Rotunda, 21
United States children, 196-97
United States hockey team (1980), 165, 168
United States Olympic Committee, 162
United States Patent Office, 97
United States Space Foundation, 95
United States Supreme Court, 75

University of Alabama, 69
University of California, 150
University of Chicago, 182
University of Colorado, 150, 227
University of Pennsylvania, 166
University of Utah, 69

Valentines, 222
Van Allsburg, Chris, 14, 123
Van Leeuwen, Jean, 176
Vancouver, British Columbia, Canada, 40
Vanderbilt, Cornelius, 48
"Vegta-fable" (story), 82
Venn diagram (fairy tales), 60
Verse activities, 207-16
Very Far Away from Anywhere Else, 121
Video History of Our Times, 25
"A Visit from St. Nicholas" (poem), 177
Visual Messages, 200
von Oech, Roger, 149-50, 155
von Goethe, Johann Wolfgang, 47

Wales, Charles, 100
Wallas, Graham, 154
Washington, District of Columbia (D.C.), 121
Washington, George, 110
Washington State, 44
Watterson, Bill, 172
Way of Life, 194
Way Things Work, 99, 123
Weighty Word Book, 13, 204
Weiner, Deborah, 95
West with the Night, 124
The Westing Game, 48, 122
What Happened When, 23
White, E. B., 176
White, T. H., 1
White House, 230
Whitney, Eli, 98
Who's Who, 78
Wiesner, David, 176
Wildlife Preservation Trust, 194
Williams, Frank, 154
Wind in the Door, 122
Winesburg, Ohio, 113
Wireless catalogue, 25
Wise Women, 60
Withycombe, Elizabeth Gidley, 25
"Wonder Years" (television program), 199
Wood, Grant, 223
World Series, 23
World War I, 167
World War II, 21, 120, 123, 167-68
World Wildlife Fund, 194
Wright Brothers, 90
Wright, Frank Lloyd, 196
Wrinkle in Time, 11, 122, 150

Writing ideas, 222-26, 235-36 (fig.)
   book sharing, 125-26 (fig.)
   creative thinking and writing, 80-82 (fig.)
   journal writing, 109-10
   mystery stories, 138 (fig.)
   understanding a word, 205 (fig.)

Yager, Craig, 109
Yamaguchi, Kristi, 161
YES! (Young Entrepreneurs Symposia), 44

"Yolanda Young's Youth" (story), 232-33
Young, Ed, 60
Your Birthday, 25

Z Was Zapped, 14
"Zebra Story," 236 (fig.)
Zebras, 235-36
Zeus, 114, 159-61
Zipes, Jack, 59
Zoo stories, 235-36

About the Author

Dr. Jerry Flack is a President's Teaching Scholar at the University of Colorado. Prior to his appointment to the School of Education at the University of Colorado (CU) at Colorado Springs in 1983, he was a classroom teacher in Michigan and Indiana for seventeen years. At CU he directs the Super Saturday Program for gifted children and a master's degree program in the education of gifted and talented children. He is the editor of the Gifted Treasury series for Teacher Ideas Press and the author of four books in the series, *Inventing, Inventions, and Inventors*; *Mystery and Detection*; *Lives of Promise*; and *TalentEd*. He is a member of the Board of Directors of the National Association for Gifted Children and the Advisory Board for Inventure Place, the home of the National Inventors Hall of Fame. He serves on the Editorial Advisory Panels of *THINK* and *Writing Teacher* magazines. In addition to receiving the lifetime title of President's Teaching Scholar from the University of Colorado, Dr. Flack has been named the National Future Problem Solving Program Teacher of the Year (1980); the University of Colorado at Colorado Springs Outstanding Teacher (1987); and the National Association for Gifted Children Early Leader (1988).

from Teacher Ideas Press

Heard About These Books?

MYSTERY AND DETECTION: Thinking and Problem Solving with the Sleuths
Jerry D. Flack

Turn your classroom into a real Scotland Yard! This unique resource ties in dozens of problem-solving and enrichment activities with mystery and sleuthing. It is divided into topical chapters on language arts, art, social studies, future studies, and crime and punishment.
Grades 5–9. *(Adaptable to other grades.)*
Gifted Treasury Series; Jerry D. Flack, Ed.
xx, 246p. 8½x11 paper   ISBN 0-87287-815-5

INVENTING, INVENTIONS, AND INVENTORS
Jerry D. Flack

Flack's exciting, mind-stretching activities illuminate a rich, interdisciplinary field of study. Investigating inventions of the past and the present, funny inventions, and inventions we may see in the future provides a natural springboard to creative thinking.
Grades 7–9. *(Adaptable for many grades.)*
xi, 148p. 8½x11 paper   ISBN 0-87287-747-7

FROM THE LAND OF ENCHANTMENT: Creative Teaching with Fairy Tales
Jerry D. Flack

Inspiring and practical, this book offers a wealth of ideas, curriculum resources, and teaching techniques that promote multiple intelligences, critical thinking, and creative problem solving, all through the common theme of fairy tales!
All Levels.
ca. 230p. 8½x11 paper   ISBN 1-56308-540-2

CREATIVE THINKING AND PROBLEM SOLVING FOR YOUNG LEARNERS
Karen S. Meador

The importance of creative thinking is widely recognized, but how can you teach creativity? With lessons based on outstanding children's literature, this book will deepen your understanding of the process of creativity and help you to recognize and nurture creativity in young learners.
Grades 1–3. (Adaptable to other grades).
ca. 150p. 8½x11 paper   ISBN 1-56308-529-1

INTEGRATING AEROSPACE SCIENCE INTO THE CURRICULUM: K–12
Robert D. Ray and Joan Klingel Ray

Demystify space with substantive information and hands-on activities that integrate space science with other curricular areas.
Grades K–12.
Gifted Treasury Series; Jerry D. Flack, Ed.
xxi, 191p. 8½x11 paper   ISBN 0-87287-924-0

For a FREE catalog or to place an order, please contact:

Teacher Ideas Press
Dept. B96 · P.O. Box 6633 · Englewood, CO 80155-6633
1-800-237-6124, ext. 1 · Fax: 303-220-8843 · E-mail: lu-books@lu.com

 Check out the TIP Web site!
www.lu.com/tip